DATE DUE

OC ~~~~ '95			
MY 14 '97			
MY 24 '01			
AE 1 1 '01			
AP 2 8 '0?			
1 5 '0?			

CRIME ON CAMPUS

CRIME ON CAMPUS

Legal Issues and Campus Administration

by
Michael Clay Smith
and
Richard Fossey

AMERICAN COUNCIL ON EDUCATION ★
ORYX PRESS ★
Series on Higher Education
1995

The rare Arabian Oryx is believed to have inspired the myth of the unicorn. This desert antelope became virtually extinct in the early 1960s. At that time several groups of international conservationists arranged to have 9 animals sent to the Phoenix Zoo to be the nucleus of a captive breeding herd. Today the Oryx population is over 1000, and over 500 have been returned to the Middle East.

© 1995 by American Council on Education and The Oryx Press
Published by The Oryx Press
4041 North Central at Indian School Road
Phoenix, Arizona 85012-3397

Published simultaneously in Canada
Printed and Bound in the United States of America

∞ The paper used in this publication meets the minimum requirements of American National Standard for Information Science—Permanence of Paper for Printed Library Materials, ANSI Z39.48, 1984.

This publication is designed to provide accurate and authoritative information in regard to the subject matter covered. It is sold with the understanding that the publisher is not engaged in rendering legal, accounting, or other professional services. If legal advice or other expert assistance is required, the services of a competent professional should be sought.
From a Declaration of Principles jointly adopted by a Committee of the American Bar Association and the Committee of Publishers.

Library of Congress Cataloging-in-Publication Data

Smith, Michael Clay.
   Crime on campus : legal issues and campus administration / by
Michael Smith and W. Richard Fossey.
      p.   cm. — (American Council on Education/Oryx Press series
on higher education)
   Includes bibliographical references and index.
   ISBN 0-89774-846-8 (cloth : acid-free paper)
   1. Universities and colleges—Law and legislation—United States. 2.
Tort liability of universities and colleges—United States. 3. Campus
crime—United States. I. Fossey, W. Richard. II. Title. III. Series:
American Council on Education/Oryx Press series on higher
education.
KF4225.S63   1995
344.73'075—dc20   95-6394
[347.30475]   CIP

Michael dedicates this book to his children, Christopher Burke, Caroline, and Leah, and his stepdaughter Missy.
Richard dedicates this book to his children, Austin and Polly.
Their safety and happiness is ever our greatest concern.

C O N T E N T S

• • • • • • • • • •

PREFACE

· · · · · · · · ·

Crime is daily fare on America's college and university campuses. It is sad but a fact that the entire catalogue of crimes and violence that plague our nation's streets can also be found at our institutions of higher learning. The news media report murders, rapes, shootings, abductions, thefts of all sorts, domestic violence, sexual harassment, and even campus hybrids such as grade tampering by computer and massive schemes to defraud student aid programs. If the culture we have enjoyed in America is to survive, we must confront and cure this pernicious social illness.

Students and would-be students, their parents, the professorate, and college and university staff members and administrators are deeply and personally affected by the problem of campus crime. This book is intended for all of them.

Especially, though, this volume is intended for college and university administrators, who must mount the front-line effort. An earlier and smaller version of this book, *Coping with Crime on Campus*, made this observation:

> Successful administration of an institution of higher education today requires a curious combination of politics, psychology, and magic, together with unerring competence in the law. Nowhere is this more true than in dealing with the crime that now rampages over our nation's campuses.

If it was true then, it is more true now. In the seven years since the earlier book was published, crime rates have continued their ascent, especially for crimes involving violence against persons. Lawsuits brought by victims of campus crime against colleges and universities—and sometimes against individual administrators—charging that their institutions failed to protect them have become common. Congress and the state legislatures have enacted hundreds of regulations designed to promote campus safety; these must be complied with in spirit and to the letter. And, campus crime has become a marketing issue, affecting decisions by students and their parents as to where, when, and how a higher education will be acquired.

The earlier version of this book was completed in 1987 and published in 1988. It is now ancient history. At the time, it was the first book in the field; it opened eyes to the breadth and depth of crime, violence, and exploitation on our campuses. Since then much has occurred. The handful of crime liability suits has multiplied to hundreds, perhaps thousands. Responding to public alarm, Congress and the state legislatures have enacted new mandates for campus operations. Fraternities, sororities, and other student-interest groups have spoken up. There has been a sea change in attitudes and the administrative environment. All of these issues are covered in this second edition.

This book is, we believe, by far the most exhaustive treatment of all issues of campus crime that is available today. In addition to presenting pertinent legal materials, the volume provides hundreds of suggestions for campus administrators as well as checklists that can readily be used to evaluate particular situations. While the book is a thorough compilation of the law in the field, it is designed for easy use by nonlawyers. The result is a volume that should be of value to college and university presidents and vice-presidents, attorneys, student affairs administrators and staff, campus housing staff, campus architects and planners, physical plant administrators, security chiefs and their police officers, and everyone else who is troubled by campus crime and wishes to do something about it.

TABLE OF CASES

• • • • • • • • •

---

*n refers to the endnote that contains the case citation.

CRIME ON CAMPUS

CHAPTER 1

......

The Campus: A Sanctuary?

Campus crime is an anomaly. A college or university campus is not a place where crime is expected. That single fact makes it enormously difficult to confront or control crime on campus. At the same time, because it visibly disrupts campus life, crime is a palpable threat to the educational mission of our institutions of higher education. For this reason, we have no choice: crime on campus must be both honestly confronted and effectively controlled.

The heart of the anomaly, of course, lies in our traditional image of campuses as bucolic, tranquil places set aside for intellectual pursuits. They have seemed the most unlikely settings for the soil and pain of crime. This paradox continues in the traditional openness of campuses. The milieu is one of freedom—intellectual, cultural, and physical—where people intermix, ideas are exchanged, and students grow to maturity. Yet, the tragic reality of crime in recent years now dictates that much campus life now must be regulated and, sometimes, closed. This, too, impedes an institution's mission.

Our campuses have been slow to come to grips with the crime problem. Sometimes this delay has been because administrators have wished to avoid untoward publicity for their institutions. In some instances, crime has been benignly ignored. In others, it has been intentionally covered up. Still, much of the slowness has resulted from the fact that it simply was not recognized as a discrete campus problem until recently. Only in the past two decades has crime become a sizable and serious phenomenon in campus life. Most people— campus administrators included—have continued to view institutions of higher learning as sedate ivory towers where problems of everyday life did not intrude. Colleges were left, in large part, to operate themselves, and the myth of the campus as a sanctuary continued.

That attitude sprang, at least in part, from legitimate historical anteced-ents. Europe's venerable institutions of higher learning, although not free from crime, had been independent of the world around them in many ways. In fact, the idea of a campus as sanctuary had its origin in the violence that was a part of the "town-versus-gown" relationship.

By the eleventh century a few of the diocesan cathedral schools, the centers of learning and professional training in their day, had grown to be recognized as *studia generalia*, institutions of regional significance that drew students from beyond their own jurisdictions. Eventually these centers be-came the great universities. These medieval universities often were at the center of a delicate balance of power between church and state, between the bishops and the princes. Just as modern communities, states, and nations have recognized that the power of education translates directly to economic and political power, so the political forces of the Middle Ages came to realize the importance of that relationship.

As there were secular political forces operative upon the universities from without, so were there ecclesiastic political forces operative within. The universities had originated in the guilds of teachers and students who banded together to protect their rights (hence the name, *universitas*, "consolida-tion"), and these interest groups continued to assert their claims. Before the end of the twelfth century the masters in some of the schools had formed guilds of liberal arts, law, medicine, and theology, because they felt them-selves fettered by the control of the chancellors who had been placed over them. The masters wanted to control their own affairs, issue licenses to teach, and appoint new members to their groups as other guilds did, and they turned to anyone who would help in their struggle for autonomy—sometimes the king, sometimes the prince, sometimes the pope.[1]

Another operative force was an enmity that often developed between the townsfolk and the students. The townspeople were vexed by the revelries of the students and by their haughtiness arising from a claim to privileged status. Sometimes the townspeople took advantage of the students. Out of all this conflict a mutual resentment grew that sometimes spilled over into violence. One of the bloodiest manifestations began at Oxford on Saint Scholastica's Day, 1354. Three days of battle between the city dwellers and the scholastics left the university pillaged and many dead, including two chaplains who were flayed alive.[2]

In response to such recurring problems and competing interests, political trading led the Crown to give special legal independence to the universities and their inhabitants. Chief among these was the right of students and faculty to be tried in ecclesiastical or university courts, rather than the towns' courts, for any charged offense. This tradition of special treatment for scholars in the law courts dates from at least the thirteenth century at Paris and the fourteenth century at Oxford.[3] The university chancellor's court grew to have exclusive jurisdiction if a student was involved in a dispute. One historian has described it thus:

> In a dispute with a scholar a townsman had not a chance. The scholar's word was always better than his; the student accused of the gravest crime was viewed with a fatherly and lenient eye; but a layman, for the pettiest offense, was cast into jail, there to kick his heels in vain.[4]

AMERICA'S LEGACY

America's colleges and universities were the heirs of this tradition of independence from governmental authority. Until recent decades there were few legal requirements affecting the administration of institutions of higher learning, as evinced by the paucity, prior to the 1960s, of cases involving higher education in the American appellate court reports and the absence of regulatory legislation at either federal or state levels. William A. Kaplin of Catholic University, a scholar in the field of higher education law, has suggested that American higher education operated like a "Victorian gentleman's club whose sacred precincts were not to be profaned" by traditional governmental authority. The higher education establishment "tended to think of itself as removed from and perhaps above the world of law and lawyers," and it was often viewed as a unique enterprise that could regulate itself through reliance on tradition and consensual agreement. "It operated best by operating autonomously, and it thrived on the privacy which autonomy afforded."[5]

The American experience differed somewhat from that of the medieval university, however. In America, the autonomy belonged to the administration, not the faculty or the students. American college presidents were autocrats with powers like the railroad presidents of their day. Even now, senior faculty at some colleges can remember when pink slips were handed out at spring commencement to those faculty members the president simply did not want back the next year. Beginning in the 1930s, the faculty began to gain power, and this beginning has flowered into the contemporary notions of "shared governance," spurred by the law explosion of due process and equal protection rights for employees, the growth of unions or unionlike organizations, the intrusion of federal standards, and other related events.

Students, however, had to wait a bit longer. Until the past few decades, students would not even have dreamed of laying claim to the sort of "rights" in higher education that are taken for granted today. Because the Constitution is fundamentally a limitation on actions by government, its applicability regarding constitutional rights of students to due process, equal protection, free speech, and so forth simply was not recognized at private colleges or universities.

In practice, the situation was little different at publicly supported institutions. Because a postsecondary education was characterized as a "privilege" and not a "right," the courts generally accepted the proposition that the institutions were free to extend or retract the privilege of attendance upon their own terms.

The decision of the United States Supreme Court in the 1934 case of *Hamilton v. Regents of the University of California*[6] typifies that approach. A group of male students at the University of California, all sons of Methodist clergy, were conscientious objectors. Their denomination's General Conference in 1928 had adopted a resolution renouncing war as an instrument of national policy, and their own Southern California Conference in 1931 further resolved that its members should not participate in the Reserve Officers Training Corps (R.O.T.C.), as it was a "preparation for war." Citing their pacifist beliefs, the students petitioned the university for exemption from R.O.T.C., which was then mandatory for male students. The request was denied, and the students then boycotted the R.O.T.C. classes and were subsequently suspended from the university. They went to court seeking readmission, alleging that the mandatory military training requirement violated their constitutional rights to freedom of religion and conscience. The Supreme Court turned them down, reiterating that attendance at a public college was a privilege and not a right, and that the university was free to establish whatever curriculum and conditions of attendance it chose, and it could expel any students who failed to comply.

This relationship between students and their colleges was grounded in the common law principles of *in loco parentis* and *parens patriae*, under which education authorities acted in the stead of parents for, it was supposed, the best interests of the students. The following quotation from a 1913 decision of the Kentucky Supreme Court typified the legal attitude:

> College authorities stand *in loco parentis* concerning the physical and moral welfare and mental training of the pupils, and we are unable to see why, to that end, they may not make any rule or regulation for the government or betterment of their pupils that a parent could make for the same purpose. Whether the rules or regulations are wise or their aims worthy is a matter left solely to the discretion of the authorities or parents, as the case may be, and, in the exercise of that discretion, the courts are not disposed to interfere, unless the rules and aims are unlawful or against public policy.[7]

Things changed drastically in the late 1960s and early 1970s. During those cataclysmic, watershed years the concept of *in loco parentis* simply evaporated from college life. Students demanded freedom and autonomy, and campus administrators quickly and quietly acquiesced. Indeed, the new attitude soon became de rigueur; conventional wisdom in the student affairs field saluted student independence as the best means for fostering maturation in students' personality and character.

Two decades later, however, in loco parentis began to make a comeback in academe, de facto if not in name. The dangerous realities of campus crime resulted in a demand from consumers—students and parents—that campuses be made safer, and, to do that, students necessarily had to surrender some freedom and autonomy. This development is discussed in more detail in chapter 4.

CAMPUS CRIME IN AMERICAN HISTORY

Perhaps this setting of governmental and judicial abstention helps to account for the lack of reported cases involving crime at our colleges and universities of yesteryear. Student conduct that might constitute a criminal offense in the outside world was handled internally, often by the deans of students, who fashioned remedies as they saw fit and were themselves the court of last resort.[8] Nonstudents, who nowadays are a major source of crime problems on many campuses, probably had little opportunity for campus crime in earlier times, given that most campuses were smaller, most students were full-time, and anonymity thus was rare.

Actually, our campuses never have been completely immune from crime; college histories from earlier decades include the occasional point-shaving scandal, murder or mayhem, and even riot. Education historians John S. Brubacher and Willis Rudy have chronicled some of the early violence. They cited, for example, the rigorous discipline of the old paternalistic college system, which discomfited many students in the first half of the nineteenth century and which caused much disruption. At the University of Virginia, where Thomas Jefferson had fostered notions of student independence and self-governance, riots by rebellious students caused the university's founder painful moments during the years before his death in 1826. Rioting continued at Charlottesville during the 1830s and 1840s, and before the riots ceased a professor had been killed and armed constables were taken onto the campus by the local sheriff to restore order.

Princeton, too, suffered stinging rioting. More than half of the student body was suspended after a particularly violent rebellion in 1807. A new wave of disturbances followed several years later. The diary of the president, the Reverend Dr. Ashbel Green, reports serious riots, the firing of a pistol at a tutor's door, the breaking of "a great deal" of glass, and an attempt to burn campus outbuildings.

Disruptions at Yale included fatal town-versus-gown confrontations. In 1841, in the "First Firemen's Riot," students bested New Haven firemen in a street fight and destroyed their equipment. In 1854, a fight between New Haven residents and Yale students ended with the death of a local bartender. Four years later, a "Second Firemen's Riot" occurred, during which a student shot and killed a fireman.

Historian William H. Prescott lost an eye during a brawl in the Harvard Commons while he was a student there around 1820. One Harvard tutor of the period incurred a lifelong limp as a result of his confrontation with student rioters. On another occasion, the college expelled more than half the senior class, including the son of John Quincy Adams, on the eve of commencement.

College authorities faced with the problem of miscreant students could expel them, but apparently were able to do little else. Thomas Jefferson had urged that a university court be established at the University of Virginia to consider all discipline cases. It was to have concurrent jurisdiction with state courts, with full power to impanel grand juries and try criminal cases. It was even to have its own jail. The Virginia General Assembly, however, refused to establish the tribunal. To the north, Harvard president Quincy called for grand jury action after a serious student riot in 1834, but nothing was done. Student misconduct apparently just did not go to court.

How is this student turmoil to be explained? Brubacher and Rudy see it as a reflection of the social fabric of America at the time. In the exuberant young nation there was an "inner conflict between an overrepressive, Calvinistic morality and a frontier pattern of heavy drinking and brutal fighting."[9] Campus violence, then, was simply the counterpart of the restlessness and impetuosity that marked the parent society. And so it may be, even today.

Another notorious instance of campus crime is the celebrated prosecution of Professor Webster, a member of the Harvard medical faculty who was convicted in 1850 of murdering a prominent Boston physician, Dr. George Parkman, from whom he had borrowed money. The case drew particular attention because the body of the victim was never found, and Webster was convicted solely on circumstantial evidence that indicated he had dismembered the body and disposed of the remains in the medical college laboratory.[10]

The image, nevertheless, of the American campus as a place where crime was a rarity probably was not inaccurate, at least until the 1960s. Still, this assumption is nothing more than an educated guess. Since there was carte blanche for institutions to police themselves, the actual extent of serious wrongdoing is somewhat obscured; modern-style crime statistics are not available to prove it one way or the other. However, the scarcity of reported court cases and the absence of material in even recent textbooks and other professional literature on higher education administration leave a strong implication that crime was not a significant problem on campus.

THE MODERN ERA BEGINS

In a physical sense, the privileged sanctuary status of the campus began to diminish in the post–World War II period. Returning veterans using the G.I. Bill of Rights were followed a decade later by the "baby boomers," and these factors, coupled with the increased need for training and credentialing in a more sophisticated world, caused an explosion in American higher education that resulted in geometric increases in numbers of institutions and students. Part-time students, "commuter campuses," cooperative programs with industry, and "enrichment" curricula for nontraditional students have also become a major part of the higher education enterprise. With the wall between academe and the world outside disintegrating, inevitably the problems of the larger culture have begun to intrude upon the academy.

That modern phenomenon sometimes called the "law explosion," then, has blown itself onto our campuses in gale force, penetrating every fissure. Most of it, of course, involves civil legal matters (the assertion of private rights against other citizens or institutions) rather than criminal offenses. Many causes can be identified for the amplification of legal matters in campus life. Among them are a greatly increased tendency in society to use formal litigation to resolve problems; the historical phenomena of the civil rights and student protest movements; the increase in employee unions on campus; the heightened awareness of employee rights in the larger society; and the increased presence of the federal government in campus life, seen in federal regulation and protection of students and employees, and federally supported programs with national standards, wages, and accountability.

Two of those factors—the civil rights movements and the Vietnam era protests—are especially significant for the phenomenon of campus crime, because their arrival brought, for the first time, widespread intentional lawbreaking and violence to the campuses, albeit lawbreaking and violence that came from ideology born of the highest moral persuasion.

By the late 1960s, thousands of criminal cases were in the courts growing out of "sit-ins" and other sorts of student demonstrations in support of political ideology.[11] In 1968, for the first time in American legal history, a grand jury returned mass felony indictments against students as a result of campus unrest. It came in the aftermath of the student occupation of the administration building at San Fernando Valley State College, where the president and other personnel had been held captive for several hours. The Los Angeles County Grand Jury indicted 24 students on kidnapping and false imprisonment charges, and all but one were convicted. In his guilty verdict,

Judge Brandle said, "We dare not and will not sanction or tolerate the use of force, violence or other illegal acts to effect desired changes. . . . College campuses are not privileged sanctuaries where disruptive, violent, felonious acts go unpunished."[12]

The state legislatures also responded to what they saw as an emergency, and put into place many statutes making it a crime to disrupt the functioning of an educational institution.[13] A survey by the National Association of State Universities and Land Grant Colleges showed that 44 states enacted statutes directly relating to campus unrest during 1969 and 1970 alone.[14]

The unrest reached its height in 1970, and then it took a lethal turn. National Guard soldiers firing into a crowd of students at Kent State University killed four and wounded nine. A few days later, police officers fired into a dormitory at Jackson State College, killing two and wounding 12.[15]

Student protests are not new. The world has seen them often. Jerome Skolnick suggests that they are a logical reflection of technological, cultural, and economic changes in our world, which necessarily require new distributions of political power. Expressions of discontent arise if political authorities are identified as agents of the status quo when such social changes occur: "Intellectuals and students are most likely to criticize established authorities because they, more than any other stratum of society, are concerned with the problem of creating and articulating new values."[16]

Still, student protests were new, by and large, to the America of the 1960s. And the organized, widespread, collective violence that accompanied them certainly was new to the American scene. President Johnson suspected that the collective violence of the period was caused by organized conspirators who held no allegiance to democratic processes. To the contrary, the National Commission on the Causes and Prevention of Violence, which Johnson appointed in June 1968, found that both student and urban group violence in the United States was caused by the failure of the existing political system either to allow for expression of legitimate grievances by disenfranchised groups or to make significant response to such grievances. The commission reported that "frustration" over material, social, and political circumstances "is a necessary precondition of group protest. Whether that frustration will erupt into violence depends largely on the degree and consistency of social control and the extent to which social and political institutions afford peaceful alternatives for the redress of group grievances."[17]

The decade of the 1960s was a watershed in American history; the cultures at both ends of that lively period were dramatically different. The crime and violence that were becoming common fare in the parent society were evident on campus as well. In addition, the phenomenon of crime in that period served as a catalyst for other sorts of profound changes in campus life and administration: the concepts of "participatory governance," in which faculty, students, and staff shared in campus decision making, and of modern student and employee "due process" rights, which were nourished in the struggles of the times as beleaguered administrators sought to retain control of their campuses. The concept of the campus as sanctuary, unfettered in governing its own affairs and unsullied by the world, was challenged on many fronts during the 1960s and 1970s. The ivy-covered walls did not come tumbling down, but there were visible cracks in the mortar.

NOTES

1. R. Freeman Butts, *The Education of the West* (1947; reprint, New York: McGraw-Hill, 1973), pp. 177-78.
2. Nathan Schachner, *The Mediaeval Universities* (1938; reprint, New York: A. S. Barnes, 1962), pp. 199-208.
3. Arthur O. Norton, *Readings in the History of Education* (Cambridge, Mass.: Harvard, 1909), pp. 86-87; Gordon Leff, *Paris and Oxford Universities in the Thirteenth and Fourteenth Centuries* (New York: John Wiley, 1968), pp. 70-71; see also Hastings Rashdall, *The Universities of Europe in the Middle Ages*, new ed., edited by F. M. Powicke and A. B. Emden (London: Oxford University Press, 1936), pp. 79-113.
4. Schachner, p. 202.
5. William A. Kaplin, *The Law of Higher Education* (San Francisco: Jossey-Bass, 1978), p. 48.
6. 293 U.S. 245 (1934).
7. *Gott v. Berea College*, 156 Ky. 376, 161 S.W. 204.206 (1913).
8. See, for instance, C. Michael Otten, *University Authority and the Student* (Berkeley: University of California Press, 1970), p. 186, and Kenneth E. Eble, *The Profane Comedy* (New York: Macmillan, 1962), p. 66.
9. John S. Brubacher and Willis Rudy, *Higher Education in Transition*, 3d ed. (New York: Harper & Row, 1976), pp. 54-57.
10. *Commonwealth v. Webster*, 59 Mass. (5 Cush.) 295, 52 Am. Dec. 711 (1850).
11. See, for example, the college-related cases of *O'Leary v. Kentucky*, 441 S.W. 2d 150 (1969); *Evers v. Birdsong*, 287 F. Supp. 900 (S.D. Miss. 1968); *In re Bacon*, 240 Cal. App. 34, 49 Cal. Rptr. 322 (Dist. Ct. App. 1966).
12. Thomas E. Blackwell, *The College Law Digest 1935-1970* (Washington, D.C.: National Association of College and University Attorneys, 1974), p. 3.
13. See, for instance, Fla. Stat. Ann. Sec. 877.13 (1969); Ohio Rev. Code Sec. 2923.61 (1970, repealed 1974), Sec. 3345.22-26 (1970).
14. NASULGC Circular No. 161.
15. *The Report of the President's Commission on Campus Unrest* (Washington, D.C.: U.S. Government Printing Office, 1970).
16. Jerome Skolnick, *The Politics of Protest* (New York: Simon and Schuster, 1969), p. 84.
17. *To Establish Justice, to Insure Domestic Tranquility*, final report of the National Commission on the Causes and Prevention of Violence (Washington, D.C.: U.S. Government Printing Office, 1969).

C H A P T E R
2
· · · · · · · · ·

The Complexion of Campus Crime Today

T
he rampant crime that now plagues America is an appalling paradox in a society that boasts of the dignity of the citizen, the freedom of the individual, and the rule of law and order. The reality of campus crime is an even greater anomaly. The campus has been set aside as the place for intellectual pursuits, discourse, and reflection; yet today it is the scene of the same sorts of violence, larceny, and criminal mischief as the parent society.

The higher education press regularly reports such things as professors shot in their classrooms, arson in campus buildings, rapes in dormitories, thefts of everything from rare books to lunchroom tickets, fraud in grants and student loan programs, sexual extortion of students by faculty members, forgery of transcripts and diplomas, and run-of-the-mill vandalism. Some campuses suffer a great deal of crime, some far less. But in many places the myth of the safe campus endures while the campus community inures itself to the undiscussed threat.

Sociologist Walter A. Lunden believes that crime on American campuses has risen for the same reasons that offenses have risen in the country as a whole: rapid growth of metropolitan centers, increased mobility, and shattered norms of conduct. It is now the norm that students' families have moved two or three times, a fact that has made it more difficult for students to identify with any group or place; moreover, social images are inconsistent. "If the outside world imprints broken and shattered patterns of conduct on the mind, it follows that the observer will have difficulty establishing a fixed standard of conduct."[1]

AMERICAN CRIME STATISTICS

In the late 1960s, the president's National Commission on the Causes and Prevention of Violence concluded that the United States was "the clear leader among modern stable democratic nations in its rates of homicide, assault, rape, and robbery."[2] On the basis of available historical information, the level of violent crime in America reached an all-time high in the 1960s, and the rate increases sustained in that decade continued throughout the 1970s.[3] America's crime rates stayed at the same high levels during the 1980s and early 1990s. In 1991, the total number of serious criminal victimizations was slightly over 35 million.[4] About one-fourth of all American households were touched by either criminal violence or theft during the year.[5] Crime victimization in rural areas was significantly lower than in cities and suburban areas; the overall rate of violent crime (rape, robbery, and assault) among city dwellers was 92 percent higher than among rural residents and 56 percent higher than among suburban residents.[6]

Who the Offenders Are

Neil Weiner and Marvin Wolfgang have analyzed the *Uniform Crime Reports* (*UCR*) and the Department of Justice's *National Crime Survey*, and can tell us much about both offenders and victims. While males make up half the population, the *Uniform Crime Reports* reveal that they comprise eight out of ten arrests for homicide and aggravated assault, and more than nine out of ten arrests for robbery.

Young adults from 18 to 24 constitute about 13 percent of the population, but they account for more than 30 percent of the homicide and aggravated assault arrests and 40 to 45 percent of those arrested for forcible rape and robbery. Older juveniles from 15 to 17 make up only 6 percent of the population, but they have accumulated approximately 10 to 15 percent of the arrests for forcible rape and 20 to 25 percent of the arrests for robbery. In addition, these older juveniles accounted for about 8 percent of the arrests for homicide and 11 percent of the arrests for aggravated assaults. While blacks comprise only about 13 percent of the nation's population, they have accumulated from 50 to 60 percent of the arrests for homicide, 50 percent of the arrests for forcible rape, 60 percent of the arrests for robbery, and 40 to 50 percent of the arrests for aggravated assault.

Who the Victims Are

The victims of crime are much like the offenders. The male victimization rate was more than twice that of females for robbery and three times that of females for aggravated assault. Older juveniles and young adults also were disproportionately likely to be victims of crime; persons in those age groups were more than twice as likely to be raped or seriously assaulted, and from two to three times as likely to be robbed. Blacks also sustained the highest proportional likelihood of being a crime victim. According to the Department of Justice's *National Crime Survey*, blacks ran a risk of rape that was one and one-half to two times that of whites, a risk of robbery that was two to three times higher, and a risk of aggravated assault that was one and one-half times greater. Overall, the risk of victimization for blacks was twice that for whites.

The poor also were more likely to be victims. *National Crime Survey* data indicate that persons who belonged to families with incomes below the poverty level were more than twice as likely as any other income group to be forcibly raped, more than one and one-half times as likely to be robbed, and more than one and one-third times as likely to be seriously assaulted. As annual family income increased, the ravages of violent crime generally decreased.

Contrary to sometimes-heard myths, crime does not tend to be interracial. More than seven out of ten violent offenses against blacks were committed by blacks, and between three-fourths and four-fifths of the forcible rapes and assaults committed against whites were committed by whites. Robbery was the exception; in more than half the incidents involving a single offender and in more than one-third of the incidents involving multiple offenders, blacks robbed whites.[7]

DATA ON CAMPUS CRIME

Only in the past few years have useful campus crime statistics become available. Prior to the late-1980s, the only numbers available were from the FBI's annual *Uniform Crime Reports*. Reporting for that federal compilation was voluntary, and only about 12 percent of the nation's 3,600 institutions of higher education participated. In the mid-1980s, the UCR typically reported somewhere around 2,000 to 2,500 crimes of personal violence on campus each year.

A far better picture of campus crime emerged in 1988, when *USA Today* conducted its own survey of 698 colleges and universities. That study found a total of 31 homicides, 1,874 armed robberies, 653 rapes, 13,079 assaults, 22,170 burglaries, and 144,717 thefts on the reporting campuses in the preceding year.[8]

Even larger numbers were reported four years later when a new federal law dealing with campus crime went into effect. The law, entitled the Student Right-to-Know and Campus Security Act (see chapter 14), was enacted by Congress in 1990 because of media and public pressure to require full disclosure from colleges about their campus safety and security records. Among other things, it made reporting of crime statistics mandatory for all American institutions of higher learning. The first round of reporting under the new law came in 1992. The results, published in 1993, include 30 murders, nearly 1,000 rapes, 1,800 robberies from persons, 32,127 burglaries, and 8,981 stolen motor vehicles.[9]

The reported numbers are large, but the cause for concern increases when it is realized that the actual number of offenses are, surely, much larger. First, the totals come only from offenses that are reported. Various studies by criminologists have revealed that only about one-half of the felonies that occur in America are reported to police, and the percentage is much lower for misdemeanors. There are many reasons why this is so: victims are too busy; they do not want the hassle; they fear retaliation; and they are unfamiliar with proper reporting processes. All of these factors are present with students— perhaps even more so than with the general population.

Another reason that the reported totals do not show the real picture is because the figures represent criminal events that occurred only within the formal boundaries of the campuses. Many aspects of student life occur off-campus. Neighborhoods around campuses often serve as the locale for social-izing. At many institutions today, large numbers of students live in privately owned dormitories or apartments near the campus. Offenses from these locations are *not* included in campus crime statistics.

Last, there have always been questions about the accuracy of campus crime statistics furnished by the colleges and universities themselves. Even after passage of the mandatory federal reporting law, some observers continue to suspect that, at least at some institutions, crime statistics may be shaded downward or intentionally understated by image-conscious campus authori-ties. One university administrator, in an editorial in *The Chronicle of Higher Education*, said her study found "widespread skepticism" among all levels of university administrators and staff members about crime rates reported by some institutions to comply with the Campus Security Act.[10]

The Towson Study: Helpful Details

One of the most useful studies of campus crime and violence was reported in 1987 by student personnel administrators at Towson State University. The Towson study consisted of a questionnaire sent to student affairs officers, campus security directors, and residence directors at 1,100 colleges and universities nationwide, selected because administrators at those institutions participated in national student personnel organizations. Responses were received from 764 institutions.

Useful data obtained through the questionnaire included the information that, overall, respondents felt only 33.6 percent of campus sexual assaults, 62.8 percent of physical assaults, and 63 percent of vandalism incidents were reported to campus police or security. In all three categories, campus security believed that a larger percentage of offenses had been reported, while residence directors felt a smaller percentage of actual offenses had been reported. Security people felt 96 percent of vandalism incidents had been reported, and residence directors believed it had been only 55.9 percent. Likewise, security felt 36.9 percent of sexual assaults had been reported, while residence directors tabbed it at 28.8 percent. As might be expected, 64 percent of residence directors felt "date rape" had been a significant part of the sexual assaults that occurred on their campuses, while only 47.3 percent of campus security so reported.[11]

Several factors may be responsible for the discrepancies between the reports from campus security and residence directors. On the one hand, the security figures may be related more to hard statistics, because those agencies do tabulate reports, while the residence director figures may be softer estimates, often based upon recollection and anecdote. On the other hand—and it would seem quite logical—residence directors may simply know more about the frequency of crime and violence than do others on campus. Residence directors surely are aware of many incidents that victims choose not to report for various reasons, among them being a sense of community among students that discourages "tattling," skepticism that the system can respond in a helpful way, unwillingness to devote time and energy to the reporting and prosecuting process, lack of awareness that a cognizable infraction has occurred, and fear of retaliation. Another beguiling statistic from the Towson study was that respondents overall felt that 29.7 percent of campus physical assaults were perpetrated by nonstudents.

Problems Caused by Nonstudents

The questionnaire did not specify whether "nonstudents" included the other campus constituencies (faculty and staff), or meant only outsiders, be they guests or intruders with no legitimate campus business. Problems caused by outsiders are significant because campus authorities have less control over variables that might affect their conduct. Campus regulations for employees and students obviously are not persuasive authority to intruders and can only have limited application with guests. The only campus policies that might affect outsiders are those that limit their access to the campus, or "target harden" campus constituencies, making them less vulnerable.

Conclusions of this sort were reached in a study of violence and firearms at Florida State University after the 1986 slaying of a football star outside the site of a campus dance. Pablo Lopez, a six-foot-five starting offensive tackle at the university, died of a shotgun blast to the abdomen during a fight with a nonstudent. After press reports of other gun problems on campus were publicized, the university commissioned a study of violent crimes at the institution. Directed by Professor Gary Kleck of the university's School of Criminology, the study concluded that the Lopez shooting was a "unique event, rather than a part of any repeated or patterned set of events." The study said there was less violent crime and much less gun ownership or possession on the campus than would be expected by reference to other communities of similar size. On the basis of the Lopez incident, which involved a nonstudent's shotgun taken from the trunk of a car by a nonstudent and used to shoot a student, and other data about campus crime, the Kleck study concluded that there was no basis for new institutional policies related to violence or guns. The study did note, however, that there was a "noteworthy problem" of *fear* of crime among the students on the campus.[12]

The Perceived Threat

Students apparently do perceive a threat. A 1986 poll by *Newsweek* magazine disclosed that 38 percent of American college students reported worrying about crime on or near their campuses "a great deal" or "a fair amount." One-sixth reported having personally been crime victims while students, most of those by theft. The survey was conducted by the Gallup organization and included 508 face-to-face interviews on 100 campuses nationwide.[13]

Comparing the Campus and the Parent Society

Comparison of data between campuses and the parent society is difficult using existing data. The *Uniform Crime Reports* (UCR) are not much help because of fuzzy boundaries and overlaps in the reporting system—often, students are counted in institutional enrollment figures and as citizens in community populations at the same time, and offenses sometimes are counted by campus authorities and reported to UCR, and are also counted by the regular police department or sheriff's office that serves the community as well. But sometimes crimes are reported only by the community police agency and not the institution. However, when the UCR is looked at, the number of offenses per population on campuses in the nation is about the same as that in the general population.

A large study by James Fox and Daryl Hellman compared the campus crime figures at 175 colleges and universities with crime statistics for the cities and towns in which the campuses were located. Their conclusion was that, on the average, the campus crime rate was only about half that, of the adjoining cities and towns (the correlation was 0.58). On the safest campus, the rate was only 1 percent of that of the community; at the other extreme, the most dangerous school had a rate three times that of the community. Only 20 of the 175 campuses had rates that exceeded those of the community.[14]

A single-campus study at the University of Alabama turned up a much higher occurrence rate than the national average. William Formby and

Robert Sigler conducted the campus study on crime and victim characteristics, comparing them to national victimization rates.[15] It examined household burglary, household larceny, robbery, and assault. The study was small; it used a stratified random sample of 1 percent of the university faculty, staff, and students, with the result that only 41 victims were interviewed. However, the study was able to conclude that the rates of crime on campus were significantly higher than national rates for all offenses examined.

Robbery and assault occurred somewhat more often on the campus, the study concluded, but the rates for household burglary and household larceny were far greater. Using national and campus average samples for 1977 and 1978, the study found that the frequency of household burglary was 103.1 percent greater than the national average, and household larceny was 98.1 percent greater. Several factors may account for the higher rates. Because the sample was small, a localized "crime wave" of burglary and theft by an active person or group during the study period might account for the difference. It would also seem quite likely that dormitory and apartment living arrangements, and student lifestyles as well, would readily lend themselves to more burglary and theft than in the society at large.

Factors Influencing Campus Crime

A beginning in the analysis of campus crime was made by Lee McPheters in a study published in 1978. He sought to identify significant variables in campus crime through econometric analysis of potentially influencing factors. For the study, he obtained budget, student population, and campus physical and location data from 38 institutions, unemployment data from the Bureau of Labor Statistics, and crime data from the *Uniform Crime Reports*. The results were not surprising. The two independent variables that seemed to result in a greater amount of crime on campus were, first, a higher proportion of students living in dormitories and, second, closer proximity to urban areas with high unemployment rates.

Comparing Campuses

McPheters felt he was unable to draw comparisons between commuter colleges and traditional, dormitory-oriented, remote campuses because the two traded one risk element for another: commuter colleges with small, or no, dormitory populations tended to be in urban areas, while isolated campuses in small towns had large dormitory populations. He did conclude that closing campuses to nonstudents would be likely to reduce crime rates, but "at the cost of a great deal of the personal freedom now associated with life in the campus community."[16] The conclusion that dormitories bring higher crime rates should be no surprise. Whether dormitory lifestyles contribute to crime is a question yet to be answered. But obviously, when students live in dormitories they and their possessions are physically present on the campus much more—24 hours a day for many months—than at a commuter college, where individual students may be on campus only a few hours a week. Not only is the time of exposure to crime much greater, but so is the amount of property that might be stolen.

The McPheters study was followed in 1985 by a large study of 222 colleges and universities conducted by Fox and Hellman, and similar conclusions were reached.[17] Using an analysis of variance framework to investigate patterns of relative safeness, the study concluded that location—rural or urban—had no apparent influence on crime rates, although a slight influence on crime mix was found, as the frequency of violent crime was somewhat higher on the urban campuses. Fox and Hellman acknowledged that the "trade-off risk" notion offered by McPheters might account for the sameness in crime rates: rural campus rates reflect the large percentage of students who live on campus, while urban rates reflect adverse urban influences offset by the small percentage of resident students.

Correlates Affecting Crime Rates

Fox and Hellman looked at 38 different correlates that they felt might have affected campus crime rates, including such things as police characteristics, density measures, scholastic characteristics, student body demographics, and even faculty salaries. In the end, they could identify only campus size and scholastic quality as positively correlating with higher crime rates. They theorized that scholastic quality might be a positive factor because higher-quality education generally costs more, and thus the economic status of the students and the value of campus assets is likely to be higher. Among student demographic factors, they found that the percentage of male students positively correlated with crime, but that the percentage of minority students, while positively correlating, was not statistically significant.

New Types of Violence

Courtship violence. Besides garden-variety fights and thefts that occur on campus, some observers are beginning to discern new types of violence in student life. Date rape and sexual harassment have been receiving considerable attention (see chapter 7), and now courtship violence and even interroommate violence are being noted. Dorothy G. Siegel, vice-president for student services at Towson State University, lamented in an editorial in the *Baltimore Evening Sun* what she and her colleagues across the nation are perceiving as a new, troubling "climate of violence" on campus: "Many believe that for every room in the dormitory in which a woman is assaulted, there are seven or eight rooms on the same dormitory floor in which students are punching each other over whose turn it is to sweep."[18]

Courtship violence is being documented. James M. Makepeace questioned 202 sociology students at a medium-sized midwestern state university and found that 61.5 percent reported personally knowing someone who had been involved in courtship violence, and that 21.2 percent reported at least one direct personal experience of it. The students were mostly freshmen and sophomores from predominantly rural and small-town backgrounds and middle-income families. Reported incidents of personal courtship violence were the following: a threat, 8.4 percent; pushed, 13.9 percent; slapped, 12.9 percent; punched, 4 percent; struck with an object, 3.5 percent; assault with a weapon, 1 percent; choked, 1.5 percent; and other, 3 percent.

The most frequently cited reason for the disagreement that sparked the violence was jealousy of one partner over the real or perceived involvement of the other with another man or woman. This situation was reported in 27.2 percent of the cases. The other most frequent causes cited were disagreements over drinking behavior, and anger over sexual denial. The most frequent place of occurrence was a home, dormitory, or apartment. Just over half the incidents occurred in such a residence, while just over one-fifth occurred in motor vehicles and another one-fifth occurred out-of-doors. The majority of males (69.2 percent) reported that they were the aggressors, while 91.7 percent of the females perceived themselves as the victims.

Makepeace examined the relationship of courtship violence to spousal abuse. Previous research has found that, for a variety of reasons, many persons subjected to spousal abuse will continue the relationship with the assailant even when the abuse has been brutal. Because of the absence of the factors often cited for spouses' staying together—economic hardship, good of the children, or to avoid the stigma of divorce—Makepeace suspected that most of the victims of courtship violence would have discontinued the relationship with the abuser. To the contrary, only about half the relationships "broke off." Nearly 16 percent reported they were still involved with the person in the same capacity, and 28.9 percent reported they had become more deeply involved with the person.

Makepeace concluded that courtship violence is a "serious social problem" for college communities, and he suggested additional study both on the links between the abuser and his or her family of orientation and, perhaps more importantly, the linkage between the premarital role and later marital roles.[19] The socializing role that courtship violence may play for later spousal abuse is quite disturbing.

Makepeace's conclusions were validated in a later study by Rosemarie Bogal-Allbritten and William Allbritten.[20] Their 1982 survey included 510 students at a medium-sized state university. Unlike Makepeace's population, there were as many juniors and seniors as freshmen and sophomores in their study, and even a 2 percent population of graduate students. Almost identical to the Makepeace report, 61 percent reported personal knowledge of another student involved in courtship violence, and 19 percent acknowledged at least one personal experience. Sixty-two percent indicated they had ended the relationship, 27 percent stated they were continuing to see the person in the same capacity, and 11 percent stated the relationship had become closer, although not necessarily as a result of the violence. Forty-eight percent of the assailants were reported to have been drinking; 17 percent of the victims were said to be under the influence of alcohol at the time of the incident.

Bogal-Allbritten and Allbritten also surveyed the directors of university housing systems listed in the directory of the Association of University Housing Offices (345 responded) and all campus counseling center directors listed in the data bank of the Association of University Counseling Center Directors (228 responded). These recited a significant incidence rate of courtship violence on their campuses, but reported few specific campus policies for dealing with the problem.

Four recommendations for campus responses were proposed by Bogal-Allbritten and Allbritten: 1) make information available to faculty and staff concerning the reasons why violence occurs, who may be an abuser, who may be abused, and why the abused individual remains in the relationship; 2) conduct surveys and informational activities through which university personnel can become aware of the frequency of courtship violence; 3) establish links with abuse shelters in the community that are able to house students and provide a community resource for abused students who do not seek shelter; and 4) conduct a media campaign to educate students (abusers, abused, and peers) about the problem and resources available for dealing with it.

Violence against resident assistants. If violence is increasing in everyday campus life, other sorts of abuses should not be unexpected. John Schuh and William Shipton studied abuses encountered by resident assistants (RAs) who oversee day-to-day operations in dormitories. In addition to the rare but tragic kinds of occurrences, such as the murder of one RA at the University of Michigan and the case of an RA at another major university who allegedly was assaulted in her room by an All-American basketball player, the study found that RAs are regularly subjected to verbal abuse and occasionally to physical abuse or the threat of it.[21]

The Schuh and Shipton study questioned 163 RAs at Indiana University-Bloomington during the 1981-82 school year. More than 50 percent of the RAs reported having an obscenity directed at them (female as well as male), half reported (again, female as well as male) receiving harassing telephone calls, and 24 percent of the men and 5 percent of the women reported they were recipients of pranks involving fireworks. Pranks against them involving fire were reported by 6 percent of the males and 3 percent of the females. Particularly troubling were reports from four female RAs (about 6 percent) that they had been subjected to sexual abuse, from six that they had been attacked with a weapon or dangerous object, and from twenty-three that they had been touched in a threatening way.

Retaliatory abuse. If RAs, who are part of the institution's administration, are themselves subjected to abuses, it should not be surprising that students who avail themselves of student judicial processes with complaints against other students are commonly retaliated against. Schuh and Douglas Oblander sampled the 78 students at Indiana University-Bloomington who had filed campus judicial complaints during the 1981-82 school year and had returned to school for 1982-83. Ultimately 45 of the students responded, and many reported being harassed or abused by the persons about whom they had filed the complaints. Twenty-nine percent reported being intentionally embarrassed in front of others, 22 percent reported having their property threatened, and 22 percent reported receiving harassing telephone calls. Eighteen percent received verbal abuse which included threats of physical harm. Over one-third of the students indicated they had received pressure to drop the charges they had originally filed.

Of even more gravity, 13 percent reported that their property had been damaged in acts of retaliatory abuse, and 5 percent reported they had suffered some form of physical abuse, including slapping, punching, kicking, pranks with fireworks, and even attacks with a weapon. Schuh and Oblander urged institutions to develop ways to deal such retaliation. Suggestions included an intervention process to notify accused offenders that reprisals would result in stiffer penalties against them and the regular publication in the campus newspaper of disciplinary case summaries, with names deleted, so that student familiarity with and confidence in the system might be heightened.[22]

CONCLUSION: THE IMPORTANCE OF CAMPUS RESPONSE

Criminal violence, theft, and vandalism clearly pervade contemporary American campus life. What would have been called student high jinks a few years ago are now being recognized for the exploitative and damaging criminal behavior that they are. The inclination of some administrators to ignore the problem in the hope either that it is not really there or that it will go away is no longer reasonable or responsible.

There are several negative consequences when criminal-type behaviors are not reported and acted upon either by the criminal justice system or campus disciplinary authorities. Among those consequences are 1) loss of the deterrent aspects of sanctions—both in providing an example for others that the conduct is not tolerated, and in limiting the ability of the offender to do it again; 2) loss of rehabilitative services to the offenders, who may be turned to a more productive course in life; 3) loss of rehabilitative services to victims—emotional, physical, and economic; 4) loss of data for rational campus planning in order to protect people and property and to ameliorate problems; 5) loss of morale among campus constituencies when offenders are not punished and standards are not upheld; and 6) ultimately the potential creation of civil liability. When public officials as well as campus administrators pass up an opportunity to identify an offender and thereby both warn others of his or her propensities and create the possibility of his or her rehabilitation, those officials might conceivably be held liable to others injured in subsequent acts of the offender that were predictable on the grounds of the earlier misconduct. That is, if you have a chance to short-circuit an offender's injurious career, you should do so.

Appropriate campus responses must be constructed and applied. Chiefly these must include 1) finding ways of persuading offenders not to commit offenses, if possible; 2) making it difficult or impossible for the offender to do it if he or she is not dissuaded; and 3) providing support and rehabilitation systems for both victims and offenders in those cases where the offense was not prevented. Education has a key role to play in all three aspects. Potential offenders may be taught that the conduct in question is unacceptable, that there are alternative ways to get along in life, and that detection and punishment for infractions is certain or highly likely. Potential victims may be educated in so-called target hardening—changing their lifestyles and practices so that the opportunity for crime is minimized. Campus administrators likewise may be educated in target hardening—modifying times, places, and types of program activities, and modifying physical plants as well, so that risks are reduced to a minimum. Education, too, about rehabilitation opportunities must be made known in order for them to be used. Crime exists only to the extent that society permits it. Crime on campus may be all too common, but it is not written in the stars that it must remain so.

NOTES

1. "A Decade of Crime on Campus," 50 *Police Chief* 66-68 (September 1983).
2. *To Establish Justice, to Insure Domestic Tranquility,* final report of the National Commission on the Causes and Prevention of Violence (Washington, D.C.: U.S. Government Printing Office, 1969).
3. Neil Alan Weiner and Marvin E. Wolfgang, "Violent Crime in America," in *American Violence and Public Policy,* edited by Lynn A. Curtis (New Haven: Yale University Press, 1985), pp. 33-34.

4. *Bureau of Justice Statistics National Update* (Washington, D.C.: Department of Justice), July 1992, p. 4.
5. *Sourcebook of Criminal Justice Statistics, 1991* (Washington, D.C.: Government Printing Office, 1992), p. 294.
6. *Bureau of Justice Statistics National Update, supra,* p. 7.
7. Weiner and Wolfgang, pp. 26-30
8. *USA Today,* October 4, 1988, p. 1.
9. *The Chronicle of Higher Education,* January 20, 1993, p. A32.
10. Ibid., February 17, 1993, p. A25.
11. "Campus Violence Survey" (unpublished compilation), Office of Student Services, Towson State University, 1987.
12. *Violence, Fear, and Guns at Florida State University* (unpublished report to the President's Committee on Student Safety and Welfare, Florida State University, January 7, 1987).
13. *Newsweek on Campus,* February, 1986, p. 10.
14. James Alan Fox and Daryl A. Hellman, "Location and Other Correlates of Campus Crime," 13 *Journal of Criminal Justice* 429 (1985).
15. William A. Formby and Robert T. Sigler, "Crime and Victim Characteristics on College Campuses: A Research Report," 7 *Victimology* 218 (1982).
16. Lee R. McPheters, "Econometric Analysis of Factors Influencing Crime on Campus," 6 *Journal of Criminal Justice* 47 (1978).
17. See article cited in n. 14.
18. *Baltimore Evening Sun,* January 6, 1987, p. 4.
19. James M. Makepeace, "Courtship Violence among College Students," 30 *Family Relations* 97 (1981).
20. Rosemarie B. Bogal-Allbritten and William L. Allbritten, "The Hidden Victims: Courtship Violence among College Students," 26 *Journal of College Student Personnel* 201 (1985).
21. John H. Schuh and William C. Shipton, "Abuses Encountered by Resident Assistants during an Academic Year," 24 *Journal of College Student Personnel* 428 (1983).
22. John H. Schuh and Douglas Oblander, "Abuses Students Experience after Filing Judicial Complaints," 25 *Journal of College Student Personnel* 343 (1984).

CHAPTER 3

The Concept of Crime and the Shape of Criminal Law

ut short and sweet, law exists as a means of social control. In more
judicial-sounding terms, it may be described as the body of principles,
standards, and rules defined by government to order the affairs of the
society. It consists, chiefly, of a collection of "thou shalt nots" that hedge in
human conduct.

The lawyers divide law into two major categories, civil law and criminal
law. Civil law, on the one hand, has to do with private rights and wrongs, in
which an individual citizen gains redress for wrong (torts or breaches of
contract) done him or her in private relationships; the usual remedy in a civil
matter is a private suit for money damages against the individual, group, or
corporation that did the wrong.

Criminal law, on the other hand, is a wrong against not just one person but
against all the people, the commonwealth of people, organized in their
government. Therefore it is the government that exacts the penalty against
the wrongdoer; the usual penalty for a crime is a fine or imprisonment. Much
egregious conduct is, at the same time, both a crime and a civil wrong, which
can subject the wrongdoer potentially to both criminal prosecution and civil
liability.

Criminal law "is at once by far the most powerful and by far the roughest
engine which society can use for any purpose," the renowned English jurist
James Fitzjames Stephen declared.[1] Not only are the criminal courts able to
take away a person's property and liberty, but criminal justice is the one
instance in which the government may lawfully use deadly violence against a
citizen. Law enforcement officers regularly use force—even lethal force when

appropriate—and one's life is at risk on a capital charge in many states now. The indignities and opprobrium that accompany even the mildest applications of the criminal law far exceed most other kinds of social sanctions. Anyone who has been arrested for just a traffic violation can testify to that.

WHAT IS THIS THING CALLED CRIME?

What, then, is crime—crime that modern, civilized society reverts to the basest and broadest powers to act against? The answer is that no one knows, at least not in terms of behavioral science. There simply is no developed critical understanding of crime or criminal violence. Even criminologists generally agree that there is no clear-cut, compelling definition of crime.[2] Probably the best answer is that crime is whatever the legislatures and the courts say it is.

Explanations for the genesis of criminal conduct fall into three general categories. The first is an economic theory, based upon a balance between need and price. Here, criminals are seen as rational actors who respond to a need in themselves which can be met by the acquisition of property or even the infliction of pain upon those whom they perceive as their enemies. They find crime an acceptable or even attractive rational choice, so long as the price they have to pay is not too high. As the likelihood of detection, prosecution, and punishment increases, this group, it is believed, is deterred. With such a concept, deterrent-oriented punishment makes sense.

A second category is the "Bad Person." This group includes theories that some people have a genetic disposition to antisocial conduct or are passing through a violent stage that is the result of adverse events or environmental influences. With this group, punishment is desirable because it incapacitates the Bad Person. As long as the person is in jail, he or she can do no harm.

The third category is the "Poor Choice." The criminal here is seen as the average citizen who simply made poor choices, possibly because of inadequate knowledge of alternatives. Rehabilitation is the prime goal of punishment for this group.

Apart from the classification schema devised by the lawyers, which will be discussed later, a workable though imprecise understanding of crime and the criminal justice processes may be drawn from the work of the social and behavioral sciencists, and the philosophers. Their thought can be seen as representations of, or variations upon, the theories of etiology of criminal behavior just discussed.

The sociologist Émile Durkheim felt that while crime is a manifestation of social morbidity, it must be counted among the "phenomena of normal sociology" because there never has been a society without it. Further, he said, the concept of crime is "necessary" and "useful" in that it provides a testing ground for moral ideas that may lead to social improvements.[3] Durkheim said society actually punishes criminals not for deterrence or rehabilitation, but because humans need a vicarious expiation for the sin of having contained the individual wrongdoer within the community. When crime goes unpunished—or punished too lightly—society feels "illness" within itself.[4] Thus, retribution may be seen to have legitimate and honorable social utility.

Richard Neely, a justice of the West Virginia Supreme Court who has been a lively interpreter and critic of American judicature, acknowledged the positivistic nature of crime and criminal law when he wrote that the criminal law system "to a very large extent consists of the members of one social class putting members of another social class in jail." He did not mean that one social class sets out to exploit the other, but only that it is mostly "poor, uneducated or stupid" people who are prosecuted for criminal activity.[5] To that extent, then, crime is a measure of the struggle between competing classes.

Vested Interests and Criminal Law

Radical criminologists, of course, long have argued that the definition of criminal offenses is a function of the economic needs of the dominant social class at any point in history. Certainly history—including much American history—is replete with examples of criminal laws being enacted and used to impose social policy upon, or preclude social change by, less powerful classes and groups. Obvious American examples include the "Jim Crow" segregation laws, the treatment of early labor movements as criminal conspiracies, and various criminal statutes drawn to enhance debt collection practices or assure the monopolies of certain business interests. The noncriminal treatment of some harmful conduct by vested interests (for instance, air and water pollution) and the lenient treatment of "white collar" crime and criminals represent the other side of that coin. The obvious problem with this sort of overall view of the criminal justice system, however, is that most actions labeled as criminal are things that are harmful to all members of society; today in America, most victims of violent crime are poor people themselves, and blacks suffer the highest victimization rates.[6] Rich and poor, establishment and nonestablishment alike enjoy the blessings of an ordered, safe society when the criminal justice system is healthy.

Few would disagree with former Attorney General Ramsey Clark's observation that crime "reflects the character of a people." Moreover, "all those qualities in life that make us what we are determine our capacity to commit crime. Heredity and environment, the interaction of individual and society, the totality of human nature and human experience—these are the elemental origins of crime."[7]

Depending upon one's basic philosophical underpinnings, however, one might disagree with Clark's suggestion that poverty is the "mother" of crime, and that the basic solution for most crime is economic—"homes, health, education, employment, beauty."[8]

Some disturbing observations on crime come from the psychiatrist Karl Menninger, who says that we are all guilty of it:

> Crime is everybody's temptation. It is easy to look with proud disdain upon "those people" who get caught—the stupid ones, the unlucky ones, the blatant ones. But who does not get nervous when a police car follows closely? We squirm over our income tax statements and make some "adjustments." We tell the customs officials that we have nothing to declare—well, practically nothing. Some of us who have never been convicted of any crime picked up over two billion dollars' worth of merchandise last year from the stores we patronize. Over a billion dollars was embezzled by employees last year. One hotel in New York lost over seventy-five thousand finger bowls, demitasse spoons, and other objects in its first ten months of operation. The Claims Bureau of the American Insurance Association estimates that seventy-five percent of all claims are dishonest in some respect and the amount of overpayment more than $350,000,000 a year![9]

Depravity and Culpability

Sympathy for such views as those of Clark, and even Menninger, seem to be on the wane today. Much more popular in contemporary America is what criminologist Samuel Walker has called the "conservative theology" of crime, which reflects both the economic and the Bad Person theories of misbehavior. It holds that criminals lack self-control; their passions get the best of them, and they break the rules. Poverty is no excuse. "If they are poor it is only because they refuse to exercise enough self-discipline to get an education and a job."[10]

Some see the etiology of serious crime as far more diabolic. Political scientist James Q. Wilson has declared that "wicked people exist. Nothing avails except to set them apart from innocent people."[11] He and Harvard psychologist Richard J. Herrnstein recently published a study reinvigorating older ideas that much criminal behavior originates in genetic factors, rather than being a product of environment, as has been widely advanced by the deterministic psychology of recent decades.[12]

CRIMINALS: WHAT DO WE DO WITH THEM?

The philosophers have spent more time deciding what to do about the criminal than trying to define crime in philosophical terms. Georg Hegel, on the one hand, felt that punishment was the appropriate response to crime because the criminal was thus "honoured as a rational being" who was responsible for his own acts; he saw deterrence and reformation as inhuman.[13]

Jeremy Bentham, on the other hand, felt punishment was never appropriate unless it prevented some greater evil. In his principle of utility, he would preclude punishment for crime unless it could prevent further mischief because "all punishment in itself is evil."[14]

Modern penology has, of course, often pretended that reformation of the criminal was its goal, but meager fiscal support (resulting from negligible public sympathy) has resulted in rehabilitation receiving little more than lip service in many jurisdictions. And, too, evaluation of convict reformation programs has not given much cause for optimism.

Probably the most significant appraisal of prison rehabilitation programs was the massive study reported by Robert Martinson in *The Public Interest* in 1974.[15] The Martinson group examined all data published in the English language about such programs from the years 1945 through 1967. Many of the studies they found had to be discarded because of methodological weaknesses; in the end, 231 studies involving hundreds of thousands of inmates were analyzed.

The conclusion was that "very little empirical evidence" could be found to substantiate the notion that a correctional facility offering a truly rehabilitative program—one that prepares inmates for life on the outside through education and vocational training—would turn out more successful individuals than a facility that merely warehoused them. With adults, no significant difference in recidivism rates could be substantiated; with juveniles, the only significant improvement occurred with the top 7 percent of the participating population—those who had high IQs, had made good records in previous schooling, and had made good academic progress in the institution. Similarly disappointing conclusions were reached about the efficacy of individual psychotherapy and even group counseling.

The conclusion was that available data "give us very little reason to hope that we have in fact found a sure way of reducing recidivism through rehabilitation." The Martinson report suggested that several conclusions could be drawn from its findings:

From this probability, one may draw any of several conclusions. It may be simply that our programs aren't yet good enough—that the education we provide to inmates is still poor education, that the therapy we administer is not administered skillfully enough, that our intensive supervision and counseling do not yet provide enough personal support for the offenders who are subjected to them. If one wishes to believe this, then what our correctional system needs is simply a more full-hearted commitment to the strategy of treatment.

It may be, on the other hand, that there is a more radical flaw in our present strategies—that education at its best, or that psychotherapy at its best, cannot overcome, or even appreciably reduce, the powerful tendency for offenders to continue in criminal behavior. Our present treatment programs are based on a theory of crime as a "disease"—that is to say, as something foreign and abnormal in the individual which can presumably be cured. This theory may well be flawed, in that it over-looks—indeed, denies—both the normality of crime in society and the personal normality of a very large proportion of offenders, criminals who are merely responding to the facts and conditions of our society.[16]

Of especial interest to educators is the biting criticism the Martinson study made of the state of criminal justice research. Much of the work had been done by academics, and millions of dollars had been spent upon it, yet the criminal justice community had failed to develop a usable process of assess-ment.

We tried to exclude from our survey those studies which were so poorly done that they simply could not be interpreted. But despite our efforts, a pattern has run through much of this discussion—of studies which "found" effects without making any truly rigorous attempt to exclude competing hypotheses, of extraneous factors permitted to intrude upon the measure-ments, of recidivism measures which are not all measuring the same thing, of "follow-up" periods which vary enormously and rarely extend beyond the period of legal supervision, of experiments never replicated, of "system effects" not taken into account, of categories drawn up without any theory to guide the enterprise. It is just possible that some of our treatment programs *are* working to some extent, but that our research is so bad that it is incapable of telling.[17]

The National Academy of Sciences reviewed the Martinson study and validated its conclusions. Subsequent studies by others have reached conclu-sions not much different from those of Martinson, and current research is being directed toward those specific rehabilitation programs that did show at least some promise—after all, Martinson did find some positive results, even if very small, in 48 percent of the programs he analyzed. Samuel Walker has recently concluded that the probation system is probably the best rehabilita-tive tool that we now have.[18]

CRIMINAL LAW AND PUBLIC POLICY

Some years ago Professor Francis Wharton gave us a traditional definition of crime for legal purposes: A crime is "the commission or omission by a person having capacity, of any act which is either prohibited or compelled by law, and the commission or omission of which is punishable by a proceeding brought in the name of the government whose law has been violated."[19] This definition reveals that crime is not a moral concept, but a utilitarian one.

A fundamental legal maxim declares *nullum crimen sine lege*—literally, there is no crime unless a law prohibits the act, whatever it is. For this reason, a criminal law cannot be vague or ambiguous. Citizens are entitled to know just what conduct is proscribed, and the courts cannot apply a law when persons of common intelligence would have to guess at its meaning. The "suspicious person ordinance" that used to be on the books of Euclid, Ohio, provides an example. It made a misdemeanant of "any person who wanders about the streets or other public ways or who is found abroad at late or unusual hours in the night without any visible or lawful business and who does not give satisfactory account of himself." One night in 1969, a Euclid policeman saw a man and a woman in a parked car. The woman got out, and went into a nearby apartment building. When approached by the officer, the man could—or would—not identify the woman, and gave several addresses for himself. He was convicted under the ordinance and sentenced to 30 days in jail. The United States Supreme Court vacated the conviction in a unanimous opinion, holding that the man could not have known his conduct was proscribed by the broad and vague wording of the ordinance.[20]

In like manner, a criminal law cannot be "overbroad," that is, it cannot go further than it needs to, and thereby stifle individual liberties, even if its basic purpose is legitimate. The city of Opelousas, Louisiana, adopted a juvenile curfew ordinance that barred youngsters under 17 from being on the public streets or in a public place between 11:00 P.M. and 4:00 A.M. on weekdays and between 1:00 A.M. and 4:00 A.M. on Fridays and Saturdays. The only exceptions arose when a minor was accompanied by a parent or other "responsible adult" or was upon an "emergency errand."

The Fifth United States Circuit Court of Appeals held that the citywide ordinance was simply too broad to withstand constitutional scrutiny. The court observed that minors are "persons" under the United States Constitution and have fundamental rights of liberty, speech, association, and travel that were impinged upon by the ordinance. The opinion noted that under the ordinance minors were prohibited from attending religious or school meetings, organized dances, theater, and sporting events, when travel to and from them would have to be made during the curfew period, and that it even prevented minors from being on the sidewalk in front of their homes, engaging in legitimate employment, or traveling through Opelousas on an interstate trip. Further, the court said, the ordinance inhibited the parental role in child rearing because it intruded upon the decision-making powers of parents in regard to such activities. In striking down the criminal ordinance, the court observed that it was not expressing any opinion on the validity of curfew ordinances "narrowly drawn to accomplish proper social objectives."[21]

The Guilty Mind

At the heart of criminal culpability lies the element of intent. The lawyers call it the *mens rea*—the guilty mind—of the wrongdoer. To be guilty of a crime in all but a few rare sorts of cases, a person must have intended a criminal act in what he or she did—though not necessarily the specific act or result that occurred.

Because of the *mens rea* requirement, children of tender years and insane persons are held incapable of crime. The modern law of insanity in crime has grown from the famous *M'Naghton's Case*.[22] Daniel M'Naghton suffered delusions that he was being persecuted by Sir Robert Peel, the British prime minister who modernized Scotland Yard and for whom the bobbies are named. In 1843 M'Naghton shot and killed Peel's secretary, believing him to be Peel. He was acquitted on grounds of insanity, and the resulting public uproar led to the pronouncement by the British judiciary of M'Naghton's Rules, an exposition on the insanity defense for future use. The doctrine announced by Lord Chief Justice Tindal proclaimed that the defense of insanity would be established if the jury believed that the accused "was laboring under such a defect of reason, from disease of mind, as not to know the nature and quality of the act he was doing, or if he did know it, that he did not know he was doing what was wrong." The M'Naghton test, then, involves cognitive function—the ability to know what you are doing, or the rightness from the wrongness of your act.

Some American jurisdictions have liberalized the rules to cover situations in which the unlawful act simply was the "product of mental disease or mental defect."[23] Others have added a volitional element, under which persons could be found insane even if, cognitively, they knew what they were doing and knew it to be wrong, but were unable to conform their actions to the requirements of the law—in other words, they were overwhelmed by an irresistible impulse.[24] Because of concern that some dangerous persons who have been found not guilty by reason of insanity are being put back on the streets, some states have adopted a new jury option of "guilty but insane." Under this verdict, the accused must serve the entire term for the crime, either in a prison or a mental hospital, as psychiatric opinion dictates.

Taxonomies of Crime

Legal scholars have broken crimes into two categories, those that are *mala in se*, that is, inherently wrong and against "natural law" (murder, rape, armed robbery, arson, assault), and those that are *mala prohibita*, wrong only because they are declared wrong by statute or ordinance (parking violations, public intoxication, tax evasion, exceeding hunting and fishing bag limits and seasons). Those that are *mala in se* usually are considered more serious and worthy of harsher punishment. But even this distinction has been criticized as culturally subjective. Wharton, for instance, has called the distinction "manifestly nonscientific," recognizing that there simply is no societal uniformity as to what is inherently wrong under the laws of nature.[25]

The most common taxonomy of crimes is by penalty. The determinant factors are the length of the term that may be imposed or the institution in which the offender may be incarcerated. Typically, a felony is punishable by one year or more in a penitentiary, and a misdemeanor is punishable by up to one year in jail. Some states, and the federal system, add a third category of petty offenses or infractions, which carry a small fine and the possibility of little or no incarceration. So-called capital offenses, in most jurisdictions, now are those which are punishable by death or life imprisonment.

Ramsey Clark has given us a useful taxonomy of crime centered upon the opportunity open to the criminal. He identifies seven basic categories: white collar crime, organized crime, crime in the streets, crimes of passion, violations of public health and safety regulations, revolutionary crime designed to alter political or economic order, and corruption in public office. "Persons capable of crime act within the range of their opportunity, their conduct shaped by their situation. Bankers rarely rob banks. There are easier, safer, more successful ways of obtaining money. The poor do not fix prices."[26]

Persons versus Property

A fundamental social principle honored by American law is that persons are more important than property. For this reason, the law has never countenanced killing simply in defense of property. A person is justified in using lethal force only in defense of self or others—including defense of a habitation—but can use only limited, reasonable physical force to protect other property or prevent its theft. Just before noon one day, two men from a finance company went to repossess a Chevrolet sedan because the woman who purchased it was two months in arrears on her payments. Knocking at the door and ringing the bell at the woman's apartment produced no result, and so the men went down to the car and raised the hood to check serial numbers. At that point, the woman leaned out of an upper window and began firing a 22-caliber rifle. A shot hit one man's leg, shattering the femur. The woman told police she had been asleep and had not heard the bell, and thought the men were trying to steal the vehicle. Her conviction for aggravated assault and battery was affirmed.[27]

Similarly, a man who planted a trap gun was convicted of assault with a deadly weapon after the gun injured a youngster.[28] Because of a past burglary, the man had placed a 22-caliber revolver in his garage, aimed and wired so that it would discharge in the direction of the garage door if it was opened. Two youngsters, apparently with theft in mind, jimmied the lock and entered the garage, and one was shot in the face by the trap. The California Supreme Court obviously was appalled by such "silent instrumentalities of death" and noted the risk of traps to innocent parties such as children, firemen, and policemen who might come on the premises.

A similar principle has been applied to the use of lethal force by law enforcement officers. In *Tennessee v. Garner*,[29] the United States Supreme Court declared unconstitutional a Tennessee statute that had given police authority to use deadly force against a crime suspect who flees or forcibly resists. In this case, a policeman had shot and killed an unarmed teenage burglary suspect as he fled over a fence in the backyard of a home he was suspected of burglarizing one night. The Court said that deadly force is justified only if an officer has probable cause to believe the suspect poses a significant threat of death or great bodily harm to the officer or others.

MODERN AMERICAN CRIMINAL CODES

We have seen that crime is difficult to define, but that criminal law can be a potent force for social control. How, then, does a particular act become a crime? What forces shape this instrument of social manipulation? A "common law of crimes" was inherited from England, but little of it remains intact today except as a skeleton around which our body of statutory crimes has been built. In America today, it is the legislative bodies that define which acts are to constitute criminal offenses and set the penalties for offenders. Because these popularly elected bodies are close to the people, the criminal codes are readily influenced by public opinion.

Crime in America is now chiefly defined in criminal codes, that is, codified definitions of crimes and their assigned punishments, which are enacted by legislative bodies. The federal Congress promulgates federal law, the state legislatures promulgate the state criminal offenses, and the city councils promulgate the ordinances that deal with minor local infractions such as traffic and parking, regulation of some business activity, and lesser health, safety, and public peace provisions.

Aside from traffic matters, by far the greatest number of criminal proceedings involve violation of state criminal laws. Most of the common crimes against people, property, and public morality are state offenses. Let us look at each of these three categories of crime in turn for the purpose of clarifying definitions and concepts that will be needed further on in this study.

Homicide

Because of the worth that our society ascribes to human life, homicide—the unlawful killing of a human being—is considered the most serious of state crimes. Homicide is commonly broken down into three categories, murder, manslaughter, and negligent homicide, depending upon the criminal intent of the perpetrator.

Murder is homicide committed with criminal malice, which is an intent to kill or injure, express or implied, although not necessarily with any hatred or ill will toward the particular victim. In most states, first degree murder occurs when the criminal premeditated the killing, that is, plotted, contrived, or determined to do it ahead of time, if even just in the few seconds before committing the fatal act.

Many states also recognize the "felony-murder doctrine," under which a person may be found guilty of first degree murder if a death resulted while the person was engaged in some other dangerous felony—typically arson, rape, burglary, or armed robbery—even though the person had no intention of killing anyone. This doctrine has had some paradoxical applications. Two would-be robbers walked into a California liquor store. One pulled a revolver while his accomplice made threats to the proprietor and demanded money. The proprietor's wife was standing nearby on a ladder, tending stock. She saw what was happening, whipped out her own gun, and fatally shot the robber who was holding the revolver. The surviving robber was convicted of his partner's murder under the felony-murder doctrine.[30] Likewise, where gunmen held up a business office at gunpoint, and the business owner died of a heart attack more than fifteen minutes after the robbers had departed, the robbers were convicted of the man's murder.[31]

Second degree murder exists where the attacker had malice—that is, an intent to kill or injure, express or implied—but did not premeditate the slaying, nor did the felony-murder rule apply. Manslaughter is the unlawful killing of another person, but without malicious intent to kill. Commonly, manslaughter includes homicides occurring in the course of other criminal acts that are not encompassed in the felony-murder rule, or through gross negligence, where a death results because a person acted carelessly under circumstances where an ordinarily prudent person would have foreseen that the act would include a high degree of risk of death or great bodily harm to others.

When one person kills another in the "heat of passion"—because of sufficient and sudden provocation such as a body blow or the discovery of one's spouse in the act of adultery—the law in some states reduces the homicide from murder to manslaughter. The theory behind the doctrine is that when a person is unexpectedly provoked to uncontrollable rage or passion, the person cannot be said to have formulated the criminal malice necessary to constitute murder. A father was informed that his adolescent daughter had been ravished by the man who was married to his older daughter. Upon confronting the errant son-in-law, the father was cursed by the young man. In an ensuing rage, the father slew him. The Missouri Supreme Court held that the offense could not be more than a low degree of manslaughter.[32] However, the doctrine of "heat of passion" is not applicable where a person, once provoked, has had time to "cool."

The lowest degree of homicide is negligent homicide, which is part of the motor vehicle code in many states. Aimed primarily at drunk and reckless drivers, such statutes typically include reckless operation of a motor vehicle evincing a wanton disregard for the safety of others.

First degree murder usually is punishable by the death penalty or life imprisonment, and second degree murder by from five to twenty years in the penitentiary. Manslaughter typically may draw from one to fifteen years of imprisonment, and negligent homicide from six months to one year.

Other Offenses against Persons

Other types of offenses against human victims include false imprisonment, which is the detention of a person against his or her will, and kidnapping, which at common law was a false imprisonment plus the element of "asportation"—the moving of the detained person from one place to another. Some modern kidnapping statutes have eliminated the asportation element, if the victim is held for some other illegal purpose, such as to extort ransom, or as a hostage.

Assault and battery are both criminal and civil offenses, and a perpetrator can be simultaneously prosecuted in criminal court and sued for money damages in a private civil lawsuit growing out of the same attack. A battery is the slightest unauthorized touching of another human being, and an assault, in criminal law, is an attempted battery while the attacker has present ability to effect the battery. In civil cases, an assault is putting someone in fear of receiving a battery. Simple assaults and batteries—made with fists—usually are misdemeanors, but aggravated or malicious assaults and batteries—performed with a weapon—are serious felonies. In some states, such batteries come under "malicious-wounding" felony statutes.

Crime Involving Property

Let us turn next to a consideration of crimes against property. Offenses against a habitation are deemed more serious than offenses against other kinds of property, because of the concomitant threat to human life. At common law, burglary was the breaking and entering of a dwelling house at night with an intent to commit a felony inside. Other lesser criminal offenses covered entries of and thefts from buildings less than a dwelling. The modern criminal codes continue to treat break-ins of homes as the most serious offenses involving property, and provide lesser burglary and "breaking and entering" statutes for other sorts of buildings, structures, and vehicles.

Other offenses against property include arson, which is the malicious burning or exploding of another's property, or one's own property if it is insured, with the intent of destroying it; trespass, which is an entry upon or remaining upon (such as remaining in a store after closing time by hiding) the property of another when the person knows that he or she is not licensed or privileged to do so; and criminal mischief, which is the malicious damaging of another's property.

Larceny is the taking and carrying away of the property of another with intent to deprive the owner of it. Embezzlement is like larceny, but under circumstances where the embezzler originally came into possession of the property lawfully. Thus, clerks or accountants who steal their employer's funds that have been entrusted to them cannot commit the crime of larceny, because they do not "take" the property. However, when they convert the funds to their own use, the conversion alone will constitute embezzlement. When one acquires title to something by trick or fraud, another hybrid of larceny is involved. In most states it is called either false pretenses or larceny by trick. Grand larceny is the theft of property over a certain dollar threshold that the legislature has established—usually from one to five hundred dollars—and it is a felony. Petit larceny, a misdemeanor, involves theft of a lesser value.

Robbery is the taking of another's possessions, from his or her person or immediate presence, against the victim's will, through force or fear of force. The robber must have a felonious intent in the taking and intend to deprive the owner permanently of the property. Because of the danger that robbery presents to persons, it is deemed a serious crime. If committed with a deadly weapon, it usually carries an extremely heavy penalty.

Forgery is the making of a false writing. It must be done with intent to defraud or injure another, and it may be accomplished by altering another's document, or making a complete counterfeit, purporting it to be something it is not. The uttering of a forged instrument is a separate crime. Uttering is the offering to another as genuine a writing known to be false. The offer itself completes the crime; it is immaterial whether the intended offeree accepts or rejects it.

Extortion and Misconduct by Public Officers

Extortion, commonly called blackmail, is the exaction of money or some other thing of value from a person through threats. It differs from robbery in that it is not "strong arm." The thing extorted need not be cash; such things as sexual favors can constitute the offense. Public administrators must be cautious that they do not use the powers of their office to encourage someone to give something of value to them or to someone else, as this might be construed as extortion. Likewise, the threat of bringing criminal charges should not be used as a club to get someone to do something. Plea bargaining, wherein a promise is made that criminal charges will not be pursued if the accused will make "restitution" to a victim, gets dangerously close to extortion. American law precludes imprisonment for debt, and use of criminal processes for private debt collection purposes is a misuse of the criminal courts and can result in a suit for malicious prosecution (see the discussion of extortion in chapter 14).

Not only is extortion a state crime, but in the Hobbs Act, Congress has made it a broad federal offense as well, outlawing the selling of any function of a public office for private gain.[33] The Hobbs Act is based on the theory that most extortion constitutes an interference with interstate commerce, and is thus an appropriate area for federal prosecution. Congress, in passing the act, recognized that corruption by local and state public officials can be a problem that local police and prosecutors may not be able—or willing—to tackle. The Federal Bureau of Investigation and Department of Justice prosecutors now devote much time and attention to catching local politicians and public employees for Hobbs Act violations such as kickback schemes and "payola."

The Hobbs Act makes it a federal felony to obstruct, delay, or simply affect commerce by extortion, which it defines as the "obtaining of property from another, with his consent, induced by wrongful use of actual or threatened force, violence, or fear, or under color of official right." The effect on commerce need be only minimal for federal jurisdiction to exist; in fact, the government has only to show that the wrongful conduct had the probability of affecting commerce in some diminutive way. The "under color of official right" portion of the act brings within its scope many inappropriate exercises of power by public employees.

The Hobbs Act clearly applies to traditional forms of extortion, such as the prosecution of the Chicago police district commander who supervised the collection and distribution among vice squad members of "protection" money paid by nightclub and bar owners.[34] The act covers less overt misuses of public office as well, such as the school board member who took airline tickets and cash from a contractor who did business with the board,[35] and the Louisiana state commissioner of agriculture who was accused of using his influence for the issuance of state auction and pest control licenses as well as for the lowering of the price of milk in the state on behalf of persons who contributed to his political campaign.[36]

One such federal extortion case has involved a college. The director of facilities at West Chester State College in Pennsylvania was convicted of demanding $2,000 in cash from a contractor in turn for the award of a bid to pave a college parking lot. The court held that the administrator's actions fell under the "color of official right" provision in the Hobbs Act because the man was a state employee and was administering public programs.[37]

Sexual and Public Morality Offenses

Rape is the carnal knowledge of a woman against her will. Females under a certain age are held incapable of consent, so a voluntary sex act with such a girl, even at a her instigation, will be called "statutory rape." The age of consent varies, but typically it is 14, 15, or 16. Many states have modernized their rape laws, placing them within comprehensive sexual assault and sexual battery schemes that outlaw other kinds of overt sexual molestation as well as forced coitus. A rape victim need not physically resist her attacker; if she submits through fear it is still a forcible rape.

Sodomy statutes in many states still prohibit anal and oral sex. However, several Supreme Court decisions in the area of marital privacy have indicated that such laws would not be enforced as to married persons.[38] The Supreme Court has not been willing to extend that protection to homosexual relations, and the Court upheld the right of a state to outlaw homosexual conduct if it chooses.[39] New York's highest court, however, has extended the privacy right to homosexual sex, and has held unconstitutional the New York statute prohibiting consensual sodomy by adults.[40]

Federal Crimes

By contrast with state courts, American federal courts have narrow and specific criminal jurisdiction, generally dealing only with offenses against the federal government or crimes that involve interstate activity. Thus, it is a federal offense to transport a kidnap victim, a stolen car, or a prostitute across a state line, or even to be a garden-variety local criminal who crosses a state line to escape prosecution. It is a federal crime to rob a bank, because banks are federally insured, or to steal federal food stamps, Social Security checks, or other federal property. It is a federal offense to use the mails to defraud or extort. And, of course, it is a federal crime to evade the payment of federal taxes. Recently, federal prosecutors have been devoting considerable time and energy to the prosecution of state and local officials for "public corruption"—the use of their public offices for personal or political gain, which is held to be an interference with interstate commerce.

Most jurisdictions have hundreds of specialized criminal statutes designed to regulate conduct in all sorts of specific fields of activity. Most of them—at least those that deal with offenses considered *mala in se*—are variations upon the general crimes described in preceding paragraphs. However, other minor regulatory laws may not fit the general mold. Some very minor offenses may even be so-called no-fault offenses that do not require any criminal intent, not even carelessness. Such criminal statutes are rare; they probably should not exist at all as criminal offenses, but if they are needed for regulatory purposes the legislatures should recast them as civil regulations with civil penalties. In any event, some do exist as crimes. The Pennsylvania Supreme Court has dealt wisely with such strict liability infractions; it has held that a "no-fault" crime cannot be the basis for depriving anyone of liberty, and the penalty for violation of such a law cannot be more than a fine.[41]

Education-Specific Offenses

There are few specific state criminal statutes that deal with higher education. Some jurisdictions have provisions outlawing the disruption of classes or other campus activities, and others commonly deal with traffic offenses and health and safety matters, such as prohibitions on smoking in buildings and possession of alcoholic beverages. Some municipalities around college campuses may have local ordinances that were designed with students in mind, such as prohibitions against drinking on public streets, but they cannot constitutionally enforce criminal ordinances singling out students for limitations that do not apply to all other citizens as well.

THE ENFORCEMENT DECISION

Once the laws are on the books, the duty of enforcing them falls first to the executive branch, in the form of the police and the prosecutors. Both have considerable discretion as to enforcement, and the exercise of this discretion often is affected by public opinion. So-called police discretion is the ability of the police officer to "look the other way"; to decline to file a charge, or to bring it for a lesser offense. It is unwritten and has no sanction in law whatsoever, but it is used thousands of times each day across our land. At the bottom line, the only real check on police discretion is for the police and the public to share common values.

Unlike police discretion, formal legal countenance is given to what is termed prosecutorial discretion, under which a prosecuting attorney may refrain from pursuing a case when he or she, in good faith and without corrupt motives, thinks that a prosecution would not serve the best interests of the state, or that the case could not be won at trial.[42]

Prosecutorial discretion is far from absolute, however. In some instances a judge may override the prosecutor's decision. Further, a prosecutor cannot arbitrarily superimpose his or her will in substitution for that of the legislature as to what conduct will be deemed criminal in the society, and for that reason a prosecutor cannot simply ignore a type or class of criminal activity.[43]

One more word is needed about the exercise of discretion in prosecuting crime. Any peace officer, public employee, or public official who ignores a criminal violation, or intentionally declines to report it to proper authorities, risks making himself or herself a criminal too. Such actions could make the person an accessory to the crime itself or could constitute the separate criminal offense of compounding a crime (discussed more thoroughly in chapter 14).

Once police officers or prosecutors decide to launch criminal proceedings, the matter goes either to a grand jury or a judge, who must find that there is probable cause both that the crime in question was committed and that the accused committed it.

Lastly, it falls to the judiciary to interpret and apply the laws once a prosecution is begun. The power to interpret is the power to rewrite. The activist courts of recent years have radically altered public policy in many areas, serving a notion like that expressed by Justice Richard Neely that the real function of the courts is to correct the flaws and fill the gaps in good public policy left by the actions (or inactions) of the legislative and executive branches.[44] It is to be remembered, though, that the judiciary—like the other branches of government—feels the need for public approbation, especially in the state courts where judges periodically face reelection.

PROCEDURE IN THE CRIMINAL COURTS

Criminal proceedings can begin either with the issuance of an arrest warrant by a judge, the filing of an information by a prosecutor, or with an indictment by a grand jury, depending upon the jurisdiction. Most begin through the warrant and information processes, usually after the police already have arrested a suspect. Charges originate with a grand jury only in complex, white-collar crimes where the grand jury has been sitting as an investigative body.

After the arrest, an accused is entitled to a prompt hearing for the setting of bail and an arraignment at which a plea is entered. After that, the procedure varies considerably depending upon whether the charge is a felony or a misdemeanor, and whether the jurisdiction is one in which there is a consti-tutional right to be indicted by a grand jury before being put on trial for a serious crime.

If the charge is a misdemeanor, it usually is set for trial following the arraignment. If it is a felony, and it did not originate through a grand jury indictment, a preliminary hearing customarily follows at which the prosecu-tion must convince a judge that there is probable cause to believe that the crime was committed and that the defendant committed it. If the judge finds that probable cause exists, the defendant is bound over for trial or to the next session of the grand jury, in those jurisdictions where a right to grand jury indictment exists. Grand jury indictment can be waived, and in some locali-ties it often is.

The preliminary hearing to determine probable cause is an important part of the procedure for the defense, because it provides a chance to look at the state's evidence. In most states and in federal courts the rules of evidence are relaxed at preliminary hearings; hearsay evidence may be received, and often only the investigating officer will testify. Defendants, on the other hand, usually hope to turn the preliminary hearing into a minitrial so that they may get a good look at the nature and extent of the prosecution's case.

If an accused felon is bound over to the grand jury, that body of citizens must decide, at its next sitting, whether to indict. The grand jury is an ancient protection for the citizen against the pervasive power of government and traces its "sifting" authority over government prosecutions all the way back to the Magna Carta. Like the preliminary hearings, rules of evidence are relaxed in grand juries; they may base their indictments upon hearsay and even evidence that was illegally obtained and that cannot be used at trial. Typically, the investigating officer is the state's only witness. Grand jury proceedings are secret, and an accused cannot be present while the government presents its case against him or her. In recent years, some white-collar defendants have elected to appear before a grand jury that they know is considering charges against them, motivated by the hope of justifying their actions and dissuading the grand jury from indicting them. Before appearing, however, defendants must waive their rights to immunity and against self-incrimination, as the law in some circumstances grants immunity from prosecution to people who have testified before the grand jury.

The Plea

Of course, a guilty plea may be entered at any stage of the proceedings, in which event the matter will proceed directly to sentencing. A defendant also may enter a plea of *nolo contendere*—meaning "no contest"—if the judge elects to accept it. Some jurisdictions limit *nolo contendere* pleas to misdemeanors. The effect of such a plea is that the defendant is treated in all respects as guilty in the case, and punishment is assigned accordingly, but the plea may not be used against the person as an admission of guilt in any other legal proceeding. This plea may be advantageous where a person is simultaneously facing criminal charges and a civil damage suit arising out of the same event, or where a defendant simply hopes to save a bit of face. Doubtlessly the world's most famous *nolo contendere* plea was the one entered by Vice President Agnew to public charges as a part of the plea bargain in which he also resigned his high office.

Discovery and Pretrial Motions

If an indicted felon pleads not guilty, the case then is set for trial at a future date. The next step is what the lawyers call "discovery," as each side tries to learn the other side's evidence and theory of the case. Generally today, the accused is entitled to discover the details of the government's case against him or her. Exceptions are the identity of some secret informants, and the prosecuting attorney's "work product" of legal research. In all events, the government is absolutely bound to reveal any evidence that might tend to exculpate the defendant. Chiefly because of the constitutional right against self-incrimination, the defendant is not required to reveal all of his or her case to the prosecution. The defense must, though, reveal the identity of the witnesses it will call at trial and give advance notice if it will claim either insanity or alibi—the factual argument that the defendant was somewhere else when the offense occurred, so that he or she could not have done it.

The last phase of the case before trial is the attempt by the defense to limit the evidence that can be used at the trial. If a confession was improperly taken, or evidence illegally seized, the defense will enter a Motion to Suppress Evidence. The judge will have to rule on the motion before the trial, so there will be no chance the jury will hear anything about it. Also, if either side suspects that irrelevant, prejudicial matters may be brought up at trial by the other side, a Motion *in Limine* may be made to obtain a pretrial disposition of the issue.

Pretrial Freedom

During the pretrial period, most defendants will be free on bail. An arrest warrant or indictment is merely an accusation, not a finding of guilt. Because a person is presumed innocent until proven guilty, a defendant is entitled to liberty on bail until the actual trial, except in a few limited circumstances where the crime was especially serious, proof of guilt is great, and there is reason to believe the defendant might flee or harm others if free. The sole purpose of bail is to ensure that the defendant returns for trial; bail is not for punishment. Accordingly, most state constitutions, as well as the federal Constitution, prohibit "excessive" bail. Bail, then, must be in an amount sufficient to ensure the defendant's return, but no more.

Often bail is provided by sureties. Family or friends may put up their homes, other property, or cash, as security from which the bail would be collected if the defendant did not appear. Or, a bail bond may be purchased from a professional bondsman, who, for a fee, posts a bond that will cover the bail forfeiture if the defendant does not return as required. Bail bondsmen sometimes have their own special ways of ensuring that their clients honor their bond requirements, some of them quite unsavory. Although the constitutional right to bail is lost once a defendant is convicted on trial, most jurisdictions also provide for release on bail pending an appeal—if the defendant is likely to return and does not pose a danger to the community.

Right to Counsel

The right to counsel is extremely important to anyone accused of crime, but the right is not absolute. At the present time, an accused has a federal constitutional right to counsel only if he or she is deprived of liberty as a result of the proceeding. Thus, in cases wherein a defendant is only fined—even though the charge carried the possibility of a jail term—the right does not attach.[45] Even in cases wherein a person faces confinement, and the right to counsel clearly attaches, questions remain as to *when* it attaches. Generally, it is said that an accused is entitled to counsel when proceedings reach a critical stage—where the defense will be prejudiced by the absence of counsel. If a defendant is entitled to counsel but cannot afford to hire a lawyer, the state must furnish counsel free of charge. This right to counsel applies to felony, misdemeanor, or juvenile proceedings,[46] but not to administrative disciplinary proceedings, because they offer no jeopardy to liberty; campus or institutional disciplinary tribunals have no power to send anyone to jail.

CRIME AND THE JUVENILE

Juveniles are treated specially by the criminal justice system, on the twin theories that they are deserving of more delicacy and more likely than adults to be turned from a criminal life by appropriate early intervention. It is true that only a small portion of college and university students are young enough to fall under juvenile jurisdiction; in most states, juvenile court jurisdiction ends when a youngster reaches 18, in others it ends at 17, and in a few at 16. But because some do fall under this jurisdiction, and because college students may occasionally be involved with younger persons, an overview of the juvenile justice system is appropriate here.

At old common law, a child under age seven could not be held responsible for criminal conduct because he or she was not capable, the law said, of formulating criminal intent. From age seven to 14, a child was presumed incapable of a criminal act, but that presumption could be rebutted by a showing that the child understood the wrongfulness of the act. If a court established that the child had such an understanding, then a child accused of crime could be tried and punished just the same as an adult. The history books record children as young as eight being hanged.

American Reforms

By the late nineteenth century, reformers were appalled that children were subjected to adult procedures and could be given long prison sentences in penitentiaries alongside hardened adult felons. They believed that society owed a special duty to its children to try to intervene and redirect them when they got into trouble, not to assure their doom. The inquiry, Judge Julian Mack wrote in 1909, should not be whether a child is "guilty" or "innocent," but rather, "what is he, how has he become what he is, and what had best be done in his interest and in the interest of the state to save him from a downward career."[47]

Accordingly, the reformers fashioned juvenile court procedures in which children who ran afoul of the law were to be treated not as criminals but as wards of the state, in need of special care and guidance. Beginning with Cook County, Illinois, in 1899, juvenile courts were established in every state. Today's juvenile courts reflect the reformers' ideals. The process is technically decriminalized: a youngster is not charged with a crime under a criminal warrant or indictment, but is the subject of a civil petition alleging a "delinquent act"; there is no trial, but an "adjudicatory hearing"; he or she is not convicted, but "adjudged delinquent"; there is no criminal record; and proceedings and records are confidential. In theory, a "disposition" of confinement is not for the purpose of punishment, but rehabilitation. And confinement must be only in a special juvenile detention facility—not an adult jail or penitentiary, most of which are extremely dangerous and are excellent postgraduate schools of criminal attitudes and conduct.

Reform of the Reform

To accomplish their lofty purposes, the juvenile courts were given almost unlimited powers to move in and take over a youngster's life until he or she reached majority. Because juvenile proceedings were not criminal, such niceties as a defense lawyer, the right to notices of charges, the right to confront and cross-examine witnesses, the right not to be a witness against oneself, and the right to take an appeal of an adverse adjudication were all deemed superfluous and were done away with.

This broad power inexorably led to abuses and unfairness. One commentator observed that the legendary powers of the Star Chamber were a "trifle" compared to an American juvenile court.

When a 15-year-old named Gerald Gault was meted six years of confinement in an Arizona reformatory for making an obscene telephone call—an offense for which an adult probably would have received, at most, a fine or a very short jail term—the United States Supreme Court intervened and ruled that the juvenile court system was denying American youngsters their constitutional right to due process of law.[48]

The Court's 1967 decision in *Gault*, followed by other similar decisions in state and federal courts, required that the states alter their juvenile codes so that juvenile offenders would receive most of the procedural safeguards guaranteed adult offenders, including the rights to counsel, to confront their accusers, to have full notice of charges, to secure appellate review, and to be able to invoke the Fifth Amendment privilege against self-incrimination. About the only constitutional safeguards that have not been extended to juveniles today are rights to indictment by a grand jury and trial before a jury of citizens (in most jurisdictions, a judge alone decides whether a youngster is delinquent).

As noted earlier, in most states today, the juvenile courts have jurisdiction over offenders who are under age 18, but some have jurisdiction under 17, and some 16. However, in most states, once the juvenile court has jurisdiction it continues to exercise it until the youngster reaches age 21, and a delinquent can be confined until that time.

Conduct Cognizable in Juvenile Court

What sorts of offenses invoke juvenile court jurisdiction? In most states, juvenile courts have exclusive jurisdiction over offenses that would be crimes if committed by adults, with the exceptions of murder and traffic offenses. Most jurisdictions handle traffic infractions in the regular traffic courts, and murder in the adult criminal courts regardless of the age of the accused. In most states, other serious—usually violent—crimes can result in a "waiver" of juvenile court jurisdiction, and the matter will be transferred to the adult criminal court. In addition to criminal-type matters, the juvenile courts also exercise jurisdiction over several types of nondelinquent cases. These include so-called status offenses—things like truancy and running away, which would not be crimes if done by an adult—and cases of neglected, abused, or ill children who need intervention and care provided by the state.

In general, a juvenile can be taken into custody the same as an adult, if the officer has probable cause to believe the juvenile is a delinquent. However, differences begin at that point. Many juvenile codes require that the police make a prompt and genuine attempt to notify the juvenile's parent(s) or guardian of the detention. In many states, a juvenile must be promptly released to parents and cannot be detained, unless the juvenile presents a clear danger to himself, herself, or others. In any event, a juvenile should never be incarcerated with adults. Failure of police to release a juvenile promptly to parents or juvenile authorities may possibly invalidate a subsequent confession given to police.[49]

While in custody, the juvenile has rights like an adult with respect to interrogation. Questioning should be conducted only after the youngster is given full Miranda warnings. Many police administrators, prosecutors, and juvenile court judges feel that it is best not to question a juvenile unless a parent or guardian is present. Any confession obtained without this safeguard might be considered invalid on the grounds that the juvenile did not understand his or her rights, or was frightened or intimidated.[50]

Searching Juveniles

Searches of juveniles and their properties and habitations also differ somewhat from adults. In general, a juvenile is entitled to all the rights accruing to any other citizen under the Fourth Amendment's prohibition against unreasonable searches and seizures, and sometimes the juvenile has even more protection than an adult. For instance, where a warrantless search is made on the grounds that it was consented to, some states require that the consent of a parent or guardian be obtained as well as that of the juvenile suspect.[51] In addition, the prosecution may have to show that a person purportedly giving consent to a police officer for a search actually knew that he or she had a right to refuse the officer's request.[52]

Juveniles, however, may have fewer protections than adults in some circumstances. Where public schools are concerned, educators have clearly been given a freer hand. In 1985, in the case of New Jersey v. T.L.O., the United States Supreme Court held that a vice-principal acted legally when he searched the purse of a 14-year-old junior high school student and found marijuana.[53] The circumstances that led up to the search began when a teacher caught the girl smoking in a lavatory, in violation of school policy. The teacher took her to the vice-principal, but the student denied smoking. The vice-principal then went through the purse; in addition to cigarettes, he found the marijuana and letters and notes that indicated she had been selling marijuana to other students. The evidence was turned over to the police.

The Supreme Court upheld the girl's delinquency adjudication, ruling that public school educators need not have full legal "probable cause" before making a search of students' property. The Court said such a search would be valid if it was "reasonable" and held that the vice-principal's actions were such. The Court said such reasonableness must be measured in two ways: the educator must have reasonable suspicion that a school rule or a law had been broken, and the search must be reasonable in scope—the search cannot be too broad or intrusive, and it must be related to the objectives of the search, in light of the age and sex of the student and the nature of the infraction. While far from giving educators carte blanche, the decision does give approbation to reasonable, justifiable disciplinary actions by school-teachers and administrators.

The decision was especially important because it settled the old question of whether school authorities are state "agents" for Fourth Amendment purposes. This point is significant because the Fourth Amendment is a limitation only on governmental action, and private citizens can make searches and seizures that violate Fourth Amendment standards and the evidence obtained still can be used in criminal courts. Had the Court held that school authorities were not state "agents," they would have had an almost unlimited power to search students.

The Court did specifically hold, however, that the Fourth Amendment is applicable to public schools and that public educators are state agents. The "reasonable" search holding derived from the T.L.O. case probably has no direct applicability to colleges and universities, because they have very different atmospheres from public schools and are dealing primarily with adults or near-adults whose presence in a schoolhouse is not compelled by the compulsory attendance laws. However, the holding that educators are state agents does have meaning for public higher education. For years, some question has existed as to the state "agent" status of student personnel administrators, dormitory resident assistants, and the like. Under *T.L.O.*, it seems highly likely that they will be deemed state agents and, thus, bound by Fourth Amendment limitations when they act in any sort of rule, regulation, or law enforcement capacity in their jobs at a tax-supported institution.

College and university administrators and security personnel should be aware of the age at which juvenile laws cease to apply to offenders and offenses in their state. Juveniles are entitled, for good reason, to be treated differently from adults when accused of wrongdoing, and an error in this regard could lead to injury to the juvenile, embarrassment for the institution, and the possibility of a civil damage suit.

AN AFTERWORD ON CRIMINAL LAW AND POLICY

We have seen that criminal law is positivistic; it is molded by people to meet society's needs for order and stability. College and university leaders should never underestimate their ability to affect what the law is and to influence changes in criminal law and procedure.

Where an anomaly or lacuna in substantive criminal law is detected or an obfuscation in procedure encountered, the situation probably can be remedied, so long as constitutional principles are not violated. State legislators can change the state code, and U.S. representatives and senators can alter federal laws. Likewise, city councils can amend local ordinance codes to give better protection to campus interests in many cases.

NOTES

1. James Fitzjames Stephen, *Liberty, Equality, Fraternity* (1873; reprint, Cambridge, Eng.: Cambridge University Press, 1967), p. 151.
2. John Kaplan and Jerome Skolnick, *Criminal Justice*, 3d ed. (Mineola, N.Y.: Foundation Press, 1982), p.1.
3. Robert Nisbet, *The Sociology of Émile Durkheim* (New York: Oxford University Press, 1974), pp. 215, 218.
4. Nisbet, pp. 222-24.
5. Richard Neely, *How Courts Govern America* (New Haven: Yale University Press, 1981), pp. 153-54.
6. Neil A. Weiner and Marvin E. Wolfgang, "The Extent and Character of Violent Crime in America, 1969 to 1982," in *American Violence and Public Policy*, edited by Lynn Curtis (New Haven: Yale University Press, 1985), p. 29.
7. Ramsey Clark, *Crime in America* (New York: Simon and Schuster, 1970), p. 15.

8. Clark, p. 43.
9. *The Crime of Punishment* (New York: Viking, 1969), p. 6.
10. Samuel Walker, *Sense and Nonsense about Crime* (Monterey, Cal.: Brooks/Cole Publishing Co., 1985), p.8.
11. *Thinking about Crime* (New York: Basic Books, 1975), p. 209.
12. *Crime and Human Nature* (New York: Simon and Schuster, 1985).
13. *Philosophy of Right* (T. Knox translation) (Oxford: Clarendon Press, 1952), p. 71.
14. "An Introduction to the Principles of Morals and Legislation," excerpt included in *The Enlightenment* edited by Peter Gay (New York: Simon and Schuster, 1973), p. 171.
15. "What Works? Questions and Answers about Prison Reform," 32 *The Public Interest* (Spring, 1974) 22–51.
16. Ibid., p. 49.
17. Ibid., pp. 48-49.
18. Walker, pp. 175-79.
19. 1 *Wharton's Criminal Law and Procedure*, Sec. 10, (Rochester, N.Y.: Lawyers Co-operative Publishing Co., 1957), pp. 11–12.
20. *Palmer v. City of Euclid*, 402 U.S. 544, 91 S.Ct. 1563 (1971).
21. *Johnson v. Opelousas*, 658 F.2d 1065 (5th Cir. 1981).
22. *M'Naghton's Case*, 8 Eng. Rep. 718 (1843).
23. *Durham v. United States*, 214 F.2d 862 (D.C. Cir. 1954).
24. *Blake v. United States*, 407 F.2d 908 (5th Cir. 1969).
25. 1 *Wharton's Criminal Law and Procedure*, Sec. 26, p. 56.
26. Clark, pp. 35-36.
27. *Commonwealth v. Emmons*, 157 Pa.Super. 495, 43 A.2d 568 (1945).
28. *People v. Ceballos*, 12 Cal.3d 470, 116 Cal.Rptr. 233, 536 P.2d 241 (1974).
29. 471 U.S. 1, 105 S.Ct. 1694, 85 L.Ed.2d 1 (1985).
30. *Taylor v. Superior Court of Alameda County*, 3 Cal. 3d 578, 91 Cal.Rptr. 275, 477 P.2d 131 (1970).
31. *People v. Stamp*, 2 Cal.App.3d 203, 82 Cal.Rptr. 598 (1969).
32. *State v. Grugin*, 147 Mo. 39, 47 S.W. 1058 (1898).
33. 18 U.S.C. 1951.
34. *United States v. Baraasch*, 505 F.2d 139 (7th Cir. 1974).
35. *United States v. Williams*, 621 F.2d 123 (5th Cir. 1980).
36. *United States v. Dozier*, 672 F.2d 531 (5th Cir. 1980).
37. *United States v. Reilly*, 456 F.Supp. 211 (D.C.Pa. 1978).
38. *Griswold v. Connecticut*, 381 U.S. 479 (1965); *Stanley v. Georgia*, 394 U.S. 557 (1969); *Roe v. Wade*, 410 U.S. 113 (1973).
39. *Bowers v. Hardwick*, 478 U.S. 186, 106 S.Ct. 2841, 92 L.Ed.2d 140 (1986).
40. *People v. Onofore*, 51 N.Y.2d 476, 434 N.Y.S.2d 947, 415 N.E.2d 936 (1980).
41. *Commonwealth v. Kocswara*, 397 Pa. 575, 155 A.2d 825 (1959).
42. 63A *Am. Jur. 2d* Prosecuting Attorneys Sec. 24, pp. 311-12 (1984).
43. *State ex rel. Ginsberg v. Naum*, 318 S.E.2d 454, 156 (W. Va. 1984).
44. Neely, pp. 21-22.
45. *Scott v. Illinois*, 440 U.S. 367, 99 S.Ct. 1158 (1979).
46. *Gideon v. Wainwright*, 372 U.S. 335, 83 S.Ct. 792 (1963); *Argersinger v. Hamlin*, 407 U.S. 25, 92 S.Ct. 2006 (1972); *In re Gault*, 387 U.S. 1, 87 S.Ct. 1428 (1967).
47. Julian Mack, "The Juvenile Court," 23 *Harvard Law Review* 104, 119-20 (1909).
48. *In re Gault*, 387 U.S. 1, S.Ct. 1428 (1967).

49. *In the Interest of Schirner*, 264 Pa.Super. 185, 399 A.2d 728 (1979.) But see *Commonwealth v. Wallace*, 346 Mass. 9, 190 N.E.2d 224 (1963) and *State v. Gordon*, 642 S.W.2d 742 (Tenn.Crim.App. 1982).

50. Steven M. Cox and John J. Conrad, *Juvenile Justice* (Dubuque, Iowa: Wm. C. Brown Publishers, 1987), p. 105. See also *State v. Michael L.*, 441 A.2d 684 (Me. 1982) and *Commonwealth v. Christmas*, 502 Pa. 218, 465 A.2d 989 (1983).

51. *In re People in the Interest of B.M.C.*, 32 Colo.App. 79, 506 P.2d 409 (1973).

52. *State in the Interest of R.H.*, 170 N.J.Super. 518, 406 A.2d 1350 (1979).

53. 469 U.S. 325, 105 S.Ct. 733, 83 L.Ed.2d 720 (1985).

C H A P T E R
4

• • • • • • • • •

College Liability Resulting from Campus Crime
Resurrection for *In Loco Parentis?*

O
n America's college and university campuses the doctrine of *in loco parentis* received a burial without honor sometime in the early 1970s. The venerable old doctrine, which for so long had justified the comprehensive authority of professor and college over student, had weakened during the 1960s under a steady decline in parental authority, but the immediate cause of death was an expanded concept of individual liberties, complicated by a lowered age of majority.

There was not even a decent funeral. The doctrine, after all, had come to be viewed as quite disreputable in its latter days. Wherever the doctrine might have been buried, most assumed the entombment would be permanent.

But in the late 1980s, a new and revolutionary line of campus liability cases, concerning victims of campus crime, began to be discerned coming from the nation's appellate courts. When institutions of higher learning fail to protect students from the ravages of campus crime, the institutions are often being held liable for damages. The courts are imposing new duties upon the institutions to expand their control over campus life and to protect students, sometimes even from themselves. Can it be that *in loco parentis* is rising to new life?

This chapter first appeared in 59 *Education Law Reporter*, 1-5 (1990). Used by permission of West Publishing Co.

COLLEGE DUTIES OF SAFETY AND SECURITY

Prior to 20 years ago, American jurisprudence was devoid of any reported case in which a college or university was held liable in compensatory damages to any person who was victimized by crime on a campus. The courts imposed no liability in such cases because the criminal act was committed by a third person who was not under the control of the college or university. The mere fact that the crime occurred on the institution's property, in itself, created no liability.

However, in recent years, the courts have crafted new legal rules concerning safety and security that are applicable to institutions which are in landlord-like relationships to especially dependent persons. The new principles are an accommodation to the changed lifestyles, housing arrangements, and crime rates of modern American society. In all states where the issue has been raised, the courts have held that college and university students stand in a "special relationship" of dependence upon their college or university. Accordingly, in situations where it is "foreseeable" that campus crime might occur, institutions—and individual administrators who fail to take adequate protective steps or give adequate warning of risks—may be liable, in damage suits, to student victims of subsequent campus criminal activities. The four leading cases in the field illustrate the new doctrine.

Probably the most significant of the leading cases is *Miller v. State of New York*,[1] a decision by New York's highest court involving the State University of New York at Stony Brook. The tragic case began when a 19-year-old female student was confronted in the laundry room of her residence hall at 6 o'clock one morning by a man wielding a large butcher knife. He blindfolded the young woman and, at knifepoint, pushed her out of the room, through an unlocked outer door of the dormitory basement, back into another unlocked entrance to the dormitory, and finally upstairs to a third-floor room where he twice raped her under the threat of mutilation or death if she made any noise. Afterward, he led her again outside to a parking lot and fled. He was never identified.

As the case developed, it was shown that prior to the attack strangers had been common in dormitory hallways, and the student herself had complained twice to residence hall advisors about nonresidents loitering in the building. There had been reports to campus security of men being in the women's bathrooms in campus residence halls. Accounts of numerous crimes in the dormitories, including armed robbery, burglary, criminal trespass, and rape, had been published in the school newspaper. Nonetheless, all 10 doors to the dormitory admittedly had been kept unlocked at all hours.

The court said that because the attack on the student had been "foreseeable," the university had owed her a duty of maintaining minimal security measures. It had not met this duty, the court ruled, and an award of $400,000 to the student was affirmed.

A similar result came in *Mullins v. Pine Manor College,*[2] a decision of the Massachusetts Supreme Court. Issues of inadequate locking systems and absence of security guards in residence hall areas were central to a verdict against the college. Like *Miller,* the case also involved a female student who had been raped in her dormitory. The decision was especially notable for campus administrators because, in addition to a judgment against the college itself, a personal verdict of $175,000 was affirmed against the college's vice-president of operations. It had been the vice-president's duty to oversee the adequacy of campus security.

In its opinion, the *Mullins* court specifically noted the demise of *in loco parentis,* but it said that did not let the college escape all responsibilities; rather, the court said, the institution owes ordinary care in protecting the well-being of its resident students, including protecting them against the criminal acts of third parties. The court declared:

> The fact that a college does not police the morals of its resident students, however, does not entitle it to abandon any effort to ensure their physical safety. Parents, students, and the general community still have a reasonable expectation, fostered in part by colleges themselves, that reasonable care will be exercised to protect resident students from foreseeable harm.[3]

Adequacy of police intervention in an argument between students was the central issue in an Arizona Supreme Court decision, *Jesik v. Maricopa Community College.*[4] Peter Jesik was registering for fall semester classes in the college gymnasium when a quarrel erupted with another student. The other man told Jesik he was going home to get a gun to kill him. Jesik told a college security guard what had happened and received assurance of help. When the other student did return later, Jesik again appealed to the guard and again received assurance of protection. The guard then talked to the student who had made the threat but did not look into the student's briefcase. Apparently satisfied, the guard walked away, and the student then pulled a handgun from the briefcase and fatally shot Jesik. The Arizona Supreme Court affirmed that the college owed the slain student a higher duty of protection than it owed the public in general, and where a college failed to exercise reasonable care to protect one of its students from foreseeable criminal harm, it would be liable in damages.

The landmark case involving the duty to warn of danger was *Peterson v. San Francisco Community College District,*[5] a decision of the California Supreme Court. It held that a student could maintain a damage suit against the institution for injuries received in an attempted rape in a college parking lot, because the college had been aware of previous assaults there but had not taken appropriate steps to warn students. The *Peterson* decision also included a verdict against an individual campus administrator.

Of course, these sensational cases reflect only a tiny part of the crime scourge on our campuses. A recent survey by *USA Today*[6] tabulated 31 homicides, and more than 13,000 physical assaults, 1,800 armed robberies, and 600 rapes occurring annually on our nation's college and university campuses. The totals came from reports from only about one-fourth of the institutions of higher education in the country. When all types of crime, including theft and vandalism, are considered, it appears clear that most campus crime is perpetrated by students.[7] One survey indicated that about 70 percent of physical assaults on campus are committed by students.[8]

CONCLUSION: RESURRECTION FOR *IN LOCO PARENTIS*?

The old doctrine of *in loco parentis* held that the schoolmaster or professor stood in the place of a parent, and thus was charged with a parent's rights, duties, and responsibilities as to the student. The doctrine was aimed at the protection and nurture of those who, because of youth or inexperience, could not protect or properly develop themselves. Apparently of English origin,[9] the doctrine was adopted into American jurisprudence and was originally understood to be applicable to college students as well as younger schoolchildren. It is worth repeating an oft-quoted enunciation of the doctrine made by the Kentucky Supreme Court in 1913:

> College authorities stand *in loco parentis* concerning the physical and moral welfare and mental training of the pupils, and we are unable to see why, to that end, they may not make any rule or regulation for the government or betterment of their pupils that a parent could make for the same purpose. Whether the rules or regulations are wise or their aims worthy is a matter left solely to the discretion of the authorities or parents, as the case may be, and in the exercise of that discretion, the courts are not disposed to interfere, unless the rules and aims are unlawful or against public policy.[10]

For years, many commentators on the higher education scene have declared the doctrine of *in loco parentis* to be dead and gone. Admittedly, little has been heard of it in the age of mixed-gender dormitories, no curfews, on-campus pubs, policies permitting overnight guests of the opposite sex in dormitory rooms, and general total freedom in the lives of college and university students.

One fact is becoming obvious, however. Colleges and universities will be unable to provide the heightened security necessary to avoid damage suit liability unless they become more intrusive into students' living arrangements and lives. Especially when it is considered that most campus crime is committed by students, a need can be seen for a return to stricter controls on student behavior.

Lawsuits often serve as quality-control devices in American society. Safety and quality standards for consumer products, automobiles, and medical care have sometimes been established by the threat of lawsuits rather than by professional or governmental regulation of the industry involved. Perhaps the threat of lawsuit liability will drive such a change in campus life.

In the campus crime liability cases, the courts have acknowledged the dependent status of students in relation to their colleges. The students often have little say about the conditions under which they must live on campus; for the most part, they simply must accept the locking systems, roommates, and social codes that they are given by the institutions. In the courts' recognition of the inevitable inability of students to fully take care of themselves, and the corresponding duty upon the institutions to protect them, the same forces are at work which gave rise, centuries ago, to the *in loco parentis* doctrine. Have we come full circle? Perhaps *in loco parentis* emanates from natural law, and an attempt to abrogate it simply will not wash in the inevitable order of things.

NOTES

1. 62 N.Y.2d 506, 467 N.E.2d 493 [19 Ed.Law Rep. 618] (1984); as to damages, see 110 A.D.2d 627, 487 N.Y.S.2d 115 [23 Ed.Law Rep. 1021] (1985).
2. 389 Mass. 47, 449 N.E.2d 331 [11 Ed.Law Rep. 595] (1983).
3. *Mullins*, 449 N.E.2d at 335-6.
4. 125 Ariz. 543, 611 P.2d 547 (1980).
5. 36 Cal.3d 799, 205 Cal.Rptr. 842, 685 Cal.2d 1193 (1984).
6. "Are Colleges Failing to Curb Crime?" *USA Today*, October 4, 1988, p.1.
7. M. Smith, *Crime and Campus Police: A Handbook for Police Officers and Administrators* 3 (1989) (Asheville: College Administration Publications).
8. "Campus Violence Survey" (unpublished compilation), Office of Student Services, Towson State University, 1987.
9. See *Powys v. Mansfield*, 3 My. & Car. 359, 6 Sim. 528 (1837), an early case adopting the doctrine.
10. *Gott v. Berea College*, 156 Ky. 376, 161 S.W. 204, 206 (1913).

CHAPTER 5

Lawsuits, Liability, and Risk Management

A
s we have said, today's college student is a consumer. As attested by their vigorous efforts at student recruitment and "enrollment management," institutions in the 1990s are keenly aware that they must sell their product. Administrators know they must treat students and potential students as customers. However, they are inexperienced customers who need some special protections, and dealings cannot proceed under the old maxim of *caveat emptor*—"let the buyer beware." And, like all sellers of a product in the marketplace, colleges and universities must be prepared to answer in the courts when they fail to meet their obligations in the deal.

This situation is all new, of course. A few years ago, the idea of a student suing his or her college or university would have seemed absurd. Today, it has come to be commonplace to sue one's college—and sometimes to sue individual administrators and officers personally—for harms suffered in campus life. Many of these lawsuits arise because of injuries from campus crime.

Like student lawsuits, campus crime itself was quite rare until recently; both statistically and anecdotally, it has been truly a phenomenon of the past three decades. The first lawsuits brought against colleges by students injured in criminal episodes were litigated in the late 1970s, and the first to be won by students were decided in the early and mid-1980s. Such litigation became routine only in the late 1980s.

Spurred by these lawsuits and a desire to avoid the attendant negative publicity, colleges and universities across the country have been taking steps to upgrade security and improve their crime warnings to students.[1]

What steps should be taken for effective risk management? A look at the theories of liability advanced by the student-victim litigants will be useful. An understanding of the types of duties of safety and protection that students have claimed to be owed by their institutions, and the treatment of these claims by the courts, is necessary for those who seek effective risk management strategies.

THEORIES OF LIABILITY

The student victim suits can be lumped into four general types of claims. Each is based upon some duty allegedly owed to students by their institutions. The courts have recognized some of these duties, but not others. The four types of claims that student plaintiffs have asserted are the following: 1) a duty to warn about known risks; 2) a duty to provide adequate security protection; 3) a duty to screen other students and employees for dangers; and 4) a duty to control student conduct. Both legislative actions and court decisions now firmly impose a strong duty on colleges and universities in regard to the first category. Some duty of the sort asserted in the second category has been recognized by the courts, but it is limited in circumstances and extent. To date, the courts have not agreed with any plaintiff's claim connected with the latter two categories.

Even where such a duty is owed, the duty is not owed to everyone in the general public; it is owed only to those persons with whom an institution has what the law calls a "special relationship." In the case of a college or university, this relationship clearly exists with regard to its students and to others who come onto the campus at the institution's behest, as its business "invitees." Trespassers or casual entrants on the premises are owed no such duty. Thus, where a college operated a day care center, and a woman was abducted from a college parking lot when she went there to leave her child, the court held the college owed her no duty of security protection. She was not a student at the institution, and because she was merely using the parking lot for her own convenience, the court said she did not come within the necessary relationship that would give rise to the duty.[2]

DUTY TO WARN OF KNOWN RISKS

Do institutions have a duty to tell students, potential students, or employees about crimes that have happened on the campus in the past? The answer is "yes" in most cases, especially if the knowledge would be useful to those persons in deciding whether they want to put themselves into that situation, or whether they should use special caution and take steps for self-protection.

On-Campus Risks

The nation's first appellate case dealing with institutional liability for campus crime was *Duarte v. State*, a 1979 decision by a California Court of Appeals.[3] It held that campus administrators must be honest when inquiries are made by potential students about campus safety. The suit was brought by the mother of a female student who was raped and murdered in her dormitory room at California State University in San Diego. The mother alleged that, before deciding where her daughter would attend college, she had visited the campus and made inquiries of university personnel about crime and safety. She was not told of prior crimes known to the university, she alleged. The court of appeals held that the university's action, if it were proven to be true, would support a suit against the school for misrepresentation and deceit.

Five years later the California Supreme Court decided *Peterson v. San Francisco Community College District*,[4] which considered a similar question. The facts were these: a student was assaulted by a man who jumped from behind thick foliage along a stairway leading from a campus parking lot. The man attempted to rape her, and she was injured. Later, the victim learned that the college had known of recent, prior attacks at the same place. The college had stepped up security patrols after the earlier attacks, but it had not publicized the incidents or otherwise warned students who used the facility. The high court ruled the college was liable for the student's injuries because it had failed to give her a timely warning of the known risk. The *Duarte* case had established the duty of college officials to be forthcoming when asked about known risks, but the *Peterson* case went beyond that to impose a positive duty on the institution to warn potential victims of foreseeable risks, even when nobody had asked.

Among students and the public there remained a widespread perception that some college officials were, at worst, covering up crimes, and, at best, being lukewarm about efforts to warn students about the possibility of crime on campus. Howard and Constance Clery, whose 19-year-old daughter, Jeanne, was raped, sodomized, slashed, and strangled in her dormitory room at Lehigh University in 1986, launched a relentless crusade to publicize campus crimes. They pressed a $25 million lawsuit against Lehigh and organized student right-to-know efforts around the country. The media joined the campaign, and in 1989 *USA Today* editorialized that colleges should be required to "open the books" on campus crime. The publication charged that "most" colleges conceal crime information to "protect their images" and the privacy of the students involved.[5]

By 1990, the legislatures of several states had passed statutes requiring colleges to make crime statistics available, but these were superseded by federal legislation in November 1990, when Congress passed the Student

Right-to-Know and Campus Security Act.[6] This far-reaching law requires every college and university receiving federal funds to report, annually, crime statistics and other data about security operations to all current and prospective students and employees. (A discussion of this new federal law is found in chapter 14.)

Warning of Off-Campus Risks

The federal and state crime disclosure laws, as well as the principles established in the *Duarte* and *Peterson* cases, deal only with risks within the geographical boundaries of campuses. What of known risks off-campus? The law is not clear in this regard, but liability may accrue in some future situations, and prudent administrators should consider the possibilities.

Of course, if the institution owns or operates the property, the same principles probably would apply as on-campus even if the facility is remote from the main campus. For instance, in 1992 a jury awarded $1.6 million to a student who was raped at an off-campus dormitory operated in Los Angeles by the University of Southern California. The suit was based, at least in part, on a claim that the university had concealed information about crime in the neighborhood.[7] The verdict later was reversed on appeal because of insufficient evidence that the university's negligence was the proximate cause of the injury.[8] The general principle of liability, however, was not altered.

True off-campus liability issues were explored in *Hartman v. Bethany College*.[9] Heather Hartman, a 17-year-old female freshman at Bethany, went to a bar near the college, Bubba's Bison Inn, where she illegally drank alcoholic beverages with two men—not students—whom she met there. Later, she went with the men to the home of one of them, where both sexually assaulted her. She sued the college alleging, among other things, that the college should have warned her of the dangers of going to the bar. Noting that there was no evidence that Bethany was aware of any prior incidents similar to the assault on Heather Hartman, District Judge Stamp ruled that the college had no obligation to warn students of dangers in their noncurricular activities when the school neither supported nor condoned such activities.

In other cases, however, the circumstances could be quite different, and a different holding could result. What of possible cases in which a college might be aware of a history of prior untoward incidents at a particular place or location, and also be aware that students—especially young, first-year students, away from home for the first time—frequent the place? An additional aggravating circumstance might be found if the college in question does not have adequate facilities to house or provide social activities for all its students and must rely on the area or facility in question to accommodate student needs. Several campus legal experts have predicted that courts may yet impose liability in some such circumstances.[10]

DUTY TO PROVIDE ADEQUATE SECURITY PROTECTION

The law imputes to colleges and universities not only a duty to warn, but also a duty to provide reasonably adequate security protection. This duty may arise in two ways: either under a "negligence" theory based upon tort law, or upon a breach of contract theory, based upon some assurance that the institution has given as to protection or safety.

Security protection, of course, takes many forms. Locks, lights, fences, police officers and security guards, the trimming or elimination of shrubbery and other hiding places, and monitoring systems are among the first level of consideration. But of equal importance, in some circumstances, are modifications to programs and architecture so that classes, research, and other regular activities are not required in remote or lonely places, and that residence halls, cafeterias, libraries, and parking lots are safely accessible and watched at all hours.

Negligence Theories

Once a school is on notice of the "foreseeability" of criminal harm because of a history of criminal incidents at a location, the institution has not only a duty to warn, but also a duty to use due care to provide reasonably adequate security protection. How much is reasonably adequate? The answer must be determined by the facts and circumstances of each individual case, given the history and location of the place and other pertinent risk data. If it comes to a lawsuit, the ultimate answer as to whether particular efforts were sufficient will lie with the decision of the jury.

The leading case illustrating the need for adequate security measures is *Miller v. State of New York*,[11] a 1984 decision of New York's highest court (also discussed in chapter 4). The case involved a 19-year-old junior at the State University of New York at Stony Brook who was confronted in the laundry room of her residence hall at 6 o'clock one morning by an intruder armed with a large butcher knife. He blindfolded her and marched her, at knife point, through an unlocked outer door of the dormitory basement, back into another unlocked door of the building, and then upstairs to a third-floor room where she was raped twice under threat of mutilation or death if she made noise. The man then led her back downstairs and outside to a parking lot. He fled and was never identified.

In court the victim was able to show that prior to her attack strangers had been common in dormitory hallways, and there had been reports to campus security of men being in the women's bathroom. The student herself had twice complained to dormitory supervisors about nonresidents loitering in the building. The campus newspaper had published accounts of numerous crimes in the dormitories at the school, including armed robbery, burglaries, trespass, and another rape. Even so, all 10 dormitory doors were admittedly kept unlocked at all hours.

The court held that the college was in essence a landlord, and it owed the same duty that any landlord owed a tenant: the premises must be kept in a "reasonably safe condition," which included a duty to maintain "minimal security measures" against foreseeable dangers. Failure to lock the doors breached that duty, the court ruled. An award of $400,000 to the student was upheld.

Foreseeability need not be based upon a history of campus crime. Other sorts of dangers may suffice. In *Mullins v. Pine Manor College*,[12] a Massachusetts college was found liable for a campus rape even though prior campus crimes had been minimal. The college's close proximity to a metropolitan area and a college official's prior acknowledgment of a crime danger were some of the factors that were held to show that the danger of rape was foreseeable.

More recently, a federal court considered a case against New York Medical College and one of its instructors involving an alleged sexual assault of a child by a psychiatric resident. The resident, who had indicated a desire to practice child psychiatry, had reportedly admitted to his instructor that he was a pedophile. In spite of the fact that the college had no knowledge of prior criminal behavior by the resident, the court ruled that the child had alleged sufficient facts to support a claim that the resident posed a foreseeable threat of harm to minor children and that the college had a duty to warn of this potential harm.[13] (This case is discussed in more detail later in the chapter.)

In another recent case, the Kansas Supreme Court considered a case against Kansas State University involving an alleged sexual assault in a coed dormitory. The man who was accused of committing the assault was a student who had been charged with rape in another coed dormitory only 35 days earlier. After the first accusation was made, the university allowed the student to move to another coed dormitory where the claimed second assault occurred. Although the man's guilt for the first incident had not yet been established in a court of law, the court ruled a fact issue existed concerning whether the university had breached its duty to protect students from known criminal dangers in the way it had responded to the first rape allegation.[14]

Adequacy of police protection has been the central issue in several cases. Recognizing the Pandora's box that could be opened, the courts have been hesitant to impose any duty to guarantee that, through policing, crime does not occur. The tone was set several years ago by the United States Supreme Court in the landmark case of *DeShaney v. Winnebago County Dept. of Social Services*,[15] which held that the due process clause does not impose an affirmative obligation upon government to ensure that citizens are not harmed through the wrongful acts of other private citizens. Campus police cases have, generally, taken the same tack. In the 1990 case of *Klobuchar v. Purdue University*,[16] the Indiana Court of Appeals reiterated that the campus police duty is the same as the police duty owed to the general public and does not give an individual grounds to sue based upon failure to protect from crime. Likewise, the Appeals Court of Massachusetts, in the 1992 case of *Robinson v. Commonwealth*,[17] cited *Winnebago* in holding that a failure of police protection will not generally constitute a deprivation of the civil rights of a person injured by a criminal.

But, if the threat is individualized enough, and a concrete security action evident, a duty may arise. In *Jesik v. Maricopa Community College*,[18] the Arizona Supreme Court indicated that, under an Arizona statute imposing upon colleges a duty to use reasonable care to protect students, a duty to provide police protection could arise in some circumstances. The case involved a campus argument that led to a shooting. The victim, Peter Jesik, had become involved in a heated argument with another student during college registration. After the other student threatened to go home to get a gun to kill Jesik, Jesik reported the threat to a college security guard. He received assurances of help and protection. The other student did later return, with a briefcase. The guard talked to the student, but did not look into the briefcase. After the guard departed, the student pulled a gun out of the case and shot Jesik to death. The Arizona high court ruled that an issue of fact was presented and remanded the case for trial.

Contractual Theories

Even though tort law imposes no duty to provide adequate protection in a given situation, it is possible that a college or university could create its own duty if it were to give assurance to its students—in catalogues, brochures, housing contracts, or the like—that it will protect them. Assurances about security practices given in university publications may be construed to be contractual obligations between the university and the student, and give rise to a breach of contract claim if they are breached.

One federal case illustrates this theory. The case is *Nieswand v. Cornell University*,[19] which was brought by the parents of a female freshman who was fatally shot, along with her roommate, in their residence hall room by the roommate's disgruntled suitor. The parents argued that leaflets and brochures sent to prospective students by Cornell gave assurances of security. Specifically, they alleged, two publications stated that residence halls were kept locked at night. This was pertinent, because the killer—armed with a rifle—had gained entrance to the residence hall when it was supposed to be locked. The university had responded in the suit alleging that the victim herself had propped open the dormitory doors. After the federal district court ruled that the matter should be decided by a jury, the parties settled the claim before trial for $200,000.[20]

In one recent case, however, the Supreme Court of Georgia was cautious about establishing liability on a claim of this sort. The case was *Savannah College of Art and Design, Inc. v. Roe*, and in it the court said that if a college is to be held liable on such a theory, the assurance would have to be clearly expressed in the document in question, not just implied. In the situation in question, the court declined to find any such implied duty just because the college's housing policy agreement contained rules that said they were intended to protect the security of dormitory residents.[21]

Duty to Protect Off-Campus

Does the duty of protection extend off-campus? Apparently not, at least under existing law. In *Donnell v. California Western School of Law*,[22] a 1988 decision, a California Court of Appeals declined to extend a college's duty of protection to off-campus property, even though it immediately adjoined the campus and was necessarily used by students. The case arose when an unidentified robber stabbed a law student as he walked back to his car after studying late in the law library. The law school occupied one city block in San Diego, and the attack occurred on the public sidewalk that ran along the side of the building. The school provided no parking, and students had to park on adjacent city streets. Even though there had been previous criminal attacks in the area, the school provided neither lighting nor security patrols on the sidewalk. The court held that because the school did not own the sidewalk, it could not control it and concomitantly owed no duty to protect its students on it.

Donnell may not be the last word on this issue, however. In several states, an off-premises duty of protection has been imposed in some noncampus cases involving commercial establishments. For instance, a federal appeals court extended an off-premises duty in a case that involved a New Orleans hotel guest, rather than a college student. In that case, *Banks v. Hyatt Corp.*,[23] decided in 1984, a man was slain by a street robber as he stood on a city sidewalk, outside the hotel's doors but under an overhang that was actually part of the hotel. The court said the hotel owed the man, its invitee, a duty of protection from foreseeable criminal assault in that location. Important to the holding was the implication that the hotel could easily have extended some protection to the location; although the hotel did not hold actual title to the real estate, the site was an integral part of its operations. Florida courts have applied this proposition to areas used by the landowner for the ingress and egress of its customers,[24] and a New York case has held that, in some circumstances, a junior high school may owe a duty of supervision and safety to its students who leave school premises during lunch hour.[25]

DUTY TO SCREEN STUDENTS AND EMPLOYEES

Do colleges have a duty to screen those coming onto campus to discover dangerous persons? *Eiseman v. State of New York*[26] grew out of an experimental program at the State University College at Buffalo that was designed to provide college opportunities for disadvantaged persons. One such applicant had been a convict in the state penitentiary. After being admitted, he was invited to an off-campus party by unsuspecting students who had befriended him. At the party, the parolee went on a bloody spree of murder and rape that left two other students dead and one maimed. In the aftermath, it was learned that the parolee had had a long and ugly history of heroin abuse, violent attacks on others, and two penitentiary sentences. Even though they had known he was incarcerated when he applied for admission, college officials had made no effort to learn whether he might pose a risk to the college community.

The trial jury awarded more than $360,000 to the family of one of the slain students, and the award was upheld by the intermediate courts. New York's highest court ultimately overturned the verdict, however, declaring that because the parole board—the "experts"—had decided the man was ready for society, the college could not be expected to do better. While this decision has left colleges, at least in New York, with no duty to screen admittees, it cannot be certain that other courts will reach the same conclusion in later cases, particularly when colleges are knowingly dealing with criminals.

Similar issues surround campus employees—particularly those who will have master keys or access to dormitories or other places where students may be especially vulnerable. Liability has been imposed in cases involving other sorts of commercial landlords. Under the doctrine of *respondeat superior*, an employer is generally liable for the acts of its employee that are incidental to the class of acts the person was hired to perform, and an employer might also be liable for negligence in hiring, retaining, or assigning a dangerous employee.

Cases involving security guards—whose roles are analogous to many campus security and housing employees—illustrate the principle of negligent hiring. Several courts have held that an employer of security personnel has a duty to use reasonable care in hiring to discover the unfitness of such employees. In a case where an apartment tenant was raped by the apartment complex's security guard, the Illinois Court of Appeals held that the landlord was negligent in failing to conduct a reasonable and adequate investigation before hiring the man.[27] In a similar case in 1988, the Illinois Supreme Court held that a failure to properly control the distribution of master keys, and failure to take reasonable precautions to prevent unauthorized entries by persons possessing those keys, could result in landlord liability.[28]

Accordingly, the prudent institutional employer will take steps to screen potential hirees for criminal backgrounds, and colleges should, within parameters of local law, ask potential students whether they have felony records. If they do, further inquiry could be made into the safety issue and, if indicated, in consultation with campus counsel, steps could be taken to keep the person from the campus community.

DUTY TO CONTROL STUDENT CONDUCT

Students commit most campus crimes.[29] The control of student conduct, then, is pertinent to campus crime liability issues. Must a college or university control its students? There is little case law on this question, and the answer is still unclear.

The first case dealing with a theory that colleges must control crime by their students, or pay the bill, is *Smith v. Day*,[30] a 1987 decision of the Vermont Supreme Court. The case grew out of off-campus actions of Kenneth Day, who was a student at Norwich University, a military school. Day fired a rifle into a passing railroad train, wounding two members of the train crew. Day was sent to jail for one year as a result of the shooting, and the wounded men, looking for a pocket deeper than Day's, sued the university. They alleged that because Day was a member of the Corps of Cadets, and his actions were in violation of various university rules and regulations, the university should pay the bill for his actions. The court held that the university owed no duty of care running to the wounded men, who were not connected with the university, and opined that it is "unrealistic to expect the modern American college to control all of the actions of its students."

However, a 1994 case, *Almonte v. New York Medical College*,[31] suggests that higher education institutions may, in some instances, be responsible for wrongs committed by their students. In this case, a 10-year-old child was allegedly assaulted by a psychiatric resident who was enrolled in the division of psychoanalytic training at New York Medical College. The parents sued the medical college and an instructor at the college, claiming that the institution and the instructor owed their child a duty to control the resident and to warn them of his allegedly dangerous proclivities.

According to the parents' allegations, the resident told Dr. Douglas Ingram, the resident's instructor and analyst, that he was a pedophile. In spite of the fact that Ingram knew that his patient intended to become a child psychiatrist, neither Ingram nor the medical college took any steps to prevent him from treating children. As a result, the resident was placed in a hospital setting where he reputedly assaulted the plaintiffs' child. A federal court ruled that the parents had alleged sufficient facts to make out a cause of action for negligence.

Almonte may not have broad application for higher education, since the case occurred in the context of a psychiatrist-patient relationship as well as an instructor-student relationship. Other cases had already established that psychiatrists have a duty to warn potential victims if they know that a patient presents a threat to specific individuals.[32] Nevertheless, *Almonte's* reasoning could be stretched to hold a college and its faculty liable for a student's wrongdoing, even outside the context of a psychiatrist-patient relationship. Indeed, the court reasoned that the doctor's duty to control the psychiatric resident was greater because the doctor was the resident's instructor as well as his analyst.

CONCLUSION

American courts are receptive to the plight of students injured by crime and are, in many instances, willing to till new legal fields to shape remedies for victims and encourage campus crime control. Effective risk management requires that campus administrators be aware of their duty to be forthcoming about foreseeable crime risks and take steps to ensure that security protection is adequate, measured against those risks. In addition, they must be cautious about the assurances they give in relation to security protection; promises not delivered upon may well increase institutional liability beyond that imputed by general law.

In a closing note, it is important to remember that many—and perhaps most—crime liability claims asserted against colleges and universities are won by the institutions. The numbers are uncertain because there is no way to tabulate how many claims are settled before going to court, or the number of cases that end at the trial court level, whether by judgment or settlement. In any event, the reported appellate opinions around the country do reveal that colleges win many such cases because 1) of a finding that the risk was not foreseeable, or 2) if it was foreseeable, that the institution took adequate steps to warn and protect, or 3) regardless of liability issues, because the institution or defendant was immune from suit because of sovereign charitable or qualified immunity principles, which vary greatly from state to state.[33]

The following checklist may be helpful in evaluating your campus. Not all campuses need all of the security equipment or practices listed on the checklist; what is needed at any campus is to be determined by the risk level, given the history of crime and violence in the area and other factors that make future crime foreseeable. Some items mentioned in the checklist are addressed in other chapters of this book.

GENERAL CAMPUS SECURITY CHECKLIST

PERIMETER

___ Is traffic flow through campus minimized?
___ Are fences adequate to discourage entry?
___ Is lighting adequate at entrances, streets?

STUDENTS (Also see chapter 14)

___ Are crime statistics furnished students regularly?
___ Is there an emergency notification procedure?
___ Is there an escort system?
___ Are drug/alcohol rules adequately enforced?
___ Does the institution screen for dangerous applicants?
___ Does it expel dangerous miscreants?
___ Are procedures in place for student complaints about security?

GROUNDS AND BUILDINGS (Also see chapter 6)

___ Is shrubbery minimized?
___ Is lighting adequate at buildings, walkways?
___ Are lights monitored for burn-outs and failures?
___ Is master key control tight?
___ Are locks changed when needed?
___ Are emergency phones available at remote areas?
___ Do closed circuit televisions monitor remote places?

POLICING (Also see chapter 5)

___ Is the number of patrol officers sufficient?
___ Are officers given adequate original and continuing training?
___ Are incident reports monitored by administration?

HOUSING (Also see chapter 6)

___ Are visitors regulated?
___ Do policies punish students or others for door propping and lock stuffing?
___ Are police patrols adequate?
___ Are new employees screened?
___ Does the institution enforce drug/alcohol rules?
___ Are deadbolt locks and peepholes provided?
___ Are keys changed periodically?
___ Are emergency phones accessible?

___ Is elevator access controlled?
___ Is there enough on-campus housing for all who want it?
___ Are students given choice of more secure dorms?
___ Are there crime education programs for students?

PARKING (Also see chapter 6)

___ Is parking safely accessible?
___ Are parking areas viewed by other people?
___ Are lots patrolled?
___ Are emergency phones in place?

NOTES

1. "Violent Crime No Stranger to Campuses," USA Today, November 29, 1990, p. 1A.
2. Figueroa v. Evangelical Covenant Church d/b/a North Park College, 879 F.2d 1427 (7th Cir. 1989).
3. 88 Cal.App.3d 473, 151 Cal.Rptr. 727 (Cal.App. 1979).
4. 685 P.2d 1193 (Cal. 1984).
5. "Open the Books on Campus Crime," USA Today, November 13, 1989, p. 10A.
6. Student Right-to-Know and Campus Security Act, Public Law No. 101-542 (1990), amended by Public Law No. 102-26, Sec. 10(e) (1991); 20 U.S.C. Sec. 1092(f).
7. "Rape Victim Awarded $1.6 Million," Sun-Herald, Gulfport, Mississippi, March 27, 1992, p. A4.
8. Nola M. v. University of Southern California, 16 Cal. App. 4th 421, 20 Cal. Rptr. 2d 97 (1993).
9. 778 F.Supp. 286 (N.D.W.Va. 1991).
10. See, "Colleges Confront Liability," USA Today, September 14, 1990, p. 6A.
11. 62 N.Y.2d 506, 478 N.Y.S.2d 829, 467 N.E.2d 493 (1984); as to damages see 110 A.D.2d 627, 487 N.Y.S.2d 115 (1985).
12. 389 Mass. 47, 449 N.E.2d 331 (1983).
13. Almonte v. New York Medical College, 851 F.Supp. 34 (D. Conn. 1994).
14. Nero v. Kansas State University, 861 P.2d 768 (Kan. 1993).
15. 489 U.S. 189 (1989).
16. 553 N.E.2d 169 (Ind.App. 1990).
17. 584 N.E.2d 636 (Mass.App. 1992).
18. 125 Ariz. 543, 611 P.2d 547 (1980).
19. 692 F.Supp. 1464 (N.D.N.Y. 1988).
20. "Parents of Slain Student," The Chronicle of Higher Education, September 28, 1989, p. A2.
21. 409 S.E.2d 848 (Ga. 1990).
22. 200 Cal.App.3d 715, 246 Cal.Rptr. 199 (1988).
23. 722 F.2d 214 (5th Cir. 1984).
24. Gutierrez v. Dade County Board of Education, 604 So.2d 853 (Fla.App.3 Dist. 1992); Marhefka v. Monte Carlo Management Corp., 358 So.2d 1171 (Fla.App.3 Dist. 1978).
25. Maness v. City of New York, 607 N.Y.S.2d 325 (A.D. 1 Dept. 1994).
26. 70 N.Y.2d 175, 518 N.Y.S.2d 608, 511 N.E.2d 1128 (1987).

27. *Easley v. Apollo Detective Agency, Inc.*, 387 N.E.2d 1241 (Ill.App. 1979).

28. *Rowe v. State Bank*, 531 N.E.2d 1358 (Ill. 1988).

29. Michael Clay Smith and Margaret D. Smith, *Wide Awake: A Guide to Safe Campus Living in the 90s* (Princeton: Peterson's Guides, 1990), pp. 4-5.

30. 148 Vt. 595, 538 A.2d 157 (1987).

31. *Almonte v. New York Medical College*, 851 F.Supp. 34 (D.Conn. 1994).

32. See *Tarasoff v. Regents of the University of California*, 17 Cal.3d 425, 131 Cal.Rptr. 14, 551 P.2d 340 (1976).

33. For instance see *Alexander v. University of North Florida*, 39 F.3d 290 (11th Cir. 1994).

CHAPTER 6

Buildings, Grounds, and Campus Crime

Criminologists always have recognized that environment is a major factor in the likelihood of crime. At the center of any security effort must be strategies for "target hardening"—prophylaxis to isolate the target from the criminal, or at least make the environment less crime prone.

Opportunity is an element of crime. The ease with which a criminal can act, the risk of interruption, and the likelihood of being identified or captured are all factors that affect a potential criminal's decision to commit the offense. Additionally, environment can create a psychological atmosphere that deters would-be criminals, empowers would-be victims, and makes users of an area feel more comfortable. These are all important factors in campus life.

DEFENSIBLE SPACE

In the early 1970s, urban planner Oscar Newman developed the theory of defensible space. While he developed it as a response to crime in public housing projects, the principles are applicable to any populated environment, and especially to a college campus. It involves far more than good lights, locks, and so forth; Newman postulated that physical design can evoke psychological reactions by residents to create a social fabric that *defends itself*.

Newman was concerned that architecture's role in America's crime problem was not being recognized. He said that modern, densely populated environments where it is easy to be anonymous were likely to produce generations of young people who would be "totally lacking in any experience of individuality, of personal space, and by extension, of the personal rights and property of others."[1] Newman's comments, made just as America's urban crime explosion was beginning, sound visionary today.

On the one hand, poor architecture—from a security standpoint—could contribute to crime. While design obviously could create physical barriers to criminals and protect potential victims, Newman said, architecture could do more than that; it could affect social and psychological factors that would discourage crime.

On the other hand, he felt that architecture could either encourage or discourage people from taking an active part in their own security—something that he believed necessary in modern, crowded environments. He was convinced that America's crime problems could not be solved by increased police force alone. Instead, he felt, community residents had to work together for their own security. "When people begin to protect themselves as individuals and not as a community, the battle against crime is effectively lost," he warned.[2]

Four major design ingredients are involved in Newman's concept. First, both real and symbolic barriers should be used to subdivide the environment into manageable zones that encourage occupants to assume territorial attitudes. Second, opportunities for surveillance of all areas, by occupants, should be maximized. Third, sites should be designed so that occupants are not perceived as vulnerable. Fourth, residential structures should be placed in proximity to safe or nonthreatening areas.

The theories of defensible space do not mean that buildings must be turned into ugly fortresses. They simply mean that community and openness are to be encouraged, and where this is done, crime and violence will be minimized. In practical terms for campuses, buildings should be placed and designed so that people do not have to use isolated areas; communal areas are overseen by many; and traffic (both human and vehicular) is restricted. In such an environment, people who belong in it will interact as a community, and those who do not belong will easily be recognized.

Traffic and Parking

Criminals must get in and get out, so restrictions on the flow of vehicular traffic may discourage many types of criminal activity. While real traffic restrictions are not possible on large university campuses, at small institutions monitoring of entrances and exits may be possible, especially at night. Required use of special parking places for visitors also can enhance security and discourage miscreants.

Parking lots and garages are offensive to the eye, so campus planners often hide them. This arrangement, of course, is antithetical to security. In fact, parking areas should be placed where as many eyes as possible will oversee them. They should be positioned so that users have ready access from their cars to the buildings they use, especially at night. If possible, traffic into and out of parking areas should be channeled so that it will be seen by a parking attendant and as many other people as possible. Lighting should be plentiful. Stairways to parking decks should be open or enclosed in glass so that attackers cannot easily hide in them. Where risks are substantial, surveillance can be enhanced with closed circuit television, emergency telephones, and alarm bells in elevators and passageways as well as parking areas. Parking areas should have regular security patrols.

Escort Services and Emergency Telephones

Where risk factors are significant, escort services should be available—and be publicized—for students and employees who must move about the campus or get to or from their cars at dangerous times. For instance, a student who arrives back at campus quite late at night may have to park a long distance from the residence hall because all closer parking spaces are taken. At most campuses, students should know that they can go to the campus police office to avail themselves of an escort.

Emergency telephones may be useful in risk areas. Good systems should be easy to use with a minimum of effort by the person seeking help. The best systems are those that are activated for a two-way conversation with security headquarters with a mere push of a button. These units have the microphone and speaker built into the box, so the caller can keep his or her hands free.

Campus Buildings and Grounds

In accord with the principles of defensible space, isolated areas should be eliminated in campus buildings. High on the list for attention in this regard are restrooms and laundry rooms, both of which are often the locale of attacks. Wherever possible, entrance to restrooms and laundry rooms should be from major common areas, and laundry rooms should be opened up as much as possible.

Shrubbery beautifies our campuses, but it also provides hiding places for assailants. In high-risk areas, shrubbery should be no more than 14 inches high, or so thin that a person cannot hide behind it. Trees should not be located immediately beside remote walkways, and shrubbery near residence halls should be located away from the building.

Residence hall security is related to policies on visitors. Newman's concept of community requires a core of people who know and look after each other. The more restrictive the dormitory policy on visitors, the more easily security can be maintained. Single-gender dormitories can be made more secure if only because male intruders (remember, males commit 90 percent of the crime in American society) can be easily recognized. Larger institutions may provide alternative residence halls with tighter visitor policies for those students who desire it.

Does the institution have adequate residence hall space for all students who desire it? Remember, whatever the crime dangers in residence halls, they usually are safer and more secure than private, off-campus apartments. While institutions are under no duty to provide housing for all, it may be a factor in selection of an institution by students who are shopping for a college.

Students who live on a campus may see security problems that the staff has missed. They should be consulted. Most institutions now have an ongoing campus safety committee, which should include student members; it should meet regularly and solicit suggestions and complaints from students and employees.

Locking Systems

Locks and keys are the starting point for most building security. The mere fact that a locking system is in place, however, does not ensure security. Many types of door locks can be quickly opened with a knife blade or plastic card. Keys are easily duplicated. Master keys exist and sometimes have been widely dispersed. Prior occupants of buildings may still have keys. An evaluation of a locking system requires a look at the hardware being used and the key control policies in place. Failure to have sound key policies may constitute legal negligence and subject an institution and its administrators to suit by crime victims. (This issue is discussed in chapter 5.)

Buildings—especially residence halls—should be designed with a minimum of entrance sites. Doors should be centrally located so they can be monitored. Ground-floor windows should be either permanently closed or modified so they can be opened only a few inches—not enough for an intruder. Security screens designed to prevent burglaries should be used where windows must be opened fully. Other possible entry sites—basements, storerooms, coal chutes—should be permanently blocked with metal grilles.

Where should locks be located? In high-risk areas, separate keys should be required for access to a building's outer doors, to call elevators, and to individual rooms. Outer doors should be kept locked 24 hours a day. Users should be instructed *not* to place identity tags on key rings. It is better to have to obtain new keys than to place in the hands of a potential criminal a full set of keys to a known address.

Types of locks. What types of locks are best? First, a lock is of little value if the door itself can be easily broken or stretched from its frame. The door should tightly fit the jamb, and the bolt of the lock should protrude well into the striker plate so that the door cannot be pried from the jamb. Steel jambs are best; some aluminum jambs can be easily bent.

Spring-loaded "night latch" type locks are convenient because they can be engaged simply by closing the door, but they are poor for security. These locks often can be opened by sliding a credit card or blade between the door and the frame. Better quality spring-loaded locks have a dead-latch plunger, which prevents the latch from being pushed back.

Dead-bolt locks, which are not spring loaded, provide the best security. They usually have a square-faced bolt that is engaged by a full turn of a knob or key. If the bolt is sufficiently long—1.5 inches or more—the door becomes almost impossible to jimmy open.

Key control. The best lock may be of no value if key control is poor. Too often, janitorial staff members are given master keys they do not need, and accounting for keys is lost with the passage of time. Campus burglaries have been committed by family members of campus employees who have taken passkeys without the employee's knowledge, used them for an illegal entry, and returned them without anyone being the wiser at the time. Where proliferation of keys is a problem because various staff members need master keys for emergencies, sequence locks can be utilized. These retain a master key in an open lock until a second key—held by another employee—is used to release it. Key boards also present problems. If duplicates of all keys are kept in one place, the opportunities for a thief are obvious. If keys are stored in this way, security surrounding the key board should be extremely tight.

Many colleges in high-risk areas now recore all residence hall locks each year, as well as every time a key is reported lost or concern is raised about an unauthorized person having a key. When locks must be changed in midyear because a student has lost a key, the student usually is charged a fee to cover the expense.

Traditional lock and key systems are now being replaced with electromagnetic card systems at many institutions. Coded cards—either notched, embossed, or encoded with a pattern of metallic flecks—replace the keys, and codes can be instantly changed, any number of times, from a remote location. While these systems are expensive at the outset, the enhanced security and the low cost of periodic changes in lock codes make them a wise investment in many situations.

In high-risk residence halls, particularly those that permit unregulated visitors, room doors should be equipped with wide-angle peepholes and interior sliding locks (which are stronger than guard chains). Sliding locks can prevent someone with an unauthorized key, or someone who has jimmied the lock, from entering the room while the occupant is asleep. Housing officials sometimes voice concern that interior sliding locks may interfere with college staff entering a room in the event of a medical emergency or other exigent circumstance; where security is a significant risk, however, it probably should take precedence. Several of the most tragic dormitory attack cases would have been avoided if interior locks had been used. Additionally, from a legal standpoint, the institution probably could not successfully be charged with negligence by a crime victim if it has provided interior door locks that simply were not used by the room's occupant.

Emergency exits. Emergency exits in residence halls present a recurring security problem. These doors usually are locked to the outside, but students often foil them to let in visitors, to get food deliveries after hours, to circulate fresh air, to take shortcuts, or because they have lost their keys. These doors can be equipped with alarm systems to call attention to an unauthorized intruder or improper use of the door by building occupants. Because they are annoyed by these alarms, students often try to destroy them, but in high-risk areas they are important. The most secure alarm systems do not stop when the door is reclosed, but continue to sound until there is a specific security response.

Student compliance with use of emergency doors is a thorny problem but a necessity in high-risk areas. Two approaches can be utilized to encourage cooperation. The first is to educate students about the risk if the doors are left open. The second is to strictly and sternly enforce student disciplinary codes against door propping or stuffing. Residence assistants should be required to report offenders, and when penalties are assessed to offenders, wide publicity should be given to that fact (of course, under the Buckley Amendment, the actual identity of the individual offender should not be revealed).

Maintenance

Maintenance of equipment is an important aspect of security, and one that sometimes is forgotten. Lights, emergency telephones, and alarm bells should be regularly checked and logs should be kept. If an institution is charged with negligence in maintenance of equipment, a log showing a regular pattern of maintenance would be most helpful in court.

Screening of Employees

A new type of lawsuit has arisen in recent years known as "negligent hiring." In essence, under this theory an institution may be held liable in a civil damage suit where it hired someone without an adequate background check and put the employee into a job through which he or she could commit some crime. Where some innocent person is harmed by the crime, the institution may be held liable if the employee had a history that would have made the crime foreseeable, and if the history could have been discovered if an adequate background check had been made. (A discussion of several cases involving negligent hiring may be found in chapter 5.)

The application to colleges and universities is obvious. For instance, where maintenance and custodial staff are to be given access to residence halls or other places where students are vulnerable, they should be screened for criminal backgrounds such as sex offenses or theft. Potential and existing employees may be asked about criminal records, and various private services now exist to provide background information on potential hirees.

SECURITY CHECKLIST

GROUNDS

   ___ Is access limited?
   ___ Is access channeled to monitored areas?
   ___ Are shrubbery, etc., minimized?
   ___ Is lighting adequate where people walk, congregate?
   ___ Is a escort service available?
   ___ Are emergency phones available?
   ___ Logged maintenance of lights, phones, alarms?

BUILDINGS

   ___ Is master key control tight?
   ___ Are employees screened?
   ___ Are security patrols adequate?
   ___ Do students have choice of more secure dorms?
   ___ Are visitors allowed in dorms? How are they monitored?
   ___ Are door proppers disciplined?
   ___ Is there student complaint/improvement system?
   ___ Are laundry and restrooms isolated?
   ___ Is elevator access controlled?
   ___ Are there emergency exit alarms?
   ___ Is there enough campus housing?
   ___ Do doors have deadbolts, peepholes, interior locks?
   ___ Are locks changed periodically?

TRAFFIC AND PARKING

   ___ Is traffic channeled for monitoring?
   ___ Are visitors identified and limited?
   ___ Are parking areas close?
   ___ Are parking areas lighted, patrolled?
   ___ Do parking areas have phones, TV?
   ___ Are parking areas viewed by others?
   ___ Are stairways open or glass?

___ Do elevators have alarms, TV?
___ Are escorts available?

NOTES

1. Oscar Newman, *Defensible Space* (New York: Macmillan, 1972), p. 4.
2. *Id.* at p. 3.

CHAPTER

7

Human Sexuality and Crime in Campus Life

I n movies and popular literature, college campuses are often portrayed as carefree havens of easy morality, where students and professors indulge in casual and harmless sexual relationships. Research studies, however, paint a very different picture of sexual behavior at colleges and universities. On some American campuses, college women run a one-in-five chance of experiencing an attempted or completed sexual assault, with freshman women being at greatest risk for rape. Far too often, college fraternities are involved in sexual misbehavior, occasionally even including sexual assault. Indeed, two popular movie comedies, *Animal House* and *Revenge of the Nerds*, portray fraternity men engaging in antics toward women that would probably be criminal offenses if they were actually to occur. Male varsity athletes often figure prominently in incidents of sexual misconduct, and research confirms that they are more likely than the average college male to be involved in various forms of rape.

Twenty years ago, few campus administrators spent much time dealing with sex crimes or sexual harassment. Sexual misconduct became a police matter only on rare occasions, with most institutions preferring to handle such incidents internally to avoid embarrassing individuals or the institution. Three developments have changed this scenario, however, and made sex crimes a central concern for most colleges and universities. First, federal laws—notably, Title IX, the Ramstad Amendment, and the Student Right-to-Know and Campus Security Act—have forced higher education institutions to assume more responsibility for stopping sexual misconduct. Second, courts have shown themselves more willing to hold institutions liable for sexual assaults that occur on college campuses and for incidents of sexual harassment against college students and employees. Third, higher education administrators, like society as a whole, are more aware that the victims of sex crimes and sexual harassment often suffer severe trauma, with long-term physical and psychological consequences. Campus decision makers are becoming increasingly aware that the atmosphere of learning and free inquiry which every college and university strives for is incompatible with a climate that tolerates sexual misconduct against any member of the campus community.

RAPE: SHOCKINGLY FREQUENT OUTRAGE

A 1982 study by Professor Mary P. Koss of Kent State University and Cheryl Oros of the U.S. General Accounting Office indicated that more than 23 percent of the 2,016 university women they surveyed had been raped, according to strict legal standards.[1] Many involved assaults by social companions who pushed things beyond expectations. This phenomenon has come to be called "date rape," and many of the subjects in the Koss-Oros study did not recognize that such assaults actually constitute the crime of rape—sexual activity achieved through force or threat of it, against the will of the victim.

In 1985, the Federal Bureau of Investigation tabulated 215 forcible rapes on the nation's campuses.[2] That figure drastically understated the incidence of campus rapes, because less than 20 percent of the nation's colleges and universities participated in the tabulation, and only offenses reported to the police were included. In 1992, the nation's colleges and universities reported nearly 1,000 rapes,[3] and even this number is probably far below the total number of campus rapes that occurred that year.

It has been estimated by one Department of Justice study that actual rapes may number from three and one-half to nine times as many as are reported.[4] Moreover, the reporting rate may be even lower when the rapist is an acquaintance of the victim. Studies have estimated that only one in a hundred acquaintance rapes gets reported to the police.[5] When all these factors are taken into account, it is clear that the number of reported rapes that occur on or near campuses constitute only a fraction of all the rapes that actually occur. Indeed, some studies have estimated that a college woman's chance of being sexually assaulted while she is a student is from 20 to 25 percent.[6] A recent study found that one in three college women had experienced nonconsensual or pressured sexual intercourse—either by physical force, drugs or alcohol, or psychological pressure, although many of these incidents might not fall within the legal definition of rape.[7]

Rape victims fail to report for many reasons. Among them are embarrassment, concern that they will receive unsympathetic treatment from police and courts, fear of reprisal by the rapist, and lack of confidence that the police can apprehend the perpetrator.[8] Alcohol is often a factor in campus rapes, and it seems likely that some victims fail to report anything because they blame themselves for having been under the influence of alcohol when the rape occurred.

The inability of the victim to recognize that she has been criminally assaulted and, alternatively, her failure to view criminal justice processes as an appropriate resolution of the matter are illustrated by a 1984 study of campus males who admitted forcing themselves upon women. Eugene Kanin studied 71 white male undergraduates who admitted having used applied or threatened force against a nonconsenting female for sexual activity. All the cases resulted in penetration. In each of the cases, the assailant was known to the victim, yet none of the incidents was reported to authorities. These incidents represented three times more rape episodes than were reported in the local community. Kanin made no claim that he had found all nonreported rapes.[9]

There is no such thing as a typical campus rape victim or a typical campus rapist, but certain kinds of students are prominent in both categories. First-year college women are at especially high risk for sexual assaults, probably because many of them are living alone for the first time and have not yet learned strategies for protecting themselves.[10] Fraternity members are more likely than nonfraternity members to engage in nonphysical coercion and to use drugs or alcohol as a means of obtaining sex, but they are no more likely than other campus males to use physical force.[11] In addition to fraternity men, student athletes are at high risk for committing rape, perhaps because of their privileged position on campus.[12] Although rapes take place in a variety of settings on or near campus, they often occur at parties, especially fraternity parties, and alcohol is frequently a factor.[13]

Another campus phenomenon that has received attention recently is gang rape. A 1985 study of campus-related gang rapes found that a majority occurred at fraternity parties, and about 20 percent involved student athletes.[14] Carol Bohmer and Andrea Parrot, in their study on campus sexual assaults, cited a 1991 study of campus gang rapes that reported similar findings. Fifty-five percent of the reported gang rapes committed by college students between 1980 and 1990 were committed by fraternity members, and 40 percent were committed by members of sports teams.[15]

Sexual aggression can have a devastating impact on the life of a college student victim. While feelings of shame, guilt, fear, disbelief, and lowered self-esteem are common, it also is not unusual for the victim to leave the college,[16] or rearrange her life so that she does not have to attend classes or extracurricular activities, use the library, or work at night.[17]

An Educational Response to the Rape Threat

Colleges and universities can help to ameliorate rape problems through education and community services. Education about sexual aggression may deter its occurrence by allowing potential "date rape" aggressors to learn what is normative and what is not in sexual relations, the harm that may result to victims, and the potential penalties for transgressions. Education likewise may avert rape by permitting potential victims to recognize dangerous situations and thus avoid them. Community services can assist a rape victim to move more successfully through the aftermath of the incident, with minimum long-term damage.

Congress, recognizing the value of rape awareness programs and special services for sexual assault victims, passed the Ramstad Amendment in 1992, requiring colleges and universities to develop campus sexual assault policies.[18] The law requires higher education institutions to adopt polices to prevent sex offenses and procedures to deal with sex offenses once they have occurred. The law specifies that the following areas will be addressed:

- education programs to promote awareness of rape, acquaintance rape, and other sex crimes;
- institutional sanctions for sex offenses, both forcible and nonforcible;
- procedures students should follow if they become a sexual assault victim, including who should be contacted, the importance of retaining evidence, and to whom the offense should be reported.

In addition, the Ramstad Amendment requires sex offense policies to state that the victim has the same right as the accused to have others present during a disciplinary hearing. Moreover, both the accuser and the accused will be informed of the outcome of any on-campus disciplinary proceeding. Institutions are also required to notify the victim that she has the option of reporting the sexual assault to law enforcement authorities and that she will receive assistance in that process. Finally, the law requires campus authorities to notify sexual assault victims about available counseling services and options for changing academic schedules and living arrangements in the wake of a sexual assault.

INSTITUTIONAL DISCIPLINE FOR SEXUAL OFFENSES

Faculty and Staff Misconduct

An educational institution necessarily holds a position of high public visibility and trust because of the role it plays in training of people, many of them young, for their roles in the larger world. The conduct of its faculty is subject to especial scrutiny, and standards are imposed that simply do not apply in more private aspects of social and economic endeavors. When faculty members are caught in sexual misconduct, formal criminal charges often are not instituted, but the employees may be discharged from their employment on grounds of moral turpitude. A review of the appellate court opinions reveals that colleges and universities have uniformly been upheld in such discipline.

In the earliest of such reported cases, a California appeals court affirmed the firing of a faculty member at Compton Junior College. The discharge occurred after a deputy sheriff discovered the instructor parked on a side street with a student. The instructor was undressed from the waist down, and the student was unclothed from the waist up. When the deputy sheriff asked the instructor for an identification, the instructor knocked the deputy sheriff to the ground, and a high-speed chase ensued. The instructor's termination was subsequently upheld based on that incident.[19]

A 1984 case involving another California institution likewise upheld the termination of an instructor who grabbed, held tightly, and kissed an 18-year-old student lab assistant at Santa Monica Community College. In holding that a college need not tolerate such conduct from a faculty member, the court admonished: "The (College Personnel) Commission and the courts have a grave responsibility not alone to respondent, but also to the appellants and their personnel, the professors, instructors, and students they embrace, and to the general public."[20]

Homosexual activities. Several cases have dealt with professors accused of homosexual activities. In 1985, the Tenth Circuit Court of Appeals upheld the dismissal of a tenured professor of veterinary medicine at Oklahoma State University after he passed notes soliciting homosexual activity to an undercover campus police officer in an adjoining restroom stall at the Student Union Building. The police officer testified that upon entering a bathroom stall he received a note wrapped around a pen from the professor, who was occupying the adjoining stall. The note, initiated by the professor in apparent response to existing writing on bathroom walls, read (the professor's admitted writing is italicized):

> *Interested in what? Did you leave the note?*
> That's why I'm here! No chains!
> *OK, let's go outside and talk.*
> There's nobody in here. What do you want?
> Ass—you?
> Sounds good!
> *OK, let's go talk.*

The professor was arrested for soliciting a lewd and indecent act, but formal criminal charges were never pressed. After his discharge the professor sued for reinstatement. In his trial, it was not controverted that the professor was considered a very good teacher with excellent research capabilities. The professor contended that moral turpitude was not involved, and that the only issue should be whether, under the guidelines of the Association of American University Professors, the incident surrounding his termination affected his teaching. He further contended that he was denied due process when terminated. The professor received little sympathy from the federal court, which held that the evidence involving the professor's actions in the restroom constituted conduct involving moral turpitude, and justified his termination.[21]

Similar reasoning was used by the Fifth U.S. Circuit Court of Appeals in a 1984 decision involving a 29-year-old graduate assistant who had sued Louisiana State University after it refused to assign her teaching duties. The court upheld the university's actions, based on the university's claim that it removed the graduate assistant's teaching duties not because of her homosexual orientation, but because of the professional impropriety of her intimate relationship with a 17-year-old freshman student, regardless of the sex of the student.[22]

It should be noted that the university employees who were sanctioned in these cases were not accused of simply engaging in private homosexual activity between consenting adults. They were charged with conduct which was otherwise unprofessional—seeking a sexual liaison in a public restroom and developing an intimate relationship with a student. Some states and municipalities have passed legislation prohibiting discrimination based on sexual orientation; and in these jurisdictions, it would be unlawful to discharge or discipline a campus employee just for being a practicing homosexual.

Moreover, decisions upholding the right of higher education institutions to sanction employees who engage in illegal homosexual behavior should not be read as support for the proposition that colleges or universities can ban all homosexual groups from campus. Gay student groups have litigated with universities since the 1970s over the issue of campus recognition, and it is now well established that public institutions violate the First Amendment if they refuse to recognize such a group based on opposition to their homosexual orientation. For example, the University of Missouri argued that it was justified in denying official recognition to a Gay Lib chapter based on the likelihood that recognition would lead to increased violation of the sodomy laws. A federal court ruled, however, that this contention was insufficient to justify the state's prior restraint on the right of a group of students to associate for the purpose of advocating the liberalization of legal restrictions against the practice of homosexuality and seeking to generate understanding and acceptance of homosexuals in society. The university was ordered to grant recognition to the group.[23] Similar rulings have been issued in cases brought by gay student groups against Texas A & M University,[24] Texas Tech University,[25] and the University of New Hampshire.[26]

In 1988, the Eighth Circuit Court of Appeals extended the recognition principle to rule that the University of Arkansas was required by the First Amendment to provide university funding for a gay student group on the same basis that funding was provided to other student organizations. The fact that homosexual activity was illegal in Arkansas did not affect the constitutional analysis. "People may extol the virtues of arson or even cannibalism," the court said. "They simply may not commit the acts."[27]

Moreover, as discussed above, several states and municipalities have passed antidiscrimination laws that specifically prohibit discrimination based on sexual orientation. These laws may limit not only the ability of public institutions to ban gay student groups, but also private colleges and universities as well. And this may be true, even if the private institution is affiliated with a religious group that is opposed to homosexuality as a tenet of religious faith.

In *Gay Rights Coalition v. Georgetown University*, a gay students organization sued Georgetown University, claiming that the university had violated the District of Columbia Human Rights Act by refusing to grant university recognition to the group and by withholding access to university facilities and services that accompanied recognition status. The act prohibited an educational institution from discriminating against an individual based on sexual orientation. Georgetown, a university affiliated with the Roman Catholic Church, argued that the human rights law violated the institution's right to free exercise of religion, since requiring Georgetown to recognize a gay student group forced it to endorse practices that are abhorrent to the Catholic faith.

A District of Columbia trial court accepted Georgetown's argument and ruled that the human rights act was unconstitutional as applied to the university since it conflicted with the Constitution's guarantee of religious freedom. On appeal, however, the trial court was substantially reversed. Although the District of Columbia Court of Appeals ruled that Georgetown was not required to recognize the gay student group, it was required to provide it with facilities and services similar to those granted other student groups. According to the court, the District of Columbia's compelling interest in eradicating sexual orientation discrimination outweighed any burden that providing these benefits might impose on Georgetown University's religious exercise.[28]

Students' Sexual Misconduct

In general, the courts have upheld colleges and universities that sanction students for sexual misbehavior. A Boston University law student was expelled for crawling on all fours under a table in the library and peeping under the skirts of women students. The dean learned that the student had been charged with a rape a decade earlier, and the dean then obtained a copy of the rape trial transcript and placed it on file for review by any interested member of the student body. The student, who had been president of the student bar association, sued for reinstatement and damages, alleging violation of his privacy and due process rights. The federal courts, however, found for the university on all counts. They noted the trial transcript was a public record, and it could not be the subject of a privacy violation claim.[29]

In a 1993 case, Tulane University suspended a male undergraduate student for allegedly engaging in nonconsensual sexual intercourse with an inebriated female companion. The student sued for reinstatement, challenging various aspects of Tulane's disciplinary procedures. In the area of student discipline, a Louisiana appellate court wrote, the court would not substitute its views for those of a private university. Although Tulane's disciplinary proceedings could be reviewed for arbitrary or capricious conduct, the court continued, Tulane had not acted arbitrarily or capriciously in the way it had imposed the suspension.[30]

SEXUAL HARASSMENT

Potential Civil and Criminal Sanctions

Although generally not as heinous as campus rape, sexual harassment in higher education is also a serious matter. An often unrecognized aspect of sexual harassment is that it may constitute a criminal as well as a civil offense. Obtaining sexual favors through some type of coercion—grades, jobs, promotions—comes within the legal definition of force or threatened force in some sexual assault statutes, just as if the act were compelled through brute physical strength. Indeed, it may be possible for the victim of serious sexual harassment to seek monetary damages against the harasser while prosecutors pursue criminal charges.

As a civil matter, sexual harassment is a form of sex discrimination, and two bodies of federal law prohibit higher education institutions from engaging in or permitting it. Title VII of the Civil Rights Act of 1964[31] prohibits most American employers, including colleges and universities, from engaging in sexual harassment against employees. Title IX of the Education Amendments of 1972[32] prohibits educational institutions that receive federal funds from engaging in sexual harassment against either employees or students.

Sexual harassment can be divided into two types. In the first type, a person in a position of authority uses that position to extort some kind of sexual activity from a subordinate. The courts refer to this kind of harassment as *quid pro quo.* In the second form, an employee is subjected to sexually offensive behavior in the workplace, usually by co-workers. This form of sexual harassment is referred to as "hostile environment" harassment.

Prior to 1992, it was unclear whether Title IX authorized a lawsuit for monetary damages. Thus, most sexual harassment lawsuits were brought in the employment context under Title VII. In 1992, however, in the case of *Franklin v. Gwinnett County Public Schools,*[33] the Supreme Court permitted a high school student to sue a Georgia school district for damages under Title IX, based on her accusation that a teacher had sexually harassed her by engaging in conduct that culminated in three acts of "coercive intercourse." Thus, in years to come, educational institutions can anticipate sexual harassment law suits brought not only by employees but also by students who accuse professors or other campus staff members of engaging in sexually offensive behavior.

Thanks to a number of federal court decisions, the contours of an institution's liability for sexual harassment have become clearer. First, when a supervisor uses his authority to extort sexual favors from a subordinate—what the courts call *quid pro quo* harassment—the institution can be held strictly liable for damages, regardless of whether it knew or should have known about the offensive behavior. When the harassment consists of a "hostile environment" —harassment by co-workers, for example—the institution is not liable unless it knew or should have known about the harassment and failed to take appropriate action to stop it.[34]

Second, a supervisor who uses his authority to obtain sexual favors is not absolved of a sexual harassment claim simply because the subordinate's participation was physically "voluntary." The Supreme Court has stated that the correct inquiry in such cases should be whether the complainant, by her conduct, had indicated that the alleged sexual advances were unwelcome.[35]

Third, a victim's failure to use an in-house grievance procedure or policy to complain about a superior's conduct will not automatically insulate an employer from liability in sexual harassment cases. This is particularly true if the grievance procedure requires the victim to file her grievance with the person who is harassing her.[36]

Fourth, a plaintiff need not show serious psychological or physical injury to obtain relief for sexual harassment. In a 1993 Supreme Court decision, Justice Sandra Day O'Connor explained that Title VII comes into play before the harassing conduct leads to a nervous breakdown. "A discriminatorily abusive work environment, even one that does not seriously affect employees' psychological well-being, can and often will detract from employees' job performance, discourage employees from remaining on the job, or keep them from advancing in their careers," Justice O'Connor wrote. "So long as the environment would reasonably be perceived, and is perceived, as hostile or abusive, there is no need for it also to be psychologically injurious."[37]

Harassment: Commonplace?

Recent research has disclosed that sexual harassment on campus apparently is far more commonplace than was recognized a few years ago. A 1983 survey of female undergraduate and graduate students at Iowa State University found that they had experienced the following behaviors from male faculty members: 6.4 percent had experienced physical advances of fondling, kissing, pinching, or hugging; 3.4 percent experienced sexual propositions; and 2.1 percent had been subject to sexual bribery that included or strongly implied promises of rewards for compliance.[38] A similar survey the same year at East Carolina University found that 8.9 percent of the female students reported patting or pinching to the point where they were uncomfortable; 4.9 percent had experienced subtle pressures for sexual activity; and 0.9 percent reported having been sexually assaulted by a male instructor.[39]

No Sympathy for Sexual Harassers from the Courts

It appears the courts have little sympathy for educators who sexually harass. Typical is a 1984 decision of the Seventh U.S. Circuit Court of Appeals that upheld the termination of a tenured associate professor of music history and musicology at Ball State University. The court found that the university had not violated the professor's constitutional rights when it fired him for making sexual advances toward his male students.[40]

A similar result came in a decision by the Fifth U.S. Circuit Court of Appeals that upheld the firing of a tenured professor of chemistry at the University of Texas at El Paso for sexual harassment. Four female students had accused the male professor of making sexual advances, and a faculty review committee had found the professor guilty. There was a question as to whether the committee had been properly constituted; the president appointed the committee in accordance with Texas Board of Regents' policy, but the professor argued the committee should have been constituted under existing rules of the University Committee on Academic Rights, Privileges, and Ethics. The appeals court said the possible failure of the university to strictly comply with its own rules would not vitiate the proceedings; technical noncompliance did not, in itself, deprive the professor of due process of law.[41]

One sexual harassment suit at Howard University grew out of the nonretention of the chairperson of the Department of Pharmacy Practice. The chairperson, a female, alleged in a suit filed after her employment was terminated that the male dean of the College of Pharmacy at Howard had subjected her to unwanted patting on the rear, suggestive comments, and sexual propositions, all in the workplace. She alleged that the nonretention was in retaliation for her rebuff of the dean. The Court of Appeals for the District of Columbia ruled that such actions would constitute a prima facie case of sexual harassment and remanded the case to the trial court for further fact-finding.[42]

One sexual harassment trial typifies the attitude of the courts in cases involving student victims. Eight female students brought a suit for damages for assault, battery, and intentional infliction of mental distress against a private dramatic arts instructor after he allegedly coerced them into a sexual relationship with him. The females, all in their twenties, charged that the instructor, who was in his mid-sixties, made them perform various sex acts, including fellatio upon him and masturbation and lesbian acts in his presence. They said they felt compelled to obey his wishes, as he had an outstanding reputation as an acting teacher who had taught many famous actors and actresses.

The jury awarded the students $2,000 each and submitted a note along with the verdict which read, "Hopefully, our decision will serve as a future deterrent in sexual abuse and harassment behavior of teacher against student." The judge found the jury's award to be inadequate, however, and ordered a new trial unless the instructor would stipulate to increasing the award to $5,000 for each student. The court's opinion said the instructor, "playing upon the emotional needs of his insecure students, actively sought to be ensconced as their trusted father figure. . . . This gross violation was not merely of their bodies but of their trust as well, an invasion so reprehensible as to cry out for the imposition of a sanction expressing the moral outrage of society."[43]

In *Lipsett v. University of Puerto Rico*,[44] the First Circuit Court of Appeals ruled that a woman surgery resident had made out a prima facie case of *quid pro quo* and "hostile environment" sexual harassment against the University of Puerto Rico. She accused the medical school staff and male residents of several instances of sexual harassment, including a statement by the chief resident that surgery was "a male preserve not hospitable to women," the display of a sexually explicit poster of her, refusal by some doctors to allow her to operate, and repeated and unwelcome sexual advances. Eventually, the woman was dismissed from the surgical residency program, and the First Circuit Court ruled that she had alleged sufficient facts to state a claim that her dismissal was because of her sex.

In a 1993 case, the University of Northern Iowa dismissed a student's sexual harassment claim against a professor, whereupon the professor sued the university for malicious prosecution. In her complaint, the student had accused the professor of kissing her during a field trip to New Orleans. The Eighth Circuit Court of Appeals ruled that the professor could not prevail on his claim since the university had probable cause to investigate the student's complaint.[45]

Finally, a recent Maine case provides an example of an interesting, although unsuccessful, defense to a sexual harassment claim. In *Winston v. Maine Technical College System*, a tenured instructor at Central Maine Technical College was discharged after he was accused of engaging in a sexually suggestive conversation with an 18-year-old female student and then kissing her. After losing a union grievance proceeding, the instructor filed suit, claiming that he had been discriminated against because of his "mental handicap of sexual addiction." The Maine Supreme Judicial Court analyzed both state and federal antidiscrimination law and concluded that the instructor's claimed disability was covered by neither.[46]

It is well that the courts take sexual harassment claims seriously, since harassment can have major long-term effects on the student victims. The impact on the victim's educational opportunity may include a lowering of academic aspirations, changing academic majors, or limiting career goals.[47] Student victims of sexual harassment also report experiencing insomnia, headaches, backaches, stomach ailments, depression, and other physical symptoms.[48]

Student-to-Student Harassment

Campus leaders may be well versed on liability issues surrounding sexual harassment by their institution's employees, but they may be surprised to learn of a trend to hold educational institutions liable when students sexually harass each other. In 1993, the U.S. Department of Education's Office for Civil Rights determined that a Minnesota school district had violated Title IX's sex discrimination provisions when it failed to stop elementary school boys from repeatedly sexually harassing a female student when she was traveling to school on a school bus.[49] A short time later, a federal court in California ruled that the Petaluma City School District could be held liable under Title IX to a high school girl who complained of sexual harassment by other students that extended over two school terms. The court said that the school district could be held responsible for student-to-student harassment that it knew about and which it failed to take effective action to stop.[50]

So far, there have been no reported court cases involving institutional liability under Title IX for sexual harassment of college students by other students. However, it is not hard to imagine situations in which such lawsuits might be brought.

For example, a case against Franklin and Marshall College, although not involving a sexual harassment claim, described the kind of student behavior that might well lead to a Title IX complaint if an institution knew about it and failed to take action. In that case a student found guilty of harassing behavior in a coed dormitory filed a lawsuit seeking to enjoin the college from suspending him. A Pennsylvania appellate court affirmed the trial court's decision in favor of the college and listed the following acts that a student conduct committee determined the student had committed: making lewd and lascivious comments about female students' dress, body, and behavior; locking two women out of their dormitory room while he went through their lingerie drawer; placing a condom on the door of a female student; loitering near the women's bathroom; following women into the bathroom; setting fire to a pair of men's underwear that was attached to the doors of two female students; pushing a woman onto a bed and attempting to pull up her night-gown; and verbally harassing two female students.[51]

A college's obligation to act in a case like the one just described seems clear; but other student behavior, even though boorish and offensive, may enjoy First Amendment protection. In *Iota Xi Chapter of Sigma Chi Fraternity v. George Mason University*, the Fourth Circuit Court of Appeals ruled that George Mason University could not sanction a fraternity for sponsoring an "Ugly Woman" contest, based on the finding that the event, as expressive speech, was protected under the First Amendment.[52] The university's argument that it had a duty to foster an educational climate that was free of discrimination was of no avail.

Campus Harassment Policies

Many campuses now have adopted sexual harassment policies; some are quite good, but some have been written by faculty committees with a clear "there but for the grace of God go I" posture. Policies that do not protect victims, or that leave the final evaluation and sanction in the hands of a secret faculty group, may do more harm than good, both legally and in the court of public opinion. An effective policy demonstrates good faith on the part of the institution and those who run it and could offset allegations that the institution had condoned sexual misbehavior. Further, the "foreseeability" doctrine of civil liability applies to sexual harassment matters; if administrators know they have an offender in their employ but do nothing about it, they and the college or university may be liable to anyone injured by subsequent abuse that might have been interdicted.

In 1986, the American Council on Education issued a report on campus sexual harassment that urged colleges and universities to adopt effective sexual harassment policies because they can help shield the institution from potential civil liability as well as address legitimate faculty and student concerns. "The entire academic community suffers when sexual harassment is allowed to pervade the academic atmosphere," the report said.[53]

The council report said that a good campus policy would contain a clear definition of sexual harassment, explain why it is important for the institution to prevent such practices, and include a grievance procedure that encourages the report of incidents, first using informal channels, but with formal channels if the informal disposition is not satisfactory. Penalties should be spelled out. Campus supervisors should be trained concerning the policy, and the written policy itself should be explained at student and employee gatherings and widely distributed, including in the institution's catalogue and student, staff, and faculty handbooks.

Each campus should have a coordinator for enforcing sexual harassment and sex discrimination policies, and he or she should be a person well respected on the campus. Complaints should be acted upon promptly and written records kept. Further, the report recommended, results of resolved complaints should be published, making certain to protect the privacy of all involved.

It also seems wise to establish a policy concerning sexual relations between students and faculty members, graduate assistants, or other campus employees in a position of authority over students. Harvard Graduate School of Education, which prohibits such relationships, adopted the following policy:

> [W]here one person's present role involves grading or otherwise evaluating the work of another, or puts the person in a position to affect the other's present performance or professional future, sexual overtures and sexual relationships, even if consensual, are inappropriate and may be grounds for disciplinary action under this policy statement.[54]

Other institutions, however, warn faculty and staff members about the inappropriateness of sexual relationships with students without prohibiting them altogether. Amherst College, for example, requires professors dating students to report their relationship to their department heads and to give up any responsibility for supervising the student's academic program.[55] Some institutions prohibit professors from dating students in the same department, without prohibiting all social relationships between faculty and students.

Although institutions have a great deal of discretion about the details of a sexual harassment policy, there can be no doubt that every college and university should have some kind of written policy. Title IX's administrative regulations require all educational institutions receiving federal funds to adopt a sex discrimination grievance procedure and to appoint a Title IX coordinator to investigate complaints about sex discrimination, including sexual harassment.[56]

RAPE, LIABILITY, AND ADMINISTRATORS

In recent years there have been growing numbers of cases in which rape victims have sued institutions to collect monetary damages for, in a sense, helping to make the rape possible. Basically, institutions of higher education owe a duty to take precautions against foreseeable dangers and to provide a reasonably safe environment for their students and employees (see chapter 5 for further discussion of liability issues). A lawsuit can be initiated for monetary damages if the institution breaches that duty and if the rape or assault might have been avoided through better security or warnings to potential victims.

In the 1984 case of *Peterson v. San Francisco Community College District*,[57] the California Supreme Court held that a student could sue the college for injuries received in an attempted rape at a college parking lot. In that case, the college had been on notice of previous assaults in the parking lot, and it had failed to warn students.

A similar result had come a year earlier from the Supreme Judicial Court of Massachusetts in the case of *Mullins v. Pine Manor College*.[58] In that case, a female student was raped on campus by an unidentified assailant who was never apprehended. On the night of the rape two guards were on duty at the school, which had a student body of 400. The student was awakened in her dormitory room by an intruder who forced her out of the building, across the courtyard, and off-campus for a time. The entire incident, including the rape, lasted for more than an hour.

The *Mullins* court held that parents, students, and the general community had an enforceable expectation, fostered in part by the college itself, that reasonable care would be exercised to protect resident students from foreseeable harm. Although in the years prior to the attack there had been no incidents of violent crime on campus, the college was in a metropolitan area and the director of student affairs had warned students during freshman orientation of the dangers inherent in being located only a short distance from bus and train lines that lead directly to Boston. The court therefore felt that the risk of a criminal act was not only foreseeable but actually had been foreseen by the school. The opinion noted that the concentration of young people, especially young women, on a college campus, "creates favorable opportunities for criminal behavior." The case does seem to present something of a "catch-22," in that, on the one hand, the college's warning to students was a factor in establishing its own liability. On the other hand, the court's real point was that because the college did appreciate the danger, it should have provided good security, and it did not.

Another dormitory rape was involved in the 1985 New York case of *Miller v. State*. The court likened the college to a landlord and said its failure to lock dormitory outer doors was a breach of its duty to maintain minimum security and that the assault had been foreseeable.[59]

A university's representations of dormitory safety led to one suit alleging deceit and misrepresentation by the institution. After a female student was sexually assaulted and murdered in her dormitory room at California State University, the victim's mother said that she had relied on the representations and the dormitory's appearance of safety and security when she decided to let her daughter live there. She complained that the school had been aware of increased violence on the campus but had chosen to ignore it. In holding that the suit could proceed, the court noted that the representation that the dormitories were safe was made by university officials "with presumed superior knowledge" of dangers.[60]

Of course, higher education institutions are not automatically liable when a student is sexually assaulted or a campus rape occurs. For example, a federal district court ruled that Bethany College, a private institution in West Virginia, was not liable for the alleged rape of a 17-year-old student that occurred at Bubba's Bison Inn, an off-campus bar. The student, who was below the legal drinking age in West Virginia, met her assailants at the bar, where she was given alcoholic beverages. Later she was taken to another location and raped.

Colleges are not required to supervise students after they leave the campus, the court ruled, nor are they required to advise students of state laws. The plaintiff had argued that the college stood in loco parentis to her on account of her age, but the court rejected this argument. "It is not reasonable to conclude today that seventeen year old college students necessarily require parental protection and supervision," the court said. "If they did, society might place many more limitations upon the ability of a minor to attend college than currently exist."[61]

Likewise, in another case involving underage drinking, the California Court of Appeals ruled that the University of California at Berkeley was not legally responsible when a first-year college student was sexually assaulted by fellow students in a coed dormitory. The assaults took place after a dormitory drinking party. All four of the assailants were university football players.

The victim argued that a shattered light bulb on the landing in a stairwell was a contributing factor, along with the fact that men and women resided together on the same dormitory floor. However, in the court's view, there was no evidence that better lighting on the stairwell landing would have prevented the attacks, some of which occurred in dormitory rooms. Nor was there any evidence that segregating the sexes on different dormitory floors would have deterred the assaults, since, as the court pointed out, the assailants knew how to use the stairs.[62]

In another California case, a woman who was raped on the University of Southern California campus won a large negligence judgment against the university, only to have the award reversed on appeal. The rape occurred when the woman had come on campus to make a deposit at the university's credit union. With the aid of an expert witness who criticized nearly every aspect of USC's security precautions, she persuaded a jury that the university had been negligent in failing to deter the attack.

The California Court of Appeals, however, ruled that the victim had not shown how any failure on the university's part had been the cause of her injury. Indeed, the court pointed out that the USC campus was far safer than the surrounding neighborhood and was better patrolled. On the night of the attack, eight USC officers were patrolling a quarter-mile area, while the Los Angeles Police Department had the same number of officers patrolling the surrounding ten and one-half square miles.

It was not enough, the California court said, for the victim's expert witness to compare USC's security measures to an abstract standard and to point out how USC could have done better. It was necessary to show how better security measures would have prevented the rape. According to the court, the attack took place in an open area of campus that could have been adequately protected, if at all, only by a "Berlin Wall." Under these circumstances, the court concluded, it was not reasonable to hold USC liable for the victim's injuries.[63]

In addition, although several courts have recognized a university's obligation to protect students from a foreseeable danger of campus rape, at least one court refused to find such an obligation when the alleged rape did not occur during a university-sponsored activity. In *Leonardi v. Bradley University*,[64] an Illinois appellate court acknowledged that Bradley University might owe a duty of care to students who were taking part in university-sponsored activities, when students would have the status of business invitees. However, in the case before it, the court ruled that a student was not a business invitee of the university at the time she was allegedly raped, which was late at night in a fraternity house.

Finally, a 1993 case, *Nero v. Kansas State University*,[65] illustrates an institution's exposure to civility liability when a student has been charged, but not convicted, of rape. In that case, a male student who resided in Moore Hall, a KSU coed dormitory, was charged with raping a female student who lived in the same dormitory. Pending disposition of the criminal charges, KSU officials transferred the accused student to an all-male dormitory on the other side of campus.

Shortly thereafter, however, the academic school year ended; and the accused student moved to Goodnow Hall, another coed dormitory and the only KSU dormitory available to students attending intersession and summer school. Thirty-five days after he reportedly raped the Moore Hall resident, the student was accused of sexually assaulting a second student in the basement of Goodnow Hall. He later plead guilty to raping the first student. In return, authorities dropped the sexual assault charge involving the second student.

The student's second alleged victim sued KSU for negligence. She argued that the university had breached its duty of care to her by failing to protect her from a foreseeable assault. Her claims were dismissed by the trial court, but the Kansas Supreme Court allowed her lawsuit to proceed. A majority of the court ruled that a factual issue existed concerning whether KSU used reasonable care in placing an accused rapist in a coed dormitory. In addition, the court ruled that there were factual issues concerning whether the second woman should have been warned of the danger that the accused rapist presented and whether adequate security measures had been taken to protect her.

Two Kansas justices dissented, and one of them pointed out the dilemma KSU faced when one of its students was accused, but not convicted, of rape:

> As the majority points out, the days of strict monitoring by a coed university of the private lives of its students is [sic] over. College students are to be treated as adults. When faced with a decision as to what to do when one student alleges sexual improprieties by a fellow resident, a university has a judgment call to make. Such a call has to be made on a case-by-case basis. The alleged impropriety herein was the subject of a criminal charge which, practically speaking, eliminates any meaningful due process proceeding by the university until after resolution of the criminal charge. It is unlikely the defense attorney would permit his or her client to tell the client's version of the events in a due process proceeding prior to resolution of the criminal charge. Yet, the University has entered into a contract with the accused resident to provide housing and cannot act arbitrarily. Thus, the University is placed in a very difficult situation.

How was KSU to have warned female students that a fellow student had been charged with rape, the dissenting justice asked. "Word of mouth? Publication in the student newspaper? Flyers? Requiring [the accused] to wear sandwich boards stating, 'I am a rapist, beware'?"[66] Even though a person is presumed innocent until proven guilty, the justice continued, the majority opinion in essence required KSU to presume guilt, treat the accused as a pariah, and ostracize him from all female students.

When one of its students was charged with rape, the dissenting Kansas justice concluded, KSU was faced with a complex situation, one that had no obvious and clear-cut solution. In hindsight, the justice acknowledged, KSU's decision to allow the accused student to move back to a coed dormitory was not a wise one, but it was the kind of discretionary decision that is normally excluded from liability under Kansas law.

What can we glean from this line of cases concerning a university's liability when a student or campus employee is raped? First, colleges and universities have a responsibility to protect the campus community from foreseeable dangers, which means they should take special precautions in areas that are known to be dangerous and to warn students and employees about these areas. Second, it does not seem likely that the courts will hold institutions liable for off-campus assaults, at least in the absence of some added factor, such as institutional sponsorship of the activity where the assault occurs.

Third, although some rapes have occurred in coed dormitories, the courts have not ruled that mixed-sex housing in itself poses an unreasonable danger for sexual assault. As *Nero v. Kansas State University* illustrates, however, some male students pose a danger to female students when they live in coed housing. Whenever a coed dorm resident is accused of sexual misconduct, that student should be moved to single-sex housing until charges are satisfactorily resolved.

Liability for Rapes Committed by Campus Employees

Colleges and universities may face an increased risk of liability if the individual who commits the rape is an employee. Courts are split with regard to whether employers are liable for an employee's sexual offenses. Some take the view that an employee who commits a sexual offense is never acting within the scope of his employment, and thus employers bear no responsibility for this kind of misconduct unless it occurred through negligent hiring or negligent supervision. In particular, most courts have refused to hold school districts liable in cases involving sexual molestation by school employees.[67] A contrary line of cases has emerged, however, in which courts have held that employers can be vicariously liable for this kind of misbehavior, even if they had no reason to suspect that the employee was a sex offender.

Most of the cases in which courts have held employers vicariously liable for an employee's sexual misconduct have involved police officers or health care workers who used their positions to commit sexual offenses.[68] In *Mary M. v. City of Los Angeles*,[69] the seminal case in this area, the California Supreme Court ruled that the Los Angeles Police Department could be held liable when a police officer raped a motorist who was stopped for a traffic violation.

Most of the cases in which courts have held employers vicariously liable for an employee's sexual misconduct have involved police officers or health care workers who used their positions to commit sexual offenses.[70] In *Mary M. v. City of Los Angeles*,[71] the seminal case in this area, the California Supreme Court ruled that the Los Angeles Police Department could be held liable when a police officer raped a motorist who was stopped for a traffic violation. Similarly, in *Samuels v. Southern Baptist Hospital*,[72] a 1992 case, a Louisiana court ruled that a hospital could be held vicariously liable for a nursing assistant's reputed assault on a 16-year-old psychiatric patient. Moreover, in a recent case, discussed more fully later in this chapter, the Louisiana Court of Appeals upheld a verdict against Grambling State University for damages suffered when a university employee allegedly raped a 15-year-old girl who was on the Grambling campus.[73] (In that case, the employee was neither a health care worker nor a law enforcement officer, but merely a summer worker hired to assist with the university's summer youth sports program.)

These cases suggest that colleges and universities should take special care when hiring law enforcement personnel, hospital workers, and mental health professionals to make sure these individuals do not have histories of sexual misconduct. Not only are institutions most likely to be vicariously liable for sexual misconduct by these categories of employees, it is these employees who, by virtue of their job responsibilities, have the opportunity to take sexual advantage of vulnerable or helpless individuals.

Additional Harm to the Institution

Another dimension to campus sex crime, beyond the aspect of civil liability, is the adverse publicity that an institution is likely to receive. When a female freshman at West Virginia University charged that she had been sexually assaulted in a dormitory by five members of the school's basketball team, the local grand jury declined to indict anyone but was highly critical of the university's handling of the matter. The grand jury's report said that "persons who hold positions of high esteem in our community and who serve as role models to many West Virginians have been involved in appalling behavior. We condemn their actions."[74] Those persons of "high esteem" were never identified, and the conjecture that raged in the press for months did the university great damage.

The grand jury's report also criticized the university's investigation of the matter, and after suggestions were made in the press that the university had sought to cover up the case to protect its athletic program, the university's acting president, Diane Reinhard, said that should another sexual assault occur on campus, she would call in state police immediately rather than rely on campus security officers.[75]

A frightened campus community may be another unwelcome by-product of a campus rape that receives publicity. When a campus secretary was repeatedly assaulted for an hour and a half one afternoon in an isolated area at Emory University's administration building, word began to circulate that the suspect was a former university employee and a football player of some renown. Rumors then added that he had a master key to university buildings, and the campus security department was inundated with calls reporting suspicious persons. Until the apprehension of the suspect, a near panic disrupted the entire campus.[76]

Protecting the Campus

Many colleges and universities have instituted vigorous programs in response to rape on campus. In the mid-1980s, for instance, Central Michigan University adopted a "provictim" stance in a broad policy that included escort service by man-woman teams and foot patrols by students, sexual assault training for dormitory advisors, increased late-night lighting, and awareness programs to help the psyche of the victim and her friends by accentuating that blame for the attack lies on the rapist, not the victim.[77] Vanderbilt University's Department of Police and Security has published two attractive booklets that are furnished to all students. One deals with rape and sexual abuse, and it explains the "myths and realties" of sexual attack, preventive measures, intervention methods, and how to deal with the aftermath of an attack.[78] The other is a general booklet on crime prevention and deals with subjects ranging from bicycle theft to purse snatching and harassing telephone calls. It even includes photographs of the campus security force and is designed to make students feel at ease with campus security programs.[79]

Institutional Responsibility Following a Rape

Preventive measures, even the most effective, will not eliminate all campus rapes. Thus, it is critical for campus law enforcement officials to have the expertise to investigate and successfully prosecute these cases when they occur. Institutions that are too small to support a sophisticated crime investigation unit should make sure that local law enforcement authorities can step in quickly to conduct a rape investigation if the need arises.

One experienced rape case prosecutor reports, for instance, that rape victims rarely are able to tell the whole story the first time, at least to regular police officers. The tendency is for victims to omit the particularly harsh, bizarre, or embarrassing details, probably because they subconsciously feel that it may reflect badly upon them. Also, if the victim was doing something that might be seen as in some way wrong in itself, such as using drugs or consenting to some lesser sexual activity, she usually will not report it in the first interview, thus hindering both the investigation and the strength and credibility of her testimony for trial. An experienced rape investigator may be able to develop a protocol that will get the "negatives" of the case out front promptly.[80]

Many student rape victims will seek medical assistance at the campus health clinic. The health care professionals who staff these clinics should be familiar with the psychological consequences of rape trauma and trained to safeguard the evidence necessary to obtain a criminal conviction. A victim may wish to change her housing situation because of the rape, and campus housing authorities should be prepared to make this accommodation quickly and with a minimum of fuss. Finally, some designated campus representative should inform the victim of internal grievance procedures as well as criminal and civil options, and this counseling should be supplemented with literature that outlines the victim's options for seeking redress and the campus services that are available to assist her.

SEX CRIMES AGAINST CHILDREN: SPECIAL CAMPUS CONCERNS

In general, the campus community is made up of adults, but an increasing number of children now visit colleges and universities on a regular basis. For example, more than a dozen states have passed so-called postsecondary option laws, allowing high school students to take college courses, either for high school or college credit.[81] Many institutions offer summer sports clinics and academic enrichment courses that attract children as young as elementary-school age. And of course, most institutions will enroll at least a few freshman students who are under the age of 18 when they arrive on campus, which means they have the legal status of children in many states.

All 50 states require educators to report incidents of child abuse that they learn about in the course of their professional duties,[82] and many of these laws are broad enough to cover higher education educators as well as public school teachers and administrators. In most states, it is a criminal offense for mandated reporters to fail to report child abuse that they know about, and some states permit civil suits against persons who violate the child abuse reporting statutes. Thus, it is essential for campus personnel who work with children to be thoroughly familiar with these laws.

Unfortunately, some adults seek child care employment in order to have opportunities to abuse children, and higher education authorities must take special care when they hire the people who operate on-campus sports and academic programs for children. For example, in a 1994 case, the parents of a 15-year-old child sued Grambling State University in Louisiana for injuries suffered when the child, who was on campus for a summer sports program, was allegedly raped by a university employee. A Louisiana court ruled that the university could be held vicariously liable for the judgment entered against the accused rapist, which was in the amount of $110,000.[83]

Many states now require school districts and child care agencies to conduct criminal background checks on prospective employees who will have contact with children,[84] and university counsel would be wise to review the legislation in their jurisdiction to determine whether these laws apply to their institutions' child-oriented programs. Higher education officials should be aware that when their institutions begin offering programs to high school and elementary school children, they assume additional responsibilities to protect this special student population from injury, including sexual abuse.

CONCLUSION: CAMPUSES MUST DEVELOP A COMPREHENSIVE PLAN FOR COMBATING SEXUAL ASSAULTS AND SEXUAL HARASSMENT

Sexual assault is a distressingly frequent occurrence on many college campuses, as well as sexual harassment in all its many forms. Institutional liability for these outrages is a growing concern for college administrators, as the courts show themselves increasingly willing to hold higher education institutions responsible for the sexual misconduct that occurs on their campuses. In some instances, federal law now dictates an institution's response with regard to both rape and sexual harassment.

Even if colleges were inclined to sweep incidents of sexual misconduct under the rug, they are no longer free to do so. Moreover, piecemeal measures and half-hearted approaches will no longer suffice to deal with sexual harassment and sexual violence. Institutions must develop a comprehensive response, involving not only campus law enforcement authorities, but also groundkeeping and maintenance departments, student services, medical staff, counselors, and housing personnel. At a minimum, the following issues should be addressed:

- A rape awareness program, using trained staff and literature, should be developed. The program should target the campus community's most vulnerable members—first year college women—and the groups that are often prominent in sexual misconduct incidents—fraternities and student athletes. Victims should know where they can go for assistance and redress, and potential aggressors should know the consequences if they use physical force, drugs, or alcohol to obtain sex. A rape awareness program should emphasize the part that alcohol plays in campus sexual aggression.

- Title IX requires higher education institutions to appoint a Title IX coordinator and to develop a grievance procedure for sex discrimination and sexual harassment complaints. The person selected as coordinator should be perceived as accessible to students and staff, committed to the elimination of sexual harassment, and energetic in pursuing complaints to equitable resolution.

- A campus sexual harassment policy that complies with the Ramstad Amendment should be developed and disseminated. This policy should state the institution's expectations with regard to faculty-student liaisons and the penalties for violating policy guidelines.

- A campus security plan should reflect the institution's efforts to prevent sexual assault. The plan should address lighting, shrubbery, police patrols, escort services, call boxes in isolated locations, and residence hall security.

- A routine procedure should be put in place to notify the campus community about serious criminal activity that is likely to be an ongoing threat to students and employees. This procedure is a requirement of the Student Right-to-Know and Campus Security Act (discussed in detail in chapter 14).

- Campus disciplinary procedures should be reviewed to make sure they are adequate to address complaints about serious sexual misconduct. All persons who participate in campus ajudicatory proceedings should be trained and thoroughly understand their roles. The institution should develop a clear policy about which kinds of sexual offenses will be handled internally, and which will be turned over to the criminal authorities.

Finally, higher education authorities should understand that an effective program to prevent campus sex crimes and sexual harassment is not something that can be put in place and then forgotten. Sex crime awareness programs need to be offered on an annual basis in order to educate first-time students, recently arrived international students, and new employees. Campus security must be constantly monitored for such problems as inadequate lighting, overgrown shrubbery, or careless dormitory security. Institutional polices against sexual harassment should be reemphasized to faculty, employees, and students on a regular basis so that everyone understands that these policies reflect institutional values and are not just empty words. In short, the task of protecting the campus community from sexual assaults and harassment must become an integral part of the institution's day-to-day mission of providing a safe and secure learning and working environment.

NOTES

1. Mary P. Koss and Cheryl J. Oros, "Sexual Experiences Survey: A Research Instrument Investigating Sexual Aggression and Victimization," 50 *Journal of Consulting and Clinical Psychology* 484-90 (1982).
2. U.S. Department of Justice, Federal Bureau of Investigation, *1985 Uniform Crime Reports* (Washington, D.C.: Government Printing Office, 1986), table 7.
3. Douglas Lederman, "Colleges Report 7,500 Violent Crimes on Their Campuses in First Annual Statements Required under Federal Law," *The Chronicle of Higher Education*, January 20, 1993, p. A32.
4. Department of Public Safety, "Selected Aspects of the Crime of Forcible Rape" (Metropolitan Washington Council of Governments, 1974), p. 1.
5. Carol Bohmer and Andrea Parrott, *Sexual Assault on Campus* (New York: Lexington Books, 1993), pp. 20-21.
6. Ibid., p. 6.
7. Colleen Finley and Eric Corty, "Rape on Campus: The Prevalence of Sexual Assault While Enrolled in College," 34 *Journal of College Student Development* 113-17 (1993).
8. U.S. Department of Justice, Law Enforcement Assistance Administration, *Forcible Rape* (1978), pp. 15-16.
9. Eugene Kanin, "Date Rape: Unofficial Criminals and Victims," 9 *Victimology* 95-108 (1984).
10. Finley and Corty, p. 116.

11. Scott Boeringer, Constance Shehan, and Ronald L. Akers, "Social Contexts and Social Learning in Sexual Coercion and Aggression: Assessing the Contribution of Fraternity Membership," 40 *Family Relations* 58-64 (1991).
12. Bohmer and Parrott, pp. 21-23.
13. Ibid.
14. Julie Ehrhart and Bernice Sandler, "Campus Gang Rape: Party Games?" Project on the Status and Education of Women (Washington, D.C.: American Association of Colleges, 1985).
15. Bohmer and Parrott p. 26.
16. Ehrhart and Sandler.
17. "The Problem of Rape on Campus," Project on the Status and Education of Women (Washington, D.C.: American Association of Colleges, 1980).
18. Public Law 102-325, § 486(c)(2), codified at 20 USC § 1092 (f)(7).
19. *Board of Trustees of Compton Junior College District v. Stubblefield*, 16 Cal. App. 3d 820, 94 Cal. Rptr. 318 (1971).
20. *Cockburn v. Santa Monica Community College District*, 161 Cal. App. 3d 734, 207 Cal. Rptr. 589 (1984).
21. *Corstvet v. Boger*, 757 F.2d 223 (10th Cir. 1985).
22. *Naragon v. Wharton*, 737 F.2d1403 (5th Cir. 1984).
23. *Gay Lib. v. University of Missouri*, 558 F.2d 848 (8th Cir. 1977), *cert. denied*, 434 U.S. 1080 (1978).
24. *Gay Student Services v. Texas A & M University*, 737 F.2d 1317 (5th Cir. 1984).
25. *Student Services for Lesbians/Gays and Friends v. Texas Tech University*, 635 F. Supp. 776 (N.D. Tex. 1986).
26. *Gay Students Organization of the University of New Hampshire v. Bonner*, 509 F.2d 652 (1st Cir. 1974).
27. *Gay and Lesbian Students Association v. Gohn*, 850 F.2d 361 (8th Cir. 1988).
28. 536 A.2d 1 (D. C. Ct. App. 1987).
29. *Cloud v. Trustees of Boston University*, 720 F.2d 721 (1st Cir. 1983).
30. *Ahlum v. Administrators of Tulane Educational Fund*, 617 So.2d 96 (La. App. 1993).
31. 42 U.S.C. Sec. 2000 et seq.
32. 20 U.S.C. Sec. 1681 et seq.
33. 112 S. Ct. 1028 (1992).
34. *Lipsett v. University of Puerto Rico*, 864 F.2d 881 (1st Cir. 1988).
35. *Meritor Savings Bank v. Vinson*, 477 U.S. 57 (1986).
36. Ibid.
37. *Harris v. Forklift Systems, Inc.*, 113 S. Ct. 1302 (1993).
38. J. W. Adams, J. L. Kottke, and J. S. Padgitt, "Sexual Harassment of University Students," 24 *Journal of College Student Personnel* 484-90 (1983).
39. K. R. Wilson and L. Kraus, "Sexual Harassment in the University," 24 *Journal of College Student Personnel* 219-34 (1983).
40. *Korf v. Ball State University*, 726 F.2d 1222 (7th Cir. 1984).
41. *Levitt v. University of Texas at El Paso*, 759 F.2d 1224 (5th Cir.), *cert. denied*, 474 U.S. 1034 (1985).
42. *Howard University v. Best*, 484 A.2d 958 (D.C. 1984).
43. *Micari v. Mann*, 126 Misc.2d 422, 481 N.Y.S.2d 967 (1984).
44. 864 F.2d 881 (1st Cir. 1988).
45. *Penn v. Iowa State Board of Regents*, 999 F.2d 305 (8th Cir. 1993).
46. *Winston v. Maine Technical College System*, 631 A.2d 70 (Me. 1993), *cert. denied*, 114 S. Ct. 1643 (1994).

47. Margaret D. Smith, "Must Higher Education Be a Hands-On Experience? Sexual Harassment by Professors," 28 *West's Education Law Reporter* 694-95 (1986).

48. "Sexual Harassment: A Hidden Issue," Project on the Status and Education of Women (Washington, D.C.: American Association of Colleges, 1978).

49. Rob Hotakainen, "U.S. Says School Violated Girl's Rights," *Minneapolis Tribune*, April 29, 1993.

50. *Doe v. Petaluma City School District*, 830 F.Supp. 1560 (N.D. Cal. 1993).

51. *Schulman v. Franklin & Marshall College*, 37 Pa. Super. 345, 538 A.2d 49 (1988).

52. 993 F.2d 386 (4th Cir. 1993).

53. "Sexual Harassment Policy Guidelines" (Washington, D.C.: American Council on Education, 1986).

54. This policy statement was kindly provided by Professor Jay Heubert of Harvard Graduate School of Education.

55. Jane Gross, "Love or Harassment? Campuses Bar (and Debate) Faculty-Student Sex," *New York Times*, April 14, 1993, p. B9.

56. Under 34 CFR §106.8(b), institutions are required to adopt and publish grievance procedures providing for "prompt and equitable" resolution of student and employee complaints alleging sex discrimination prohibited by Title IX. 34 CFR §106.8(a) requires educational institutions to designate at least one employee to coordinate its efforts to comply with and carry out the institution's responsibilities for complying with Title IX. That employee is also responsible for investigating complaints about sex discrimination and sexual harassment.

57. 685 P.2d 1193 (Calif. 1984).

58. *Mullins v. Pine Manor College*, 449 N.E.2d 331 (Mass. 1983).

59. *Miller v. State of New York*, 478 N.Y.S.2d 829, 467 N.E. 493 (1984).

60. *Duarte v. State*, 88 Cal. App. 3d 473, 151 Cal. Rptr. 727 (1979).

61. *Hartman v. Bethany College*, 778 F.Supp. 286, 294 (N.D. W. Va. 1991).

62. *Tanja H. v. Regents of the University of California*, 278 Cal.Rptr. 918 (Cal.App. 1991).

63. *Nola M. v. University of Southern California,*, 16 Cal. App. 4th 421, 20 Cal.Rptr 2d 97 (1993).

64. 625 N.E.2d 431 (Ill. App. 1993).

65. 861 P.2d 768 (Kan. 1993).

66. *Id.* at 789 (McFarland, J., dissenting).

67. *Bratton v. Calkins*, 870 P.2d 981 (Wash. App. 1994); *John R. v. Oakland Unified Sch. Dist.*, 769 P.2d (Cal. 1989); *Bozarth v. Harper Creek Board of Education*, 288 N.W.2d 424 (Mich. App. 1979).

68. See, for example, *Samuels v. Southern Baptist Hospital*, 594 So.2d 571 (La. App. 1992) (nursing assistant); *Simmons v. United States*, 805 F.2d 1363 (9th Cir. 1986) (social worker); *Marston v. Minneapolis Clinic of Psychiatry & Neurology, Ltd.*, 329 N.W.2d 306 (Minn. 1982) (doctor); *Appelwhite v. City of Baton Rouge*, 380 So.2d 119 (La. App. 1979) (police officer).

69. *Mary M. v. City of Los Angeles*, 814 P.2d 1341 (Calif. 1991).

70. See, for example, *Simmons v. United States*, 805 F.2d 1363 (9th Cir. 1986) (social worker), *Marston v. Minneapolis Clinic of Psychiatry & Neurology, Ltd.*, 329 N.W.2d 306 (Minn. 1982) (doctor); *Applewhite v. City of Baton Rouge*, 380 So.2d 119 (La. App. 1979) (police officer).

71. *Mary M. v. City of Los Angeles*, 814 P.2d 1341 (Calif. 1991).

72. 594 So.2d 571 (La. App. 1992).

73. *Dismuke v. Quaynor*, 637 So.2d 555 (La. App. 1994).

74. "WVU Mess," *The Charleston Gazette*, November 7, 1985, p. 6A.

75. *Charleston Daily Mail,* November 9, 1985, p. 2B.
76. 15 *Campus Law Enforcement Journal* 5-7, 11 (July-August, 1985).
77. *The Chronicle of Higher Education,* December 11, 1985, pp. 1, 27.
78. "Rape and Sexual Abuse" (Nashville: Vanderbilt Office of University Publications, 1984).
79. "Crime Prevention: How You Can Help" (Nashville: Vanderbilt Office of University Publications, 1985).
80. Interview conducted by Michael Clay Smith, March 7, 1986. The prosecutor requested anonymity.
81. Richard Fossey, *School Choice Legislation, a Survey of the States,* Occasional Paper published by the Consortium for Policy Research in Education, Rutgers University (1992).
82. See National School Board Association, Council of School Attorneys, *Child Abuse: Legal Issues for Schools* (Alexandria, Va: author, 1994), p. 175, for a list of state child abuse reporting laws.
83. *Dismuke v. Quaynor,* 637 So.2d 555 (La. App. 1994).
84. James Davidson, "Protection of Children through Criminal History Record Screening, Well-meaning Promises and Legal Pitfalls," 89 *Dickinson Law Review* 577 (1985).

CHAPTER 8

Searching, Seizing, and Confessing

K ing George's officers had been so abusive in their unbridled searches of people and homes in the colonies that the American constitutional framers responded by making the Fourth Amendment one of the most precise limitations on governmental power found in the Bill of Rights: "The right of the people to be secure in their persons, houses, papers, and effects, against unreasonable searches and seizures, shall not be violated, and no Warrant shall issue, but upon probable cause, supported by Oath or affirmation, and particularly describing the place to be searched, and the persons or things to be seized."[1] The amendment sets forth the norm that both searches and arrests of citizens are to be made upon a warrant issued by a judge.

SEARCH AND SEIZURE ON CAMPUS

The issues of search and seizure confront college and university officials most commonly when questions about searching dormitory rooms arise, but sometimes concerning the propriety of searching motor vehicles, lockers, or even individuals themselves, including their clothing, purses, or bookbags. The "exclusionary rule" precludes evidence that was unconstitutionally seized from being used against a person in a criminal trial,[2] but in some circumstances such evidence may still be used in lesser civil matters, such as campus disciplinary proceedings.

The exclusionary rule is a limitation on governmental action only, and does not apply to actions by private citizens.[3] Thus, evidence unconstitutionally seized by private citizens may still be used against an accused criminal, unless the police requested or encouraged the illegal search. As might be expected, questions arise as to whether college officials or security guards are governmental agents for purposes of the exclusionary rule; the answer turns on many factors of the public/private question.

Of course, any place can be searched, and any evidence seized, if a valid search warrant is first obtained from a "neutral and detached" judicial officer, usually a judge or magistrate.[4] It has been suggested in some quarters that a college or university official whose regular duties are not involved with campus security functions might be a sufficiently impartial magistrate to meet constitutional standards for issuance of a valid search warrant, but such a procedure would be fraught with peril; the prudent course would be to use established judicial procedures of the state court system.

Before issuing the warrant, the judicial officer must be given under oath reliable evidence showing that there is a probable cause to believe that a crime has been committed and that needed evidence will be found. Hearsay evidence can be used but there must be assurance that it is reliable. In a marijuana case stemming from the search of a dormitory room at McNeese State University, the Louisiana Supreme Court upheld a search warrant affidavit based on hearsay from a person identified only as a source who is "a responsible citizen of the utmost character and integrity, and has a great interest in the youth of Lake Charles, Louisiana."[5] The warrant itself must describe with particularity the place to be searched and the things to be seized.

When a Warrant Is Not Needed

There are exceptions to the search warrant requirement. First, as has been noted, it does not apply to action by private individuals, but only to governmental policing functions. Other common exceptions provide that a warrant is not necessary 1) if the evidence sought is in "plain view," that is, can be seen and seized by a person looking on from a place where he or she has a right to be; 2) if the search is made pursuant to an otherwise lawful arrest (police can search the immediate area around an arrested person to check for weapons, to inventory personal effects, etc.); 3) in some types of health or safety emergencies; 4) in exigent circumstances where evidence is likely to be destroyed if not seized immediately, including searches of entire automobiles—even car trunks and closed containers—where officers have probable cause to believe criminal evidence is in the car; and 5) with the consent of the individual involved, so long as it is freely and voluntarily given.

Likewise, there are exceptions to the arrest warrant requirement. A court held that University of Nebraska-Lincoln police officers were not required to obtain an arrest warrant before arresting an ex-campus security officer when the police were already in the suspect's home pursuant to a valid search warrant, and their search had produced sufficient evidence to justify an arrest.[6] Similarly, a court ruled that Brown University police did not need a warrant to arrest a suspect found hiding in his girlfriend's closet. The court ruled that the police had probable cause to make the arrest, even if they didn't know the defendant's complete name or residence. Since the defendant had given a false name and his girlfriend's address, the police were not required to obtain a formal warrant before taking him into custody.[7]

A review of the recent college and university cases in the area of search and seizure reveals that they involve myriad issues, some typical of crime in the parent society, and some peculiar to the campus. The following analysis of the cases by category may be helpful.

Fourth Amendment Applicability Issues

Private searches and the *T.L.O.* decision. As has been noted, the Fourth Amendment and the exclusionary rule do not apply to purely private actions. This point is poignantly illustrated by the case where an off-duty police officer searched his daughter's apartment and found stolen merchandise. The evidence was allowed in a subsequent prosecution because, at the time, the officer was acting as a concerned parent and not as a policeman.[8] Likewise, where security guards at the Rochester Institute of Technology, a private institution, conducted a dormitory search that did not meet Fourth Amendment standards, they were able to turn the marijuana that they found over to police, who then prosecuted the students. Ironically, the search had been instigated because one of the students wrote his girlfriend about his recent purchase of a pound of marijuana, and the letter was intercepted by the girl's mother, who turned it over to the police. Because the police did not instigate the search, the court held it valid.[9]

For years, there has been some question about whether administrators and security officers at public higher education institutions who do not hold explicit police powers would be encompassed within the exclusionary rule doctrine. Although the United States Supreme Court has yet to answer that question directly, it now seems likely that the courts are going to treat them as state officers and require them to comply fully with the Fourth Amendment insofar as gathering evidence to be used in a criminal case is concerned.

That was the holding some years ago by a federal district court in *Morale v. Grigel*.[10] In that case the court said that dormitory resident assistants at the New Hampshire Technical Institute were acting as governmental officers when they searched a student's room, and therefore they had to meet Fourth Amendment standards if the evidence was to be used in a criminal prosecution. In its 1985 decision in *T.L.O. v. New Jersey* (partly delineated in chapter 3), the United States Supreme Court held that public school administrators are acting as officers of the state when they search students because they "act in furtherance of publicly mandated educational and disciplinary policies."[11] This decision upheld the search of a student's purse based upon "reasonable" suspicion by a vice-principal that the purse contained cigarettes, a prohibited item at the junior high school. The search yielded marijuana, and the student was prosecuted.

The central holding of *T.L.O.* was that school authorities are state officers and thus subject to the Fourth Amendment, but that they are not held to the police standard of having to have "probable cause" to believe evidence will be found. Rather, their searches will be valid if authorities have "reasonable grounds for suspecting" that the search will turn up evidence of a violation of the law or a school rule. The court said that "reasonable" suspicion must be more than a mere "hunch"—it must be particularized suspicion based upon some reason. Further, to be valid, the search must be limited to a reasonable scope, considering the age and sex of the student and the nature of the infraction.

What does *T.L.O.* mean for higher education? The same "state action" that the court said brought public school officials within the Fourth Amendment's restrictions is certainly present at tax-supported, state-operated colleges and universities—probably far more so. However, much of the similarity between public schools and higher education institutions ends there. The *T.L.O.* court based its lower "reasonableness" standard on the need to "maintain order" in the public schools, and it recognized that "the preservation of order and a proper educational environment requires close supervision of schoolchildren, as well as the enforcement of rules against conduct that would be perfectly permissible if undertaken by an adult." College and university students are more like adults than schoolchildren; they attend voluntarily and do not have to be policed like children in the public schools. Their expectation of privacy thus is higher, and the courts may require that college and university authorities meet the full "probable cause" standard for valid searches, rather than the lower public school standard of "reasonableness."

Even though officers at private colleges may be able to search and seize evidence under circumstances in which police or officers of public institutions could not, this allowance will not hold when it is only a subterfuge for governmental action. If the police procure the search by private persons, or set into operation a chain of events that leads to a private search, the evidence will be precluded from criminal proceedings unless it meets Fourth Amendment standards.

Accordingly, when administrators at Hofstra University invited police to help survey dormitories because of concern about the increased use of marijuana, the university administrators lost their private standing for Fourth

Amendment purposes. While two administrators and police officers were in a dormitory hallway, they smelled the odor of marijuana. They traced the smell to a dormitory room and entered it without permission or a warrant. In the marijuana prosecution that followed, the evidence was suppressed, and the charges were dismissed.[12]

In another instance, when state police narcotics investigators tipped campus security at the Rochester Institute of Technology that a quantity of marijuana was in a dormitory room, and college officers then made a search that did not comport with Fourth Amendment standards, the evidence seized was allowed in the trial of the room's occupant. The court said that under those facts, the state police had not expressly or impliedly requested the search, and thus it was a search by private citizens.[13]

Likewise, when the dean of students at a private college ordered a warrantless search of a student's dormitory room, a Virginia court ruled that the marijuana that was seized was admissible evidence in the student's criminal trial. Although the dean told a police detective that she intended to conduct the search, the detective asked the dean not to do so, fearing a search conducted by college officials would jeopardize an ongoing police investigation. When the dean proceeded anyway, the court ruled that the search was initiated by private citizens and the Fourth Amendment was not implicated.[14]

The exclusionary rule in disciplinary proceedings. Another issue is whether the exclusionary rule is applicable to campus disciplinary proceedings. The answer seems to be that it is not, although the cases are not unanimous. One federal district judge grappled with the issue in the 1970 case of *Speake v. Grantham*.[15] Declaring that "this court finds some merit in the view that disciplinary punishment short of irrevocable expulsion of students should not be required to conform inexorably to the rules, safeguards and procedures of criminal law," Judge Walter Nixon nevertheless applied full Fourth Amendment standards in considering the propriety of the suspension of students from the University of Southern Mississippi. Even so, the suspensions were upheld. The case had arisen in connection with civil rights demonstrations in Mississippi. As a part of their civil rights advocacy, the students had become involved in the distribution of false notices that university classes would not meet. The notices were found when campus security officers pulled over a vehicle that failed to stop at a traffic sign and they saw the leaflets protruding from under a seat in "plain view."

In *Keene v. Rodgers*, another 1970 case, the dismissal of a student from the Maine Maritime Academy was upheld even though evidence against him was gained through a search that did not comport with Fourth amendment standards. Academy officials were distressed because a midshipman seemed to be improperly displaying American flags in his Volkswagen. The academy security officer directed the student to open the vehicle, and the officer's ensuing search turned up a quantity of marijuana. The federal district court ruled that strict standards would not be applied because "[q]uite plainly, the search was conducted solely for the purpose of enforcing the Academy Rules and Regulations and of insuring proper conduct and discipline on the part of a cadet."[16]

In a 1968 case from Alabama, *Moore v. Student Affairs Committee of Troy State University*, a federal district court upheld a blanket right of university officials to search dormitory rooms and use the evidence garnered in disciplinary proceedings.[17] A university policy had reserved a full right to inspect rooms, baggage, and other personal material, and had published it in the college bulletin and student handbook. The court said that the regulation was enforceable "in aid of the basic responsibility of the institution regarding discipline and the maintenance of an 'educational atmosphere' . . . despite the fact that it may infringe to some extent on the outer bounds of the Fourth Amendment rights of students." It is to be noted that the case dealt only with campus disciplinary proceedings, not criminal prosecution.

Two 1976 federal cases likewise held the exclusionary rule inapplicable to campus disciplinary proceedings. In *Ekelund v. Secretary of Commerce*, a midshipman at the United States Merchant Marine Academy sought to restrain the academy from dismissing him because of marijuana discovered in his room.[18] The court held that academy superiors had the right to search the room under institutional policies, and that the exclusionary rule and Fourth Amendment standards were inapplicable to an academy hearing. The court noted "how dubious is the principle of exclusion even as applied in criminal cases and the further damage to the search for truth that must flow from uselessly extending it to civil cases."

In the other 1976 case, *Morale v. Grigel*, a federal court in New Hampshire held that such a "drastic" measure as the exclusionary rule was unneeded in campus disciplinary proceedings.[19] The court said that it understood the ruling of the United States Supreme Court in *United States v. Calandra*[20] to mean that the exclusionary rule is limited to criminal proceedings and that only a criminal defendant may invoke its protections. The *Morale* court upheld the suspension of a college student for marijuana.

A year before *Morale*, another federal district court had held that evidence gained in contravention of Fourth Amendment rules could not be used in a college disciplinary proceeding. The case, which has received much attention, is *Smyth v. Lubbers*.[21] It involved a marijuana search in a dormitory at Grand Valley State Colleges. The court reasoned that were the exclusionary rule not applied, "the college authorities would have no incentive to respect the privacy of its students." *Smyth* remains the exception, however, and subsequent cases have declined to apply the exclusionary rule in civil disciplinary proceedings.

Dormitory Searches

Oversight, safety, and maintenance. Two theories advanced by colleges and universities for allowing warrantless searches of dormitories are that institutional rules provide for routine searches and that students have agreed to searches by terms of their room rental agreements. The theories have met mixed results.

In *Piazzola v. Watkins*, a criminal prosecution stemming from the same dormitory search that was the subject of the *Moore* dismissal case (discussed earlier in this chapter), a federal appeals court held that while a university policy allowing searches might be valid for civil disciplinary proceedings, such a policy would not be sufficient to authorize a search of dormitory rooms for criminal evidence. Thus, the court said, even though students might be held to have consented to the search provision for civil, educational purposes, evidence gained in such a manner could not be used in a criminal prosecution because the policy would be "an unconstitutional attempt to require students to waive their protection from unreasonable searches and seizures as a condition to their occupancy of rooms."[22]

Like reasoning was used in the *Smyth v. Lubbers* case (discussed earlier in this chapter). The court said the state "cannot condition attendance at Grand Valley State Colleges on a waiver of constitutional rights. . . . A blanket authorization in an adhesion contract that the College may search the room for violation of whatever substantive regulations the College chooses to adopt and pursuant to whatever search regulation the College chooses to adopt is not the type of focused, deliberate, and immediate consent contemplated by the Constitution."[23] The *Smyth* court held searches pursuant to the college regulation invalid for both criminal prosecution and student discipline purposes.

The *Morale* court (discussed earlier in this chapter) held terms permitting health and safety inspections in a student residence contract to be insufficient to meet constitutional standards for seizure of criminal evidence, though, as noted earlier, sufficient for campus disciplinary purposes.[24]

Several other cases have upheld institutional policy as the basis for searches. *Ekelund* (discussed earlier in this chapter) held that the Merchant Marine Academy had the blanket right to search rooms and use the evidence in disciplinary proceedings, and in *State v. Kappes*, an institutional policy of routine monthly dormitory inspections led to the conviction of an 18-year-old female freshman for possession of marijuana. In *Kappes*, the Arizona Court of Appeals held that where Northern Arizona University had a policy of inspecting dormitories monthly for cleanliness, safety, or need for repairs and maintenance, and the policy was set forth in a dormitory rental contract that the student had signed, the discovery of marijuana in the room by a resident advisor during such an inspection was not an unlawful search and the evidence found could be used against the student in criminal court.[25]

A number of cases have analogized a dormitory room to a person's home and have extended full constitutional protection to it, at least for criminal evidence purposes. In *Smyth v. Lubbers,* the court said that a student's dormitory room "is his house and home for all practical purposes, and he has the same interest in the privacy of his room as any adult has in the privacy of his home, dwelling, or lodging. Because of the material and psychological importance of a man's home, the college dormitory room is not in the least like a licensed business establishment."[26]

In *People v. Cohen,*[27] a case involving a private institution, the court said that university students are adults, and the dormitory a home. "To suggest that a student who lives off campus in a boarding house is protected but that one who occupies a dormitory room waives his constitutional liberties is at war with reason, logic and law." In the case, Hofstra University officials had accompanied police officers into the student's room. The court said that even if the student had impliedly consented to entry by the university officials, they could not share it with or delegate it to the police.

The Supreme Court of Ohio adopted much the same view in *City of Athens v. Wolf.*[28] The court said: "Although few people who have ever resided in a college dormitory would favorably compare those living quarters to the comfort of a private home, a dormitory room is 'home' to large numbers of students." The court overturned the drug conviction of an Ohio University student whose room had been entered from an adjoining room by a municipal police officer.

Even in a case in which a search warrant had been used, a Pennsylvania court overturned the conviction because the officers had not given notice of their identity and purpose prior to entering the dormitory room to execute the warrant.[29] The court said a dormitory room is analogous to "an apartment or a hotel room," and that officers should announce themselves prior to entry. The court appeared to be bending over backwards to reverse the conviction.

However, a recent decision by the Utah Court of Appeals demonstrates that the notion that university students have strong privacy interests in their dormitory rooms is by no means universally accepted. In *State v. Hunter,* a 1992 case, the Utah court relied on a university policy, reserving the right to search residence halls at any time, to uphold a warrantless, room-to-room search by Utah State University officials and a campus police officer. The court upheld a student's theft conviction based on the discovery of stolen property during the search, which was conducted while the student was absent.

It is worth noting that the university's search was not a routine inspection for safety or cleanliness; rather, university officials conducted the search for the specific purpose of finding evidence of student vandalism. In defense of the university's actions, the court pointed out that the student had signed a housing contract acknowledging the university's right to inspect his room. The searchers had not circumvented constitutional restrictions on police searches, the court reasoned, since the search was instituted for university purposes, not at the behest of law enforcement officials. The university police officer only came along, the court concluded, "to provide assistance in the event that [the housing director] confronted problems that he was not able to handle on his own."[30]

Michael L. Keller, writing in the *Journal of College and University Law*, has suggested that the United States Supreme Court's decision in *Washington v. Chrisman* (discussed later in this chapter) displays a lack of commitment by the high court to the dormitory room-private home analogy. In *Chrisman*, the court upheld a "plain view" search by a police officer who accompanied an arrested student back to his room to retrieve his identification. In the article, Keller suggested that, at a minimum, "the failure to accord any special weight to the privacy interests in the room argues against the rigid procedural guidelines mandated by the *Lubbers* court."[31]

Searches incident to an arrest. Searches made incident to (meaning flowing out of) a lawful arrest have always been an exception to the requirement of a search warrant. After public safety officers at the University of Georgia told a group of young men that they could not go to the roof of a certain building (they said they wanted to view the sunrise), they went there anyway. Later, when officers spotted them and effected arrests for trespass, a pat-down search uncovered on one member of the group a plastic wrapper containing a creamy brown powder. Laboratory analysis confirmed that it was "speed." The Georgia Court of Appeals upheld the young man's conviction on the basis that the search was a valid incident to the arrest for trespassing.[32]

When material that clearly is criminal evidence is in plain view, such as on the seat of an automobile, or on an open porch, or otherwise visible to a person who is in a place where he or she has a legal right to be, the evidence may properly be seized without a warrant. Where officers had obtained a valid search warrant to enter a student's dormitory room to look for marijuana, which they had probable cause to believe was there, they properly seized contraband phenobarbital pills that were in a desk drawer with the marijuana because it was in plain view.[33]

In a case that has received much attention in higher education circles, *Washington v. Chrisman,* the United States Supreme Court validated the lawful arrest and plain view doctrines in relation to campus arrests and dormitory activities.[34] A Washington State University police officer observed a student leave a dormitory carrying a bottle of gin, and because he suspected the young man was underage, took him into custody. The officer accompanied the student to his dormitory room so that he could retrieve his identification, and through the open doorway saw the student's roommate with what he believed to be marijuana seeds and a pipe. In an opinion written by Chief Justice Warren Burger, the court said that once the officer had placed the youngster under lawful arrest he was authorized to accompany him to his room, and that what the officer saw there was in plain view and could be seized.

Consent: coerced or voluntary? Consent of the person whose possessions or premises are to be searched has always been valid authority for making a search without a warrant. However, the consent must be voluntarily and intelligently given. In State v. Wingerd, the Ohio Court of Appeals upheld the conviction of an Ohio University student on drug charges that resulted from the student's voluntarily turning over to university officers five bags of marijuana and other drugs. Several university residence hall officers had gone to the student's room and asked for permission to enter, which was given, and then they told him that they "had reason to believe that he had drugs" and asked him to turn them over to them. The student did, and he was charged. The court said the defendant had agreed to the search "without a word of complaint or objection and in a setting which is not to be equated with the aura of oppressiveness which oft pervades the precincts of a police station."[35]

In a case involving Washington State University, an undercover police officer made arrangements by telephone to go to a student's room to buy drugs from her. She had told him to call for an escort when he arrived at the women's dormitory, but he, accompanied by other officers, went without an escort to the woman's room, where another person let him in and sold him cocaine. Dormitory rules required an escort for males coming up to women's rooms, and the defendant sought to have evidence of the cocaine purchase excluded from court because the officer had no search warrant and had violated the escort rule. However, the Washington Court of Appeals affirmed the conviction, holding that there was no "expectation of privacy" because the student had consented to the search by inviting the officer to the room to make the sale.[36]

Where consent is coerced in some way, the courts will not recognize it. In one landmark case, the United States Supreme Court held that where police demanded entry to premises under color of their office, the consent was given "in submission to authority rather than as an understanding and intentional waiver of a constitutional right."[37]

When campus police officers at Illinois State University demanded consent from the inhabitants to search a dormitory room, stipulating that otherwise the room would be "sealed" until a search warrant could be obtained
(which, the court said, might have been more than 24 hours), the consent
was held to be coerced. The officers had first obtained consent from a
roommate of the suspect when they awakened him at 2:00 A.M. on a Sunday
morning and told him the room would be sealed if he did not consent. After
the roommate consented, the suspect did likewise, and the ensuing search
turned up stolen merchandise. The court said consent to a search had to be
unequivocal and specific, freely and intelligently given, and that "a more
crystalline case of coercion can scarcely be imagined."[38]
    It is well settled that where two or more persons have the joint use or
occupancy of certain premises, the consent to a search by either party is
binding upon the other.[39] Therefore, one roommate may give valid consent in
the other's absence to a search of their premises, at least as to jointly
controlled areas where the other had no reasonable expectation of privacy.[40]
    Just as consent cannot be coerced, it cannot be obtained by deceit or
trickery. When two state liquor agents received complaints that beer was
being sold illegally at the Pi Kappa Alpha house at the University of Cincinnati, they went to the fraternity to investigate. The agents met the house
manager outside the house and told him that one of the agents was a fraternity
brother from Georgia whose younger brother would be attending the University of Cincinnati in the fall. One agent asked to see the house to be certain he
wanted his younger brother to join. The story was untrue, and the men never
revealed that they were liquor control agents and that their real purpose was
to determine if beer was being sold illegally.
    During a tour of the house, one agent saw a soft drink machine that
dispensed several kinds of beer. He asked if he could buy a can, and the house
manager gave permission. The agent inserted 50 cents into the machine and
received a can of beer. The agents left, taking the beer with them. They used
the can of beer to obtain a search warrant for the house, which was searched
the next day. On the basis of evidence found, the fraternity was charged with
various alcoholic beverage violations.
    The fraternity said the search was illegal and sought to suppress all the
evidence. The state contended that the officers had a "privilege" under state
law, and they were entitled to use deception to gain admission. The Supreme
Court of Ohio agreed with the fraternity. The court said the fraternity house
was not a commercial center, and the agents had not been invited into the
premises for the purpose of selling them beer. Further, even though the beer
was in plain view inside the house, the court said that because the initial
intrusion had been made through deceit, the invitation was not freely given.
The evidence was suppressed.[41]

The Pi Kappa Alpha case is to be distinguished from a line of cases that permits covert agents to gain access to places of substantial activity through subterfuge. The United States Supreme Court has ruled such searches without a warrant to be valid, but only where the premises are a "commercial center of criminal activity," and the agents are invited onto the premises to do criminal business.[42]

Other Types of Searches

While the Fourth Amendment protects a person's "effects" as well as body and home from unreasonable searches, the courts generally accord particular sanctity to a person's home, as has been seen in the foregoing cases. A review of the cases involving searches of other places reveals considerably less protection by the courts.

Suitcase. When a job corpsman returned to his dormitory after a leave, an administrator at the center called him into his office and told him, "I would like to look at the contents of your suitcase." The youngster testified that he did not want to allow the inspection but felt he had no choice. A quantity of marijuana was found, and the federal district court allowed it to be used against the corpsman in a criminal prosecution, explaining simply that the search was reasonable as an exercise of the institution's authority "to maintain proper standards of conduct and discipline at the center." The court noted that to "promote proper moral and disciplinary conditions at the centers, standards of conduct and deportment are to be provided" the corpsmen.[43] The case certainly has a flavor of the old *in loco parentis* doctrine.

Locker. The Supreme Court of California upheld a warrantless search of a student's library carrel locker at Stanford University after library employees noticed a noxious odor that "smelled as if someone had vomited in the room." A maintenance employee opened all the lockers in the room and found in the last a briefcase from which an odor like "sweet apples" emanated strongly. He opened it and found 38 packets of marijuana. The odor apparently had come from a preservative added to the marijuana. The court upheld the criminal conviction of the student, declaring that the search had been justified without a warrant because the odor problem constituted an "emergency."[44]

More recent cases, involving secondary schools, not higher education institutions, have consistently upheld locker searches by school authorities under the relaxed standards for conducting school searches articulated by *T.L.O.*[45] In a 1993 case, a Milwaukee high school student was unable to suppress evidence of a gun found in his school locker during an inspection by school officials. The Wisconsin Supreme Court pointed out that the school district maintained ownership and control of the lockers, as evidenced by the fact that the district kept pass keys to student lockers and prohibited students from using their own locks. Moreover, the district warned students that the lockers were subject to inspection. Under these circumstances, the court concluded, students had no reasonable expectation of privacy in their lockers, and thus the inspection was not a search for Fourth Amendment purposes.[46]

Purse. When a student at Pima Junior College left her purse in a classroom after an evening class, a custodian found it and turned it over to security officers. When officers looked for identification in the purse and then made an inventory of it, they found amphetamines. She contended that once the identification was found, the officers had no right to proceed to look through the purse. The Arizona Supreme Court upheld her conviction, declaring that the officers had a right to inventory the entire purse for safeguarding of valuables once it had come into their lawful possession, just as with an abandoned or seized automobile.[47]

Mail. The interception of a student's mail containing a quantity of marijuana was upheld in a civil damage suit against a municipal police officer in Iowa. A special delivery package had been sent to the student's residence hall, and the receptionist noted that it had a strong odor and felt like "hay." A residence hall director suspected it contained marijuana and called police, who used a specially trained dog to affirm the presence of the drug. Criminal proceedings were dropped due to a technicality, but the federal appeals court held that the police officer's actions did not violate the Fourth Amendment, and the student lost his damage suit.[48]

Electronic monitoring and eavesdropping. "Trapping" of telephone call origination numbers in response to bomb threats at California State University at San Jose led to the conviction of a student on two counts of explosives violations. After the university had received a series of bomb threats, a "trap" was placed on university telephone lines to record the number from which calls originated. Interestingly, the defendant had already become a suspect before the trapping, because one of the calls had warned a certain biology professor that some students would be hurt by a bomb unless he canceled the genetics examination he had scheduled for the next day; the defendant was on a list that officers had requested, naming students whose grades at the time were "significantly below average." The fact that one of the calls came from the defendant's telephone number cumulated the evidence against him.[49]

While it is illegal under federal law to "eavesdrop" electronically on a telephone call unless one of the parties to the call has consented,[50] it is not a violation of Fourth Amendment rights to use equipment to record the fact that a call was made, or to trace the number to which, or from which, it was made. Fourth Amendment protection extends only to the content of the call, not the fact that it was made. However, Congress has recently required that court orders be obtained before police use "pen register" devices to note numbers dialed from a certain telephone, or "trap and trace" devices to follow calls back to a specific telephone.[51]

Films. Search warrants must themselves be based upon a showing of probable cause to believe that criminal evidence will be found in the requested search. That probable cause must be shown by reliable evidence. Where civic authorities had sought to prevent a student activities programming committee at the University of North Dakota from showing the film *Deep Throat*, the state's highest court held that a search warrant for the film was defective because it was based on such remote hearsay about the film's content that it did not meet the probable cause requirement of the Fourth Amendment.[52]

Research data. The courts protect the privacy of witnesses to crimes, as well as the rights of defendants, and this concept has had unusual application in the higher education field. A federal district court in New York upheld a special privileged status for the research notebook of a doctoral student at the State University of New York at Stony Brook, even though it potentially contained evidence about a crime. The student was working on a dissertation entitled "The Sociology of the American Restaurant" and had compiled the notebook while he worked as a waiter in a restaurant for eight months. After a suspicious fire broke out at the restaurant, a federal grand jury subpoenaed both the student and his notebook, but the student interposed an objection to turning the notebook over on the legal theory that the scientific research within it was confidential and should be accorded a privilege against forced revelation in the courts.

   A federal trial court agreed with the student, comparing the research to a journalist's qualified privilege not to reveal documents or confidential sources. The court said that compelling production of the research might inhibit the researcher's access to sources, thus obstructing the flow of information to the researcher and limiting or precluding the ultimate benefit that the public could realize from the study.[53]

   Unhappy with the trial court's ruling in favor of scholar's privilege, the U.S. Attorney's Office appealed to a considerably more skeptical federal appeals court. The appellate court ruled that the record was too sparse to determine whether a scholar's privilege existed, and if it did, whether it should apply to the student's research about restaurants. To qualify for a scholar's privilege, the court wrote, a researcher must make a threshold showing consisting of "a detailed description of the nature and seriousness of the scholarly study in question, of the methodology employed, of the need for assurances of confidentiality to various sources to conduct the study, and of the fact that the disclosure requested by the subpoena will seriously impinge upon that confidentiality."

Since the doctoral student had provided none of this information, the appellate court remanded his privilege claim back to the trial court to permit the student to amplify the record. During that process, the appellate court instructed, the student was required to make the diary available to the trial court for the judge's private inspection (known as an "in camera inspection"). Regardless of how the lower court ruled after the record was supplemented, the appellate court made clear that actual observation of criminal activity was not subject to a claim of privilege.[54]

Testing students and employees for drug use. The United States Supreme Court has held that urinalysis drug testing by a public agency is a search, subject to Fourth Amendment safeguards. However, in two 1989 decisions, the Court upheld regulations authorizing urinalysis testing of public employees in certain circumstances without a warrant and without individualized suspicion of wrongdoing. Specifically, the Court upheld regulations requiring drug tests for train crew employees who were directly involved in railroad accidents[55] and for U.S. Customs Service employees seeking promotions to jobs involving the interdiction of illegal drugs, the carrying of firearms, or access to sensitive information.[56] Lower courts have upheld random drug testing of public employees in a variety of employment settings where there is a governmental interest in safety, preservation of workforce integrity, or protection of classified material.

In the college or university setting, there have been several lawsuits challenging drug-testing programs for student athletes, but the legality of these programs has not been clearly determined. In a decision that was reversed for lack of federal jurisdiction, a federal court in Washington ruled that the National Collegiate Athletic Association's drug-testing program was not an unconstitutional search in light of student athletes' diminished expectations of privacy and the compelling interest of the University of Washington and the NCAA in curtailing drug use in intervarsity athletic competition.[57] Similarly, student athletes at Northeastern University were unsuccessful when they challenged that university's drug-testing policy. In a 1989 decision, the Massachusetts Supreme Judicial Court ruled that the Northeastern program did not violate the Massachusetts State Civil Rights Act or the state's right to privacy statute.[58] Likewise, in a 1994 decision, the California Supreme Court ruled that the NCAA's drug-testing policy for college athletes did not violate the California constitutional guarantee to privacy. The California court determined that the privacy provision applied to the NCAA but that the NCAA's interest in maintaining the integrity of varsity athletic competition outweighed the privacy interests of individual athletes.[59] However in a 1993 decision, the Colorado Supreme Court ruled that the University of Colorado's policy of drug testing intercollegiate athletes by urinalysis violated the students' right to be free of unreasonable searches under both the United States and Colorado constitutions.[60]

Urinalysis drug testing of high school athletes has been upheld by one federal appeals court and struck down by another. In *Schaill v. Tippecanoe County School Corporation*,[61] a 1988 decision that predated the Supreme Court's rulings on drug testing by public agencies, the Seventh Circuit Court of Appeals ruled that a school district's random urinalysis testing program was justified in light of the students' diminished right to privacy when they participated in athletics and by evidence that some drug-impaired students had been injured during athletic competition. On the other hand, in *Acton v. Veronia School District*,[62] the Ninth Circuit reversed a federal district court in Oregon when it ruled that drug testing of high school athletes by an Oregon school district was unconstitutional. The Ninth Circuit ruled that the school district's interest in reducing drug use by student athletes was not so compelling as to justify the intrusion required by random tests of students' urine.

Colleges or universities that are considering a program for random urinalysis drug testing of student athletes would be well advised to design the program to minimize the invasion of privacy that occurs when urine samples are collected and to include safeguards against incorrect test results. Such a policy should have an appeal process that a student can use to rebut positive test results and a procedure for protecting the confidentiality of a student's medical history, including the use of prescription drugs. Moreover, to pass constitutional muster, university officials cannot undertake drug testing at the behest of law enforcement officials.

CONFESSING

The Fifth Amendment to the Constitution provides that no person "shall be compelled in any criminal case to be a witness against himself." Since this right would have little value if a court could infer guilt from silence, the fact that a defendant "stood mute" or claimed his privilege against self-incrimination may not be used against him in a criminal trial.[63] Of course, a person can waive the Fifth Amendment's protections and freely and voluntarily make a confession that can be used in criminal court. Moreover, the Fifth Amendment's protections are considerably constricted in an administrative setting. An administrative hearing body is entitled to draw an adverse inference from the fact that a party refuses to testify.[64]

Coerced confessions always have been prohibited. "The rack and torture chamber may not be substituted for the witness stand," the Supreme Court said in 1936.[65] The law of confessions was revolutionized in 1963, however, with the Supreme Court's ruling in *Miranda v. Arizona*.[66]

The *Miranda* Warnings

In that landmark case, the court held that before any confession is taken from a person in custody, he or she must be advised of the right to remain silent, the right to a lawyer, and the possibility that any statement given may be used against him or her. Unless these procedures are followed, admissions by a suspect usually cannot be used against the person in a criminal case. The rule clearly does not apply, however, to civil matters, including campus disciplinary proceedings.

Even in criminal matters, there are many limitations upon the *Miranda* doctrine. First, it applies only to interrogation, that is, express questioning. Thus, when two police officers who were driving a murder suspect to the police station engaged in a conversation between themselves about the case, and the suspect chimed in to tell them where the shotgun used in the murder was hidden, the admission was validly used against him in court. The United States Supreme Court ruled that the conversation between the officers was not interrogation, and the confession was admissible even though *Miranda* warnings were not given.[67]

Private security guards and *Miranda*. Moreover, *Miranda* applies only to "custodial" interrogation—that is, when someone is deprived of freedom, under arrest. In effect, then, it is a limitation only upon the police. It does not apply to confessions heard by private citizens, unless they are set up as agents of the police, and it does not apply to governmental employees other than police, if they do not have arrest power. Accordingly, the courts have held that private security guards and even state welfare investigators, both of whom have no arrest powers, are not governed by *Miranda*.[68] An analogy easily can be drawn here to security officers on some campuses, especially at private institutions, who have no legal power to arrest, and thus no ability to conduct true custodial interrogation. A caution is necessary, however: some courts have ruled that the custodial question is to be decided on a subjective basis, examining whether the accused believed he or she was free to go. In this way, it would be possible for *Miranda* to be applied to circumstances where the suspect was, in fact, free to go, but believed to the contrary because the security guard looked and acted like a policeman conducting custodial interrogation.

Documents, Physical Characteristics, and the Fifth Amendment

The privilege against self-incrimination applies only to communications that are "testimonial" in nature and not to physical characteristics. Therefore, a suspect can be compelled to give blood samples, breath samples, fingerprints, handwriting exemplars, and voiceprints; to be photographed; and even to stand in a lineup and speak certain words.

In addition, documents generally do not fall under the self-incrimination privilege because they are not "testimonial." A person's tax return form has been held by the Supreme Court to be nontestimonial, even though in completing such a form the taxpayer is answering questions propounded by the government and is compelled to complete and file the form under threat of powerful sanctions.[69] The concept is illustrated in one campus case. An officer in the corps of cadets at Texas A&M had helped to formulate a list of physical exercises for cadets to use, then commanded two cadets to perform the exercises at two o'clock one morning. After performing the exercises, one of the cadets fell gravely ill and died. When police asked to see the exercise list, the student officer tore it up. When he was subsequently prosecuted for obstructing justice by tampering with evidence, he asserted that the list was protected by his privilege against self-incrimination. The Texas Court of Appeals disagreed and affirmed his conviction.[70]

SUMMARY: THE CAMPUS AND THE FOURTH AND FIFTH AMENDMENTS

The right of citizens to be free from unreasonable governmental searches and seizures of their bodies, effects, and properties, and from compelled confessions against themselves, extends to college and university campuses and to students, regardless of age. Under the exclusionary rule, evidence acquired as the result of an illegal search or seizure cannot be used in criminal court against an accused offender, but it sometimes can be used in campus disciplinary proceedings. Legal limitations on searches and seizures, however, are limitations on governmental action only and not on those of private citizens. Evidence gained by purely private searches often may be used even if gained through a procedure that would not pass constitutional muster. For this reason, private colleges and universities have a somewhat freer hand in searches than do public institutions.

As we have seen, a clear split exists between jurisdictions as to whether dormitory rooms are to be accorded the same sanctity as a house for search warrant purposes, and many different factors affect whether a search warrant is needed. A search warrant is unnecessary when a search is made 1) as an incident of a lawful arrest, 2) in some emergencies, 3) if the evidence is in plain view, or 4) if valid consent to the search is given. Admissions of guilt usually can be used against a person in a civil proceeding, such as a campus disciplinary hearing, and in many criminal cases when it was voluntarily given. However, a confession given to police officers usually cannot be used in criminal court if it was made after a person became a suspect but before the person was informed of, and waived, rights to silence and counsel. Such rules, however, do not apply to confessions taken by purely private security guards or citizens.

Campus administrators should be aware of the legal status of their institution and its security force so far as search and seizure issues are concerned. With assistance from legal counsel, the campus security force and administrators who oversee security operations should acquaint themselves with permissible procedures for the lawful acquisition of evidence that will be usable in campus disciplinary proceedings and, in appropriate cases, in the criminal courts.

NOTES

1. United States Constitution, Amendment IV.
2. *Mapp v. Ohio*, 367 U.S. 643 (1961).
3. *Burdeau v. McDowell*, 256 U.S. 465 (1921).
4. *Johnson v. United States*, 333 U.S. 10 (1948); *Coolidge v. New Hampshire*, 403 U.S. 443 (1971).
5. *State v. Boudreaux*, 304 So.2d 343 (La. 1974).
6. *Mahlberg v. Mentzer*, 968 F.2d 772 (8th Cir. 1992).
7. *State v. Harris*, 609 A.2d 944 (R.I. 1992).
8. *People v. Wolder*, 4 Cal.App.3d 984, 84 Cal.Rptr. 788 (1970).
9. *People v. Boettner*, 362 N.Y.S.2d 365 (Sup.Ct. 1974).
10. 422 F.Supp. 988 (D.N.H. 1976).
11. 105 S.Ct. 733 (1985).
12. *People v. Cohen*, 292 N.Y.S.2d 706 (D.C. 1968); see also *People v. Fierro*, 236 Cal. App. 2d 344 (1965).
13. See *People v. Boettner*, n. 9.
14. *Duarte v. Commonwealth*, 407 S.E.2d 41 (Va. App. 1991).
15. 317 F.Supp. 1253 (S.D. Miss. 1970), aff'd, 440 F.2d 1351 (5th Cir. 1971).
16. 316 F.Supp. 217 (D. Maine 1970).
17. 284 F.Supp. 725 (M.D. Ala. 1968).
18. 418 F.Supp. 102 (E.D.N.Y. 1976).
19. 422 F.Supp. 988 (D.N.H. 1976).
20. 414 U.S. 338 (1974).
21. 398 F.Supp. 777 (W.D.Mich. 1975).
22. 442 F.2d 284 (5th Cir. 1971).
23. 398 F.Supp. at 788.
24. 422 F.Supp. at 999.
25. 550 P.2d 121 (Ariz. App. 1976).
26. 398 F.Supp. at 786.
27. 292 N.Y.S.2d 706 (N.Y.D.C. 1968).

28. 313 N.E.2d 405 (Ohio 1974).
29. *Commonwealth v. McCloskey,* 272 A.2d 271 (Sup. Ct. Pa. 1970).
30. 831 P.2d 1033, 1038 (Utah App. 1992), *cert. denied,* 843 P.2d 1042 (1992).
31. Michael Keller, 12 *Journal of College and University Law* 415 (1985).
32. *Singer v. State,* 274 S.E.2d 612 (Ga. App. 1980).
33. *State v. King,* 298 N.W.2d 168 (Neb. 1980).
34. 455 U.S. 1 (1982).
35. 318 N.E.2d 866 (Ohio App. 1974).
36. *State v. Dalton,* 716 P.2d 940 (Wash. App. 1986).
37. See *Johnson v. United States,* n. 4.
38. *People v. Wahlen,* 443 N.E.2d 728 (Ill. App. 1982).
39. 1 *Wharton's Criminal Procedure,* 12th ed., Sec. 182, p. 392.
40. *State v. Radcliffe,* 483 So.2d 95 (Fla. 1986).
41. *State v. Pi Kappa Alpha Fraternity,* 491 N.E.2d 1129 (Ohio 1986).
42. *Lewis v. United States,* 385 U.S. 206 (1966).
43. *United States v. Coles,* 302 F.Supp. 99 (D. Maine 1969).
44. *People v. Lanthier,* 488 P.2d 625 (Cal. 1971).
45. See, for example *Commonwealth v. Snyder,* 413 Mass. 521, 597 N.E.2d 1363 (1992); *S. C. v. State,* 583 So.2d 188 (Miss. 1991).
46. *In the Interest of Isaiah B.,* 176 Wis.2d 639, 500 N.W.2d 637 (1993).
47. *State v. Johnson,* 530 P.2d 910 (Ariz. App. 1975).
48. *Garmon v. Foust,* 741 F.2d 1069 (8th Cir. 1984).
49. *People v. Suite,* 161 Cal.Rptr. 825, 101 Cal. App. 3d 680(1980).
50. 18 U.S.C. 2511.
51. 18 U.S.C. 3121.
52. *State v. Spoke Committee,* 270 N.W.2d 330 (N.D. 1978).
53. In re Grand Jury Subpoena Dated January 4, 1984, 583 F.Supp. 991(E.D.N.Y. 1984).
54. In re Grand Jury Subpoena Dated January 4, 1984, 750 F.2d 223 (2d Cir. 1984).
55. *Skinner v. Railway Labor Executives Assn.,* 489 U. S. 602 (1989).
56. *National Treasury Employees Union v. Von Raab,* 489 U. S. 656 (1989).
57. *O'Halloran v. University of Washington,* 679 F. Supp. 997 W.D. Wash. 1988), *rev'd,* 856 F.22d 1375 (9th Cir. 1988).
58. *Bally v. Northeastern University,* 532 N.E.2d 49 (Mass. 1989).
59. *Hill v. National Collegiate Athletic Association,* 865 P.2d 633 (Cal. 1994).
60. *University of Colorado v. Derdeyn,* 863 P.2d 929 (Colo. 1993).
61. 864 F.2d 1309 (7th Cir. 1988).
62. 23 F.3d 1514 (9th Cir. 1994).
63. *Miranda v. Arizona,* 384 U.S. 436 (1966).
64. *Baxter v. Palmigiano,* 425 U.S. 308 (1976); *Labor Relations Com'n v. Fall River Educ. Ass'n,* 416 N.E.2d 1340 (1981).
65. *Brown v. Mississippi,* 297 U.S. 278, 285 (1936).
66. 384 U.S. 436 (1966).
67. *Rhode Island v. Innis,* 446 U.S. 291, 100 S.Ct. 1682 (1980).
68. *State v. Graves,* 291 A.2d 2 (N.J. 1972); *McBride v. Atlantic City,* 370 A.2d 69 (N.J. Super. 1974); 31 A.L.R.3d 567, 666-669.
69. *Garner v. United States,* 424 U.S. 648, 96 S.Ct. 1178, 47 L.Ed.2d 370 (1976).
70. *Cuadra v. State,* 715 S.W.2d 723 (Tex. App. 1986).

C H A P T E R

9

• • • • • • • • •

Fraud, Theft, Payoffs, and Other Campus Mischief

L ife at our institutions of higher learning includes every sort of criminal offense commonly experienced in the parent society, ranging from vandalism to mayhem and murder. The campus has its own hybrids as well—forged transcripts and diplomas, point shaving by athletes, stolen research data, and the theft of ideas themselves.

In one study of a cross-section of American campuses, researchers had expected to find a broad student acceptance of certain types of "destructive behavior" (defined as ranging from graffiti to rape) on campus, particularly destructiveness directed against the college or university itself rather than individual students. They found instead that students overwhelmingly disapproved of such conduct. Ninety-eight percent disapproved of stealing student property, 97 percent disapproved of the destruction of campus property, 88 percent disapproved of stealing institutional property, and 75 percent disapproved of graffiti. Students reported that they believed destructiveness was most often group behavior, and that often participating students were under the influence of alcohol.

The researchers also had expected to be able to profile student offenders, but failed. They found that offenders were not significantly different from other students in terms of their academic majors or grade point averages, and breakdowns by college class indicated equivalent distributions.[1] Similarly, a study of college students who were shoplifters failed to identify characteristics that distinguished them from students in general. The researchers found that student shoplifters were not delinquent and had neither criminal personalities nor psychopathic tendencies, and that they stole for a variety of reasons, including the acquisition of attractive goods while saving money for other purposes.[2]

A 1990 study likewise found little difference between students who stole or mutilated library materials and those who did not. Few students believed that the behavior was an expression of hostility toward the institution. Most students explained book theft and page ripping as acts of thoughtlessness that could best be remedied by providing free copying service for library users.[3]

Of course, not all campus crime originates with students. Administrators, faculty, and noninstructional staff all have laid claim to campus delicts, and outsiders frequently use campuses for criminal activity at the point of either a gun or a pen.

FORGERY AND FRAUD: NOT ALWAYS WHAT THEY SEEM

A college football coach forged a high school official's signature to an unqualified athletic recruit's eligibility form. An undergraduate forged higher grades and more advanced courses on his transcript to gain entrance to medical school. A poor woman forged another person's signature to a check to buy food for her children.

The three cases are modeled after real events. The coach was fired. The student was denied his M.D. Only the woman was charged in the criminal courts with forgery, yet all might have been so charged. With academe's privileged status receding and the legal processes intruding deeper and deeper into campus life, criminal responsibility may come to lie at the doorstep of people like the coach and the student in coming years.

Sir William Blackstone defined forgery as "the fraudulent making or alteration of a writing to the prejudice of another man's rights." In his day, serious forgery was punished by "forfeiture to the party grieved of double costs and damages, by standing in the pillory, and having both ears cut off, and his nostrils slit and seared; by forfeiture to the crown of the profits of his lands, and by perpetual imprisonment."[4] The definition remains the same today, but the penalty has lightened considerably. Not only is it a crime to forge an instrument, but it is also a crime to "utter" a forged instrument, that is, to pass along or offer a forged instrument to another person with knowledge of the falsity of the writing and with intent to defraud.

Bogus Diplomas

The value of a college education becomes more evident with each passing year, while the earning power of noncollege-bound high-school graduates continues to shrink.[5] It is not surprising then, that a thriving business has developed in selling bogus college diplomas.

In their study of the subject, David Stewart and Henry Spille pointed out that so-called diploma mills come in two varieties. The first variety is a mill that simply sells a diploma, either its own or a forged copy of a legitimate institution's diploma. Such an enterprise might properly be called a "diploma factory." The second and more common variety "is a diploma mill that will grant a degree while posing requirements that emulate but are far less demanding than those ordinarily specified at legitimate colleges and universities."[6] According to an FBI estimate, there were about 100 institutions that could be called diploma mills in 1984, selling an estimated 10,000 to 15,000 bogus degrees.[7]

Diploma mill operators are subject to prosecution by state and federal authorities. For example, in 1985, two men pleaded guilty to federal charges in connection with the operation over a number of years of organizations known as American Western University and the Northwestern College of Allied Science, fictitious collegiate institutions from which individuals could purchase degrees from baccalaureates through doctorates for hefty price tags and with no academic work whatsoever. One undercover FBI agent purchased a master's degree in business administration for $510 and a master's degree in business management for $830. Both degrees were accompanied by transcripts reflecting numerous courses and grades, even though no course work was ever assigned nor any completed. Testimony at the sentencing hearing indicated the operation had sold about three thousand phony diplomas at a price tag of $2.3 million.[8] The major operator of the scheme pleaded guilty to mail fraud charges, but anyone who used one of the phony diplomas to gain something of value—a job, a raise, or the like—by holding the diploma or transcript out to represent actual academic work would likely fall under state laws against uttering forged instruments or obtaining property through false pretenses.

A case in New York led to the indictment by the Manhattan Grand Jury of four persons for conspiring to obtain fraudulent medical degrees from a school located in the Caribbean. The four included a professor at the New York Institute of Technology in Westbury, a physician's assistant, a medical records clerk, and a workman who had some training as a chiropractor. The attorney general of New York reported they paid from $5,000 to $27,000 each for their phony degrees, which would have qualified the four for medical residencies in hospitals in the United States. The indictments were part of a larger investigation that resulted in 21 arrests involving phony diplomas from Santo Domingo.[9]

Though no criminal charges were brought, a college professor was fired and denied unemployment compensation benefits after it was learned he had obtained his teaching position at Loretto Heights College by using a forged transcript which represented that he held a B.A. from Hunter, an M.A. from the University of New Mexico, and a Ph.D. from New York University. In fact, he held no college degrees. The evidence in the case, however, indicated that the man had performed satisfactorily as a teacher.[10]

College transcripts and admission documents likewise have often been the object of forgery or fraud. Even classroom work may be the setting for such misconduct. Some states now have "paper mill" statutes making it criminal to sell research papers that will be used by students to fulfill course requirements, and other forgery or fraud statutes might encompass attempts to use bogus academic work for credit.

Even though a medical student successfully completed the curriculum for an M.D. at the medical school of West Virginia University, he was denied his degree because he had falsified his admission documents. The Committee on Student Discipline at the university found unanimously that the student had willfully supplied the school with false material relating to his undergraduate grade point average and courses taken, degrees earned, and even birth date and marital status. West Virginia Chief Justice Neely observed that, after eight years of skillful legal maneuvering in the courts by the student's lawyer, their final appeal ignored "what is fundamental knowledge among all students of higher education, namely, that a person who cheats to get into school and gets caught will be expelled." The court refused to interfere with the university's denial of the medical diploma.[11]

Bogus Claims by Faculty

Other sorts of forgery than that of diplomas and credits, of course, enter college and university life. Some involve fraud through use of documents that misrepresent facts or work performed. For example, a psychology professor at California State University at Sacramento was terminated after he pleaded guilty to defrauding the state's Medicaid program. Medi-Cal investigators had claimed the psychologist billed for 119 services that were actually performed by his wife, who was not licensed to bill Medi-Cal; that he had billed for hours in excess of those actually worked; and that he had billed for rendering psychotherapeutic services to children he had not actually seen. The plea came in response to a 17-count information charging him with various false billings. The charges had related entirely to the professor's private practice, which he conducted on his own time, and a faculty committee found no nexus between the criminal offense and his teaching duties and therefore recommended only a reprimand. The university president disagreed, however. He found that the evidence of dishonesty and unprofessional conduct had an impact upon the man's ability to teach, and he dismissed him. The California Court of Appeals upheld the termination.[12]

Turning in fraudulent expense claims is a recurring crime in the university setting. The former associate athletic director at the University of New

Mexico was convicted of making or permitting a false public voucher in connection with his request for reimbursement of $82.44 for a meal. Evidence was submitted showing that he had written the names of people who had not attended the dinner on the back of the credit card receipt.

The conviction was later dismissed after the defendant completed the requirements of an order deferring sentence, but the former employee appealed anyway. He argued that no public monies were involved because reimbursement for the voucher was made from a discretionary account funded by athletic boosters. He also argued that he had not intended to defraud the university, in that he had already received approval from the athletic director for incurring the meal expense.

These arguments were unavailing. The New Mexico appellate court ruled as a matter of law that funds made available to the university become public funds, regardless of the source. Moreover, the fact that a superior had approved an expense that the employee knew to be in violation of university policy would not shield the employee from criminal culpability.[13]

WASTE, FRAUD, AND ABUSE IN FEDERAL GRANTS AND STUDENT LOANS

While the actual number of dollars available to higher education have fluctuated in recent years, federal money has become a way of life for most colleges and universities in research efforts and especially in the matter of student financial aid. These big programs reach so many people that fraud and abuse are bound to be present, and so they are.

Student Aid Scams and Defaults

Student financial assistance programs, including federally guaranteed loans provided by private lenders, have been defrauded through a variety of schemes, resulting in major losses to the federal government. Indeed, by the early 1990s, the United States Department of Education was losing between three and four billion dollars each year to waste, fraud, and defaults in higher education student loans, more than 10 percent of the department's annual budget.[14] Nonstudents have used fraudulent names and social security numbers to obtain loans and grants, usually intending neither to use the funds for educational purposes nor to repay them. Aliens, who generally are not eligible for such programs, have falsified their immigration status to obtain the monies. Students who otherwise were eligible have collected the funds, then quit school and used the monies for other purposes.

One source of abuse, the student who finances his college education with federally guaranteed loans and then immediately files for personal bankruptcy, has been adequately addressed. In 1978, Congress amended the U.S.

Bankruptcy Code to prohibit a debtor from discharging student loans through bankruptcy until at least five years after the debt becomes due, unless the debtor can show undue hardship. In 1990, the waiting period was extended to seven years.[15] In addition, Congress has abolished the statute of limitations for bringing suit on student loan debts.[16]

Medical students who promise to serve needy areas after they complete their studies in return for federal financial aid while in medical school are penalized severely if they renege on their obligations. Federal law permits the government to assess triple penalties for doctors who accept federal scholarships and then refuse to report to their public service post. Thus, one doctor who received $46,726 in scholarships and then declined an assignment in South Dakota found herself facing a debt of $379,485.74 after interest and penalties were attached, more than eight times the federal aid she originally received. When she tried to discharge this huge sum in federal bankruptcy court, a sympathetic judge cut the debt in half, ruling that it would be almost impossible for her to discharge the entire debt. The Third Circuit Court of Appeals, however, reinstated the obligation in full, pointing out that the doctor could still discharge the debt by accepting a public service assignment.[17]

Institutional Abuse of Student Loan Programs

Of course, a large percentage of defaulting student debtors, perhaps the majority, assumed their debts in good faith and were simply unable to repay their loans when they later became due. Indeed, it has been dishonest institutions, not individual students, that have been responsible for the biggest portion of the fraud and abuse in federally guaranteed student loans. Most of the abuse was perpetrated by for-profit trade schools, some of which are apparently operated for the express purpose of collecting student loan and grant money, while providing little if any useful training or job skills. The U.S. Department of Education recently estimated that 76 percent of its defaulting student loans come from the for-profit trade schools.[18]

In its series of investigative articles on student aid abuses, the *New York Times* reported on one trade-school recipient of federal money that allegedly paid its owners annual salaries of $1 million apiece while only finding employment for 10 to 20 percent of its students. According to persons who testified at a Senate investigatory hearing, the school had only 23 instructors but 70 loan processors.[19]

The same Senate investigation produced a report in which investigators accused several Judaic Studies schools in New York of using "ghost" students and falsified student grant applications to collect millions of dollars in Pell Grant funds. According to the report, some of these schools artificially inflated tuition levels to enable Pell Grant recipients to draw the maximum award. The report cited one Jewish seminary in which all but 10 of its 1,507 students had received Pell Grant awards.[20]

Misconduct Involving Federal Research Grants

In addition to student financial assistance programs, the federal government distributes about $9 billion annually in research grants to various institutions of higher education.[21] Not surprisingly, there have been a number of instances in which federal research money was misdirected, stolen, or fraudulently obtained.

Perhaps the most publicized incident involving misuse of federal research funds grew out of a federal audit of Stanford University's research grants. By the time the university had resolved this matter, Stanford's president and two top administrators had resigned, a criminal investigation of the university's federal grants had been launched, and Stanford's centennial celebration had been marred by nationwide negative publicity.

Like most universities receiving federal research funds, Stanford had billed the government for the indirect costs associated with its federal research—items like use of facilities, utilities, libraries, and administrative expenses. When federal investigators began investigating Stanford in 1990, the university's indirect costs were quite high—variously reported at from 74 to 78 percent. In 1991, federal auditors announced that Stanford overbilled for its indirect costs and owed the government more than $200 million for excessive charges made during the 1980s.

Although it was little noted at the time, Stanford's indirect costs were not the highest in the country. Three universities' costs were higher, and the average indirect cost for all federally funded university research was about 49 percent.[22]

What outraged the public and some congressional leaders, however, was not so much the amount of Stanford's billings, but the fact that Stanford had sought reimbursement for items that were clearly inappropriate. It was revealed, for example, that Stanford had billed the government for the maintenance expense of a 72-foot yacht, an antique commode, flowers for the president's home, and upkeep on the university founder's tomb.[23]

By the end of 1991, congressional hearings and audits of other universities' research grants had uncovered more abuses. For example, the *Washington Post* reported that Syracuse University had charged the government $1.4 million for cheerleaders, bands, and a club called the "Sour Citrus Society"; Pennsylvania State University had billed $15,000 for advertisements and billboards at Hershey Amusement Park; and Harvard University Medical School had sought reimbursement for athletic facility memberships, legal fees, and alumni mailings.[24]

These events led Stanford's president, Donald Kennedy, to resign and tarnished Stanford's reputation. Nevertheless, had the university not taken fast corrective action, the damage might have been considerably worse. First, the university readily acknowledged that some federal reimbursements were inappropriate and refunded about $2 million in federal grant funds without protest.[25] Second, the university used the media effectively to tell its side of the story. For example, Stanford officials explained that many of the disputed costs had previously been approved by government grant administrators in more than 100 separate, written agreements. The university also released documents showing that it had repeatedly asked the government to audit the university's research grants, after the government had delayed in doing so.[26]

Third, Stanford undertook a comprehensive accounting overhaul to prevent improper billings in the future. The university established a written code of ethical behavior and a procedure for supporting employees who reveal suspected fraud or who take action to eliminate inappropriate charges to government accounts.[27]

Finally, the university never let itself appear to be combative or defensive, even after it was announced that navy investigators were launching a criminal investigation.[28] Peter Van Etten, who was named as Stanford's chief financial officer after the scandal broke, established the tone of Stanford's response to the criminal probe. "We ourselves feel quite confident that criminal indictments will not be brought," Van Etten said, "but I can't say clearly what will happen in the future." He pointed out that many of the university's problems with its internal controls had been corrected, and he expressed optimism about a positive resolution of the university's dispute with the government. "Our goal," Van Etten said, "is to come to a settlement that's fair to the government and fair to Stanford, and we're confident that we'll be able to work that out in the next few months."[29]

Stanford's problems with federal research grants did not entirely end within a few months; the 1991 scandal created budgetary pressures as a result of changes in federal grant funding policies and the university's refunds of overcharges. As a public relations problem, however, the scandal had largely subsided by the spring of 1992, when virtually all media coverage of the issue had ceased.

Penalties for Fraud Involving Federal Grant and Research Funds

Criminal penalties. Faculty members who fraudulently obtain public funds or expend those funds improperly are subject to criminal penalties.[30] For example, college and university employees can be prosecuted under the criminal False Statement statute for making a written or oral false statement that is capable of influencing a decision of a federal agency that relates to the performance of its function. One commentator has pointed out that it is not necessary for the false statement to be made under oath to sustain a conviction. Furthermore, a prosecutor need not show that anyone relied on the false statement in order to pursue a criminal action.[31] Higher education employees may also be subject to the federal False Claims statute for making a fraudulent claim for federal research funds.[32] Each false demand for payment is a separate offense. The penalty for violating this statute can be up to five years' imprisonment.[33]

From time to time, education officials and higher education employees who misuse federal funds are convicted under one of the various federal criminal laws. A former employee of the Massachusetts Department of Education was sentenced to 30 months in federal prison and required to pay up to $80,000 in restitution after he pleaded guilty to defrauding the state government of funds for an adult education center.[34] A faculty member of the University of California pleaded guilty to defrauding the federal government of more than a half-million dollars. Under a plea agreement he agreed to pay $1.6 million in fines and penalties and to resign his faculty position.[35]

It is quite clear that federal grant funds retain their federal character for purposes of a criminal prosecution, even after the funds have been given to a state agency. In a 1979 decision, a federal appellate court ruled that federal funds that had been received by a college and put into its work-study budget continued to have the character of "money . . . of the United States," and thus stealing it from the work-study program was theft of public property.[36] More recently, an associate professor at Northwestern State University, a state institution in Louisiana, was convicted of the theft of federal government funds, even though the funds had been received by the university from a state agency set up to administer a federal program. The funds retained their federal character, the court ruled, in light of the control exercised by the federal government over ultimate disposition of the money.[37]

These decisions have implications for many other federally funded programs in which monies are received by institutions and commingled in state and institutional accounts. They are especially significant because federal auditing and investigatory processes have been far more vigorous and sophisticated than state oversight in recent years, and it appears this vigilance will continue.

Civil penalties. In addition to criminal penalties, persons who fraudulently obtain federal funds can be subject to civil liability, and the institutions that receive these wrongfully spent funds may be liable as well. A Justice Department official recently described the civil False Claims suit as "the government's primary weapon for fighting fraud."[38]

Indeed, the civil False Claims Act is a particularly powerful weapon for combating fraudulent activities in connection with federal research funds, since the legislation permits recovery of treble damages. Damages may be reduced to not less than double the actual damages, if the grantee discovers the fraud before the federal government does, voluntarily discloses it, and cooperates in the federal investigation.[39] Moreover, the act permits private litigants to sue federal contractors on the government's behalf and encourages them to do so by giving these "whistle-blowers" a share of the money that is collected if the suit is successful.[40]

The False Claims Act was originally passed in the nineteenth century and amended in 1986 to establish tougher penalties. Since that time it has typically been used against federal defense contractors.[41] However, in 1991, a False Claims Act suit was brought against Stanford University in connection with the research grant controversy that was discussed earlier in this chapter. The plaintiff in the suit was one of the federal auditors who claimed that Stanford had overcharged the government for indirect costs in connection with research grants. By filing the suit on the government's behalf, the auditor hoped to benefit financially if the allegations he had made against Stanford were sustained in court.[42]

The whistle-blower's incentive provision of the False Claims Act has been criticized because it has the potential for encouraging an individual with a grudge against an institution to file a treble damages action "as a convenient means of retribution and potential enrichment."[43] Nevertheless, the provision remains in effect as a substantial danger to any higher education institution that makes a false claim in connection with a federal grant.

PETIT LARCENY AND VANDALISM

Larceny—the taking and carrying away of another's property with intent to deprive the owner of it—is a common campus occurrence. One 1985 survey found that theft of personal articles from students—purses, wallets, knapsacks—was the most frequent campus crime, and following it in frequency were thefts of cameras and jewelry from unlocked and unoccupied dormitory rooms, thefts of equipment from motor vehicles, and theft of bicycles.[44]

Campus morale is affected when such stealing is rampant and seemingly ignored. The only apparent response to such petit theft would seem to lie in education of the victims so that opportunity is minimized. Students can be informed of the problem and given techniques for theft avoidance during orientation sessions and in campus publications. Property-marking equipment can be made available. Recognition and discussion of the problem might also lead to wider student participation in spotting and reporting thefts.

Vandalism, too, is a significant problem on some campuses, though statistics on its frequency are not available because most vandalism does not generate a police report. One college president has likened campus vandalism to "a cancer of bricks and mortar," and her institution has responded by vandal-proofing where possible. Plexiglas is used instead of glass, tough vinyl instead of lighter fabrics, and heavy oak furniture is built in campus shops for use in problem areas.[45]

Theft on the Job by Faculty and Staff

Theft of institutional property is yet another problem area. Clearly, the theft of institutional money, such as embezzlement of college funds by a bookkeeper, is illegal[46]; but thefts of other things of value, such as secretarial time and long distance telephone services, likewise can come under theft statutes in most states. Administrators, too, can become criminals by misusing the property entrusted to them. Thus, a state adjutant general was convicted of charges stemming from his use of a National Guard airplane for visits to his girlfriend.[47] But a federal appeals court overturned the conviction of an executive of the U.S. Department of Health, Education, and Welfare (now the Department of Health and Human Resources) for conversion of government property when he had his secretary spend many hours typing documents for his private business. The court acknowledged that the officer appeared to have "misused his position and violated his obligation to render loyal service to his employer," but said the government had failed to prove that any other work failed to be done because of the typing—it was done in a slack period between shifts in programs—and thus no loss to the government was shown so as to constitute a criminal offense.[48]

COMPUTERS, BUGGING, AND ELECTRONIC CRIME

America has become an "information society." Not only must colleges and universities conduct much of their own information processing on computers, but they must see that students are trained to use these "engines" of the new age. Estimates of loss through computer theft range from hundreds of millions of dollars to $40 billion annually, and our campuses obviously are ripe targets for such theft.[49] Likewise, the technology of electronic eavesdropping has grown geometrically in recent years, and the opportunities for misdeeds are legion.

Computer Mischief

Data within computer memories can be covertly pilfered, altered, or destroyed with the push of a single key. Computer-to-computer communications can be intercepted through wiretaps, and despite the best efforts of electronic surveillance equipment and personal security in areas of input and transmission, one commentator has said that "real security measures" against wiretaps have not yet been developed.[50]

In many instances, use of computer time without permission of its owner is itself a crime, and, for those with access to a computer, three methods of theft or interference have been described. One such method is the "Trojan Horse," in which an improper operation is hidden within the main program and the unauthorized activity (generation of reports, or alteration or transfer of data) is accomplished while the system seemingly performs the legitimate task. Another is the "Salami Technique," in which an applications program is placed into computer memory to siphon off almost indistinguishable amounts of data. An example would be the rounding off of all bank deposits to the lowest ten cents and crediting the odd pennies to the thief's account. The third method is "Super Zapping," which employs a micro-utility program to modify or destroy the computer's memory without trace of tampering.[51]

Computer criminals may be separated into two categories: "hackers" and adult criminals. A typical hacker is a juvenile with a home computer who uses a modem and computerized bulletin boards to gain illegal access to computer systems.[52] It has been suggested that hackers are performing a public service by helping to divulge the serious weaknesses in computer systems,[53] but their activities are not always benign. For example, some hackers employ their computer skills to obtain stolen credit card numbers, which they use to obtain goods and services by theft. Even if hackers do no economic damage, their activities constitute a modern form of trespass and an invasion of privacy.

Adult computer criminals run the gamut from disgruntled employees who use their computer skills to wreak havoc on their employer's business activities to embezzlers, drug offenders, and child pornographers. A typical adult computer criminal is a bright, motivated male who holds a position of trust at his job, has no previous criminal history, and works alone. On the surface, the computer criminal may appear to deviate little from social norms; and he may justify his computerized crime as simply a "game."[54]

Increasing system security. The American Society for Industrial Security suggests five criteria for increased system security: 1) separation of knowledge through job rotations, division of responsibilities, physical isolation, and the like; 2) written program instructions with threat monitoring and audit trails built in; 3) careful accounting of all input documents; 4) periodic changes in access codes and passwords; and 5) scramblers and cryptographic applications.[55]

New criminal statutes. In recent years, Congress has enacted the Counterfeit Access Device Act,[56] the Computer Fraud and Abuse Act,[57] and the Electronic Funds Transfer Act[58] in an attempt to meet the modern hybrids of crime made possible by computers. Other federal statutes prohibiting theft from the government or its contractors, banks, or through use of the mails also have applicability.[59] One legal expert has declared that development of the law dealing with computers "is about three years behind technology."[60]

An example is the case of *Lund v. Commonwealth*, in which the conviction of a doctoral student at Virginia Tech on computer theft charges was overturned by the state's highest court.[61] The student, who was pursuing a degree in statistics, had not obtained permission to use the institution's mainframe computer for his massive research project. Instead, he went ahead with the project using access keys assigned to other people. The university, which leased the mainframe from IBM, established the value of the computer time taken by the student to be $26,384.16, though the actual physical property that he had taken—computer cards and printouts—was of negligible value.

The student was found guilty of grand larceny, but the Virginia Supreme Court overturned the conviction because the Virginia larceny and false pretenses statutes covered only theft of goods and chattels, which the court said could not be stretched to include computer time or services. The Virginia legislature passed a specific computer theft statute in response to the court's decision, and most other states now have done likewise.[62]

However, even a well-drafted computer trespass statute may not prohibit the kind of computer misconduct that a university wishes to discourage. In *State v. Olson*, for example, a campus police officer at the University of Washington was convicted of computer trespass after it was discovered that he had obtained information about female university students from the police department computer. On appeal, the officer argued that the evidence did not support a conviction for computer trespass, because he had authority to use the computer when he obtained the data about the female students. The Washington Court of Appeals essentially agreed. When the officer had gathered data about the university women, the court reasoned, he may have done so without authority, since the data was not part of an ongoing police investigation. Unauthorized use of data, however, was not prohibited by the Washington computer trespass statute. Accordingly, the court of appeals reversed the conviction.[63]

Over the years, university computers have been used for various kinds of mischief. For example, a grade-tampering scheme involving university computers resulted in a guilty plea by a former employee of the University of Southern California and the expulsion of 14 students. The former employee of the university's registration and records office allegedly took payoffs from students ranging from $500 to $2,000 to change course grades. He pleaded guilty under a California computer crime statute.[64] At the University of Tennessee, 19 students were suspended after the Office of Student Conduct determined that they had been involved in a scheme to use university computers to add courses that were already full or drop courses after the drop deadline.[65]

Computer evidence searches. When criminal activity involving a computer is suspected, a search for a program or data files within the suspect's computer system sometimes is necessary. Because of the difficulties in acquiring a search warrant and performing such a search, the Federal Bureau of Investigation has compiled a guide for computer evidence searches. Presearch considerations include identification of the equipment to be searched, so that appropriate technical assistance, hardware, and materials (perhaps specially written investigatory software to retrieve the desired data) will be available. The search itself must be conducted under tight physical security to ensure that remote terminals are not available to permit erasure or alteration of data before it can be seized. An activity log, on which the computer records all activity during the search, also is recommended. Safe storage for the seized items likewise must be arranged well ahead of time.[66]

Electronic "Bugging"

Another aspect of electronic crime is so-called bugging. A federal statute[67] makes it a felony to use any sort of "bug" or wiretap to intercept or overhear anybody else's private conversation, unless one of the parties to the conversation consents. However, if any party to the conversation consents, it may be overheard or recorded, and the other parties to it need not be informed. (This subject is discussed more thoroughly in chapter 8).

One campus electronic crime case involved the athletic director at Louisiana State University, Robert Brodhead, who pleaded guilty to federal charges that he used illegal bugging equipment in his own office. The equipment had been installed, apparently, to allow Brodhead to overhear conversations between LSU athletes and investigators from the National Collegiate Athletic Association, which was looking at LSU programs.[68] In the plea bargain with federal prosecutors made by Brodhead in mid-1986, he pleaded guilty to one count of conspiracy to intercept radio communications.[69] He resigned his post at LSU shortly thereafter.

Higher education administrators should be aware that state privacy laws may be more restrictive than federal law with regard to recording private conversations. For example, the Washington Privacy Act prohibits any individual, including a state employee, from recording a private telephone conversation or private face-to-face conversation without the consent of all the parties engaged in the conversation.[70] To avoid possible civil or criminal penalties, college and university officials should familiarize themselves with state electronic eavesdropping laws before recording any private conversation to which all the parties have not consented.

CRIME AND INTELLECTUAL PROPERTY

Federal law has long protected intellectual property as an encouragement and reward for individual creativity. While trademarks[71] and patents[72] on products and processes can be enforced through civil lawsuits, the other type of intellectual property protection, copyright, can be enforced in federal criminal courts as well.[73]

The copyright laws protect original works of authorship that have been expressed in a tangible way (writing, film, painting, sculpture, photographs, computer programs, sound recording, and many radio and television broadcasts). The owner of a copyright has the exclusive authority to reproduce the copyrighted work, to prepare derivative works, to distribute copies, and to perform or display the work publicly. Protection affixes once original material is recorded in tangible form, and formal registration has not been necessary since the Copyright Act was revised by Congress in 1976. Registration is, however, necessary before a copyright suit can be maintained in federal court.

Fair Use

Copyright protection is not absolute, however. Material that otherwise is protected can be reproduced under the "fair use" exception for some educational activities; scholarly, literary, and social criticism or parody; and free speech and press activities protected by the First Amendment, such as news reporting. The fair use exception is limited, and presupposes good faith and fair dealing by those who claim it. While it is impossible to give a single clear definition of fair use for classroom purposes, it can be said that the doctrine generally provides that small quantities of limited portions of a work may be reproduced for classroom use where no charge is made for the copies, the economic loss to the copyright holder is not significant, the material was not originally prepared specifically for educational purposes, and there is no intent to republish or display it publicly.

Prior to the 1976 revisions, the act itself did not mention fair use; the doctrine had been developed in court rulings to meet needs of a changing society. The 1976 act, however, provided criteria for courts to use in determining fair use, considering the facts of each individual case. They include considering the purpose and character of the use, the nature of the copyrighted work, the proportion of the material used, and the economic effect upon the copyright owner.[74] These criteria were an attempt by Congress to codify the general principles of fair use that the courts had developed, and thus the cases predating the 1976 act still carry much authority.

The matter is confused even more because when Congress adopted the 1976 act, it included within the published legislative history certain "guidelines" for copying materials for classroom use in not-for-profit educational institutions. The guidelines offer specific totals on amounts of copying that can be done, and time periods within which material can be taken from one work.[75] These guidelines resulted from attempts by congressional committees to have the constituencies that had special interest in the copyright legislation—authors, publishers, and educators—come together and express consensus as to what the new law should be. The process did not work smoothly, and the guidelines that resulted contained many compromises.

The guidelines are not actually a part of the law, however. Under general rules for construction of statutes, courts may look to legislative history to aid in interpreting unclear portions of statutes, and therefore the guidelines carry some legal weight, although it is not yet certain how much. Further, and unfortunately, the guidelines are not clearly drawn, and in some instances contradict the act itself. As a result, the definition of fair use may be even more illusive than it was before the congressional action.[76] Still, they do provide some parameters, and the educator who follows them most likely is within permissible fair use and, in any event, could claim good faith. The courts may yet hold, however, that other matters that exceed the guidelines fall within the statutory "fair use."

Perhaps more understanding of fair use can come from examining the cases dealing with it. Of four significant cases that have dealt with fair use in an educational setting, three resulted in judgments for the copyright owner. In the first, *Macmillan v. King*, a 1914 case in Massachusetts, the court held for the book publisher in an injunction suit against a Harvard professor who had copied substantial portions of an economics textbook to produce an outline for his students. The nature of the work—a text whose market was colleges—and the large extent of the copying outweighed the educational and nonprofit purposes asserted in the defendant's unsuccessful claim of fair use.[77]

A 1978 civil case in New York, *Encyclopaedia Britannica Educational Corp. v. C. N. Crooks*, addressed the issues of systematic copying and effect upon the market, and likewise held that an educational and nonprofit purpose was insufficient to establish fair use. The case involved an educational support agency that had copied videotapes made by Encyclopaedia Britannica and distributed them to schools. The court noted that the only market for the tapes was just where they were used—in education—and granted Britannica's request for an injunction.[78] In a subsequent trial, the court reiterated its earlier ruling that the agency's copying activities did not constitute fair use.[79]

In the mid-1970s, in *Williams and Wilkins v. United States*, the federal Court of Claims and the United States Supreme Court upheld the fair use defense as applied to the copying of journal articles by the National Library of Medicine, a federal agency. In the case, a publisher of scholarly medical journals had sued for damages for copyright infringement because the library distributed some 85,000 copies of journal articles each year, a large number coming from the plaintiff's journals, in response to requests from physicians, medical researchers, and other libraries. The library contended that its activities, in the specific context of the case, were "fair use" and not an infringement. Ultimately the position of the library was vindicated, but by votes of only four to three in the Court of Claims and by a divided four-to-four vote in the Supreme Court (which resulted in automatic affirmance of the Court of Claims).[80]

Finally, in *Basic Books, Inc. v. Kinko's Graphic Corporation,* a 1991 case, a federal district court in New York interpreted the fair use doctrine in a copyright infringement case brought by several publishing companies against Kinko's Graphics Corporation, a private copying company. The publishing companies accused Kinko's of violating the copyright laws by reproducing portions of copyrighted works as anthologies for college professors who then used these compilations as reading materials for various college courses. In all, Kinko's reproduced portions of 12 of the plaintiffs' copyrighted books, including portions of six books for a course in which only three students were enrolled.

Kinko's asserted a fair use defense, which the federal court analyzed by applying the four factors for determining fair use that are codified in the Copyright Act. As discussed above, those factors are 1) the purpose and character of the use, 2) the nature of the copyrighted work, 3) the amount and substantiality of the portion used, and 4) the effect of the use on potential markets for or value of the copyrighted work.[81]

After weighing all four factors, the court found that the copying company did not meet the criteria for fair use. In particular, the court was influenced by the fact that the copying company had engaged in a substantial amount of copying and had done so for profit. The court was also persuaded that the sale of the anthologies assembled by the copying company had an adverse impact on the sale of the publishing companies' books.

The court then considered whether Kinko's activities qualified as fair use of the plaintiffs' materials under the Classroom Guidelines. Here again, the copying company was unsuccessful. The court held that Kinko's status as a for-profit corporation, and its profit-making intent, rendered it outside the purview of the Classroom Guidelines. Moreover, the court added, even if Kinko's was entitled to review under the guidelines, the copying company's activities violated the guidelines' requirements.

The court acknowledged that the guidelines permitted a teacher to make multiple copies of copyrighted material if the copying met the tests of brevity, spontaneity, and cumulative effect and so long as each copy includes a notice of copyright. However, according to the court, Kinko's met none of these tests.

First, under the guidelines, brevity in prose was defined as "a complete article, story or essay of less than 2,500 words," or an excerpt of "not more than 1,000 words or 10 percent of the work, whichever is less."[82] Kinko's copies did not meet the brevity standard.

Second, for the copying to meet the guidelines' spontaneity standard, "the inspiration and decision to use the work and the moment of its use for maximum teaching effectiveness [had to be] so close in time that it would be unreasonable to expect a timely reply to a request for permission."[83] The copying that Kinko's engaged in was not spontaneous, the court found, since it coincided with the start of each semester and began after Kinko's obtained a list of course materials from professors.

Third, the guidelines' cumulative effect test prohibited more than nine instances of multiple copying for one course during a class term. Of the five court packets under review, the court pointed out that four of them contained more than nine items.

Finally, Kinko's had included copyright notices on none of the copies that were in dispute. Thus, this requirement of the Classroom Guidelines had not been met.

In addition, the court observed that Kinko's violated the guidelines' mandate against copying to create, replace, or substitute for anthologies, compilations, or collected works as well as a prohibition against copying as a substitute for the purchase of books. Although the court declined to hold that all unconsented anthologies violate the copyright laws, it concluded that the fact that Kinko's had engaged in the publication of anthologies weighed heavily against its fair use argument.

The *Kinko's* case is highly significant for higher education institutions because it addresses a practice that has become quite common in the university classroom—the reproduction and distribution of professor-compiled anthologies as teaching materials. Although the defendant was a private copying company, not a college or university, one commentator has argued that the standards applied by the court in *Kinko's* would apply to a university print shop as well.[84] As *Kinko's* attests, the penalty for exceeding fair use in the compilation of anthologies can be quite high. In that case, the court awarded statutory damages of $510,000.

Criminal Sanctions

While persons who feel their copyrights have been violated may bring private suit for injunctions or damages, willful infringements of the Copyright Act also may result in criminal proceedings instituted by the United States Attorney.[85] There have been few such prosecutions through the years, however; most have dealt with fraudulent schemes to violate copyrights for commercial gain. The recent cases have involved piracy of records, films, and sound and video tapes. Under the 1976 act, general copyright infringement or fraud can be a misdemeanor offense punishable by up to one year's imprisonment and a $25,000 fine, but record and tape piracy come in for much harsher penalties of five years and $250,000, together with broad governmental rights of seizure and forfeiture.

The Copyright Remedy Clarification Act of 1990

Because they feared that lawsuits against states for copyright violations might be barred by the Eleventh Amendment, software designers, publishing companies, and other copyright owners lobbied Congress to pass legislation abrogating the states' immunity to damages suits for copyright infringement. They argued that without the ability to sue state entities for damages when they violated the copyright laws, copyright owners stood to lose substantial revenues.[86]

Persuaded by these arguments, Congress passed the Copyright Remedy Clarification Act in 1990.[87] Although, previous law had permitted copyright owners to get injunctions against state agencies that infringed on copyrights, the new law allows the copyright holders to obtain money awards against them as well. As a result, state colleges and universities that use their own copying facilities and print shops to prepare anthologies for professors could be liable for damages for copyright infringement if a court were to determine that the copying exceeded fair use. Moreover, state universities and their employees can be liable not only for actual damages, which often are quite small, but statutory damages as well. In cases where the infringement was committed willfully, a court may award up to $100,000 in statutory damages for each violation.

Avoiding Trouble

Although *Basic Books, Inc. v. Kinko's Graphics Corporation* provides some guidance about the scope of the fair use doctrine and the Classroom Guidelines, many questions about classroom copying remain unanswered. Thus, it is difficult to give advice for dealing with copyright issues. The best advice is for educators to have a copy of the guidelines handy, and to consult with counsel on any matters not clearly permitted by them. The following prudent principles for general classroom and research applications should be kept in mind:

1. The fact the use is nonprofit is immaterial.
2. The fact the use is educational is immaterial.
3. Copying should not substitute for the purchase of original materials, except in extremely limited circumstances.
4. Copying should not be required by superiors; copying should be done only at the inspiration of the individual teacher.

5. No charge beyond actual reproduction cost should be made to any student to whom a copy is furnished.
6. The smaller the amount of material copied the better. It should be no more than a sample portion from a writing or recording, with no copy from the same work more than once in a term, and no copying of complete chapters.
7. Notice of copyright should be on every copy distributed.
8. No copying of "consumable" workbooks, tests, or the like is allowed.
9. Copying should not be done to create anthologies.

NOTES

1. Robert Leslie, "Campus Destructiveness in the 1980s: A Survey of American College Students," paper presented at the annual meeting of the Association for the Study of Higher Education, March 25-26, 1983, ERIC ED 232 555, p. 16.
2. Richard H. Moore, "College Shoplifters: Rebuttal of Beck and McIntyre," 53 *Psychological Reports* 1111-16 (1983).
3. Terri L. Pederson, "Theft and Mutilation of Library Materials," 51 *College and Research Libraries*, pp. 120-28 (1990).
4. IV *Blackstone's Commentaries* 247, 248.
5. Richard Murnane and Frank Levy, "Why Today's High-School-Educated Males Earn Less than Their Fathers Did: The Problem and an Assessment of Responses," 63 *Harvard Educational Review*, 1-19 (1993).
6. David W. Stewart and Henry A. Spille, *Diploma Mills, Degrees of Fraud* (New York: Macmillan Publishing Company and American Council on Education, 1988), p. 11.
7. Ibid., p. 37, citing Ellie McGrath, "Sending Degrees to the Dogs," *Time*, April 2, 1984, p. 90.
8. *United States v. Geruntino*, U.S. District Court, Western District of North Carolina, Charlotte, No. C-CR-85-22.
9. *Criminal Justice Report*, May 1985 (Washington, D.C.: National Association of Attorneys General), p. 8.
10. *Denberg v. Loretto Heights College*, 694 P.2d 375 (Colo. App. 1984).
11. *North v. Board of Regents*, 332 S.E.2d 141 (W.Va. 1985).
12. *Samaan v. Trustees of the California State University and Colleges*, 197 Cal. Rptr. 856, 150 Cal. App. 3d 651 (Cal. App. 3 Dist. 1983).
13. *State v. Hearne*, 813 P.2d 485 (N.M. App. 1991).
14. Michael Winerip, "Billions for School Are Lost in Fraud, Waste and Abuse," *New York Times*, February 2, 1994, sec. A, page 1.
15. 11 U.S.C. Sect. 523. For a good discussion of the treatment of student debts under the U.S. Bankruptcy Code, see Darrell Dunham and Ronald A. Bunch, "Educational Debts under the Bankruptcy Code, 22 *Memphis State University Law Review* 679 (1992).
16. 20 U.S.C. Sec. 1091a.
17. *Matthews v. Pineo*, 19 F.3d 121 (3rd Cir.), *cert. denied*, 115 S.Ct 82, 130 L.Ed.2d 35 (1994).
18. Winerip, *New York Times*, February 2, 1994, p. 1.
19. Ibid.

20. Jim Zook, "Jewish Seminaries Said to Have Bilked U.S. out of Millions in Pell Grants," The Chronicle of Higher Education, November 3, 1993, p. A29.
21. Steve Gordon, "The Liability of Colleges and Universities for Fraud, Waste, and Abuse in Federally Funded Grants and Projects," 75 West's Education Law Reporter 13, 14 (August 13, 1992).
22. John Wildermuth, "Federal Auditor Suing Stanford," San Francisco Chronicle, September 24, 1991, p. A13; "Despite Furor over Research Fees, Stanford Plans Similar Rate Again," New York Times, July 5, 1991, sec. D, p. 6.
23. "Stanford to Return U.S. Funds for Upkeep of Tomb," Los Angeles Times, September 6, 1991, part A, p. 3; "U.S. Schools Favored Other Nations while Overbilling Own Government for Research Costs," San Diego Union-Tribune, January 30, 1992, p. A2.
24. Mary Jordan, "Rep. Dingell Says New Audits Show Widespread Abuse of U.S. Funds," Washington Post, January 30, 1992, p. 1.
25. "Stanford Investigated On New Overbilling Charges," Los Angeles Times, November 16, 1991, sec A, p. 27.
26. Louis Freedberg, "Stanford May Owe US Hundreds of Millions, Research Grants Have Not Been Audited since 1980," San Francisco Chronicle, November 27, 1991, p. A11.
27. Anthony DePalma, "Stanford to Alter Its Accounting of Overhead on Research Grants," New York Times, July 23, 1991, sec. A, p. 14.
28. For an excellent discussion on managing public relations crises, see David Kuechle, "Negotiating with an Angry Public, Advice to Corporate Leaders," Negotiations Journal, October 1985, p. 317.
29. Carolyn Lochhead, "Stanford Faces Criminal Probe of Overbilling, U.S. agencies also examining records of two other col[leges]," San Francisco Chronicle, January 30, 1992, p. A1.
30. 18 U.S.C. Sec. 1001.
31. Gordon, pp. 13, 16–17.
32. 18 U.S.C. Sec. 287.
33. Gordon, pp. 17-18.
34. "Former Dukakis Advisor Sentenced to Prison,"The Chronicle of Higher Education, May 4, 1988, p. 2A.
35. "Professor Found Guilty of Research Fraud," The Chronicle of Higher Education, February 28, 1992, p. A6.
36. United States v. Smith, 596 F.2d 662 (5th Cir. 1979).
37. United States v. Long, 996 F.2d 731 (5th Cir. 1993).
38. Gordon, p. 14, citing Corporate Crime Reporter, Vol. 4, No. 35, September 17, 1990, pp. 10-11.
39. 31 U.S.C. Sec. 3729.
40. 31 U.S.C. Sec. 3730.
41. Howard Mintz, The Recorder, October 9, 1991, p. 1.
42. "Transfer of Stanford Auditor Urged," Los Angeles Times, December 20, 1991, part A, p. 40.
43. Gordon, p. 24.
44. Lawrence J. Fennelly, "Crime Problems on College Campuses," Security Management, September 1985, p. 122.
45. "Taming Campus Vandals," American School & University, October 1980, p. 44.
46. Seaman v. State, 225 So. 2d 418 (Fla. 1969).

47. *United States v. May*, 625 F.2d 186 (8th Cir. 1980).
48. *United States v. Wilson*, 636 F.2d 225 (8th Cir. 1980).
49. Michael C. Gemignani, *Computer Law* (Rochester, N.Y.: Lawyers Cooperative Publishing Co., 1985), p. 491.
50. Diana Smith, "Who Is Calling Your Computer Next? Hacker!" 8 *Criminal Justice Journal* 89 (1985).
51. Gemignani, pp. 525-36.
52. Catherine H. Conly, *Organizing for Computer Crime Investigation and Prosecution* (Washington, D. C.: U.S. Department of Justice, National Institute of Justice, 1989), p. 7-8.
53. Smith, p. 94.
54. Conly, pp. 5-6.
55. Smith, pp. 109-10.
56. 18 U.S.C. Sec. 1029.
57. 18 U.S.C. Sec. 1030.
58. 18 U.S.C. Secs. 1341-1343.
59. See Donn B. Parker, *Computer Crime: Criminal Justice Resource Manual* (Washington D. C.: National Institute of Justice, U. S. Department of Justice, 1989), pp. 96-109, which lists federal criminal statutes that could apply to computer crimes.
60. Kim Uyehara, "Let the Operator Beware," *Student Lawyer*, April 1986, p. 30.
61. 232 S.E.2d 745 (Va. 1977).
62. The computer crime statutes of 48 states are listed in Conly, p. 155.
63. 735 P.2d 1362 (Wash. App. 1987).
64. *The Chronicle of Higher Education*, July 30, 1986, p. 2.
65. Beth Kinnane, "More than 200 students involved in drop/add computer fraud case," *U*. April, 1990, p. 1.
66. *Criminal Justice Report* (Washington, D.C.: National Association of Attorneys General, February, 1986), p. 1. A good discussion of the special considerations involved in gathering computer evidence is contained in Conly, pp. 66-74.
67. 18 U.S.C. Sec. 2510, 2511.
68. *Sports Illustrated*, November 18, 1985, p. 22.
69. United States District Court, Middle District of Louisiana, Criminal No. 86-29-A.
70. Wash. Rev. Code Sec. 9.73.030.
71. 15 U.S.C. Sec. 1051 et seq.
72. 35 U.S.C. Sec. 101 et seq.
73. 17 U.S.C. Sec. 506.
74. 17 U.S.C. Sec. 107.
75. H.R. Rep. 94-1476, 94th Cong., 2d Sess., pp. 68-70.
76. See Gail Sorenson, "Impact of the Copyright Law on College Teaching," 12 *Journal of College and University Law* 509 (1986); "Copyright and Fair Use: Implications of Nation Enterprises for Higher Education," 12 *Journal of College and University Law* 489 (1986); Eric Brandfonbrener, "Fair Use and University Photocopying: Addison-Wesley Publishing v. New York University," 19 *Michigan Journal of Law Reform* 669 (1986).
77. 223 F. 862 (D. Mass. 1914).
78. 447 F. Supp. 243 (W.D.N.Y. 1978).
79. *Encyclopaedia Britannica Educational Corp. v. Crooks*, 542 F. Supp. 1156 (W.D.N.Y. 1982); attorney fees, 558 F. Supp. 1247 (1983).

80. 487 F.2d 1345 (Ct. Cl. 1983); aff'd by equally divided ct., 420 U.S. 376 (1975).
81. 17 U.S.C. Sec. 107.
82. 758 F. Supp. at 1537, quoting the Classroom Guidelines.
83. Ibid.
84. Eileen Wagner, "Beware the Custom-made Anthology: Academic Photocopying and *Basic Books v. Kinko's Graphics*," 68 *West's Education Law Reporter*, 16 (1991).
85. 17 U.S.C. Sec. 506; 18 U.S.C. Sec. 2319.
86. Jennifer J. Demmon, "Congress Clears the Way for Copyright Infringement Suits against States: The Copyright Remedy Clarification Act," 17 *Journal of Corporate Law* 833, 852-54 (1992).
87. 17 U.S.C. Secs. 501 & 511.

C H A P T E R
10

Alcohol and Drugs as Campus Crime

runkenness of American college students was a problem even in
colonial times,[1] and in our day one of the highest courts in the land
has taken judicial notice of the obvious: "Beer drinking by college
students is a common experience."[2] With the recent proliferation of marijuana and other drugs in our culture, substance abuse by students has become
a significant criminal justice concern. A 1989 Gallup Poll on education listed
drug abuse as the American public's top education concern, as well as the
factor most responsible for crime.[3]

Drug abuse by athletes has drawn many recent headlines. Colleges and
universities are now grappling with the competing values of drug-testing and
privacy, and one National Collegiate Athletic Association official has warned
that drugs and gambling "threaten the very existence of college sports." That
official said that game fixing by some athletes is a result of their drug abuse
problems.[4] At least one study, however, found that drug use by college
athletes has declined somewhat.[5] It may be that the random drug-testing of
student athletes has had a positive effect in discouraging the use of drugs.[6]

Student drinking has commonly been tolerated on most college campuses,
and during the 1970s some college officials took a laissez-faire attitude toward
drug use as well. Several recent factors, however, have changed that posture.
One is the general societal disapproval of and crackdown upon illegal drugs
that occurred during the mid-1980s. Another is the concomitant toughening
of attitudes toward drunken driving, spurred by considerable media attention
and special interest groups that have made it a local political issue in the
election of judges, sheriffs, and other officials in many communities. A third
factor is the liability insurance crisis that recently has swept the country.

With insurance exorbitantly priced or unavailable, partying styles and attitudes toward them have been metamorphosing.

Implications of substance abuse for the college and university decision maker fall into three general categories. First, the existence of true criminal activity on the campus must be addressed as a very serious problem that requires cooperation with law enforcement agencies. Second, more minor sorts of substance abuse must be dealt with as a campus disciplinary issue. Third, campus administrators must be vigilant in avoiding the imposition of civil liability (in the form of adverse monetary judgments) upon their institution and its agents and administrators because of injuries resulting from substance abuse.

ALCOHOL, DRUGS, AND CRIMINAL ETIOLOGY

Alcohol and drug use frequently accompany criminal activity on campus. Indeed, when Congress passed the Crime Awareness and Campus Security Act (discussed in detail in chapter 14), it cited a survey finding that 95 percent of all violent campus crimes were alcohol or drug related.[7] On campus, about half of the assailants in courtship violence have been drinking, and campus law enforcement officers regularly report, anecdotally, that alcohol is a factor in a very large part of campus violence.[8] A study issued by the Center for the Study of Crime and Prevention of Campus Violence at Towson State University reported that nearly two-thirds of students who admitted to having committed crimes said that they had been under the influence of drugs, alcohol, or both at the time the crime was committed.[9]

Moreover, the risk of being a crime victim increases for students who use drugs or alcohol. The Towson State study revealed that student crime victims drank and used drugs more frequently than nonvictims, had lower-than-average grades, and tended disproportionately to be fraternity or sorority members.[10] "Though over 90 percent of campus crime is alcohol-related," a Towson State professor said, "chances of becoming a victim of crimes other than theft are remote if you avoid drugs and drink infrequently and sensibly."[11]

Drunken Conduct in Public and Behind the Wheel

The criminal law long has regulated alcohol abuse. It is not illegal to be drunk in private, but if drunken conduct spills over to endanger, or even bother, other persons, the law is empowered to step in. In all states, it is illegal to drive while one is intoxicated. The state may attempt to prove violation of drunken driving laws by two kinds of evidence. The first test comprises an officer's observations of erratic driving, the smell of alcohol on the driver's breath, or the driver's failure to pass "field tests" of walking a straight line or touching the tip of the nose with a finger. Such evidence can constitute sufficient proof, although whether that evidence will be sufficient to convince the jury of guilt beyond a reasonable doubt is another issue.

The second and more common way of proving drunk driving cases is by use of the "Breathalyzer" or blood tests. Most states now have provided by statute that it is illegal to operate a motor vehicle when the operator's blood alcohol content exceeds 0.10 percent by weight volume, and several have reduced the level to 0.08 percent. This level may be measured by chemical analysis of breath, blood, or urine, and drivers are legally deemed to have consented to such tests by exercising the privilege of driving on the public roads. The United States Supreme Court has held there is no Fifth Amendment right against having blood or breath sampled[12]—the privilege against self-incrimination applies only to "testimonial" types of spoken or written evidence, and not to one's body appearance or its physical characteristics.

In addition, one must actually drive to violate the drunk driving laws. When an intoxicated man climbed into the driver's seat of a parked car, and it accidentally rolled or "drifted" and struck the car in front of it, the man was held to be not guilty of drunk driving.[13]

All states also ban public drunkenness, although some require that it be both in a public place and in the presence of others. The Mississippi statute, for instance, requires that two or more other persons must be present to constitute the offense.[14] Thus, when a police officer finds a drunk, he cannot arrest him for public drunkenness unless at least one other person is there. Privately owned but publicly frequented property, such as a restaurant, will be a public place under most such statutes. Some states also prohibit open containers of alcoholic beverages in motor vehicles, and many municipalities ban the carrying of open alcohol containers in a public place.

Regulation of the sale of alcoholic beverages is universal. In most places, it is illegal to sell alcohol after certain specific hours, and everywhere it is illegal to sell it to minors or to sell it without a proper state license. The latter provision has been used by at least one campus area police agency to close down boisterous student parties. At Normal, Illinois, the home of Illinois State University, the police began sending undercover officers into large student revelries so that they could buy a beer from the party hosts, who had purchased the keg for the party and were reselling the beer by the cup to those in attendance. Because the hosts did not hold beer sales permits, the officers then were able to arrest them, confiscate the beer, and close down the party. It worked effectively for ending the parties, but not unexpectedly created a sizable community relations problem.[15] Students, like the rest of us, do not like to have pleasurable activities interrupted.

Drunkenness and Culpability

Should drunken people be responsible for their crimes? Although an affirmative answer probably seems logical, it becomes less so when we consider that criminal imputability is founded upon criminal intent—the *mens rea*—formed in the mind of a guilty person. An act that is neither intended nor the result of carelessness cannot be a criminal act, and for this reason the law does not hold insane persons responsible for crimes. Why, then, should an act performed by a person whose good sense has been stolen by alcohol be held to be a criminal?

The law has had to accommodate to the reality of drunkenness to formulate the universal legal rule that drunkenness is not an excuse for, or a defense to, crime. It is founded on the premise that drunkenness is itself voluntary. But with alcoholics this may not really be the case. Likewise, even the moderate social drinker is subject to the occasional unintentional overindulgence, in which the intoxication steals up on the drinker and is not recognized until the next morning—and certainly was not intentional in the usual sense of the word.

The law does recognize two rare exceptions to the principle that drunkenness is not a defense. One is when the drunkenness was truly involuntary—when the person was deceived or forced to drink alcoholic beverages or drank the beverage not realizing that it contained alcohol. Also, some states have recognized a "diminished capacity" defense for persons whose long-term alcohol abuse has so destroyed their mental powers that they are held incapable of formulating the specific intent necessary for the highest degrees of serious crime.[16] In such states, if the jury finds that the defendant suffered "diminished capacity," a murder charge can be reduced to a manslaughter conviction. Other than those two exceptions, drunkenness simply is not a defense to criminal culpability, and it will not support a claim of not guilty by reason of insanity.[17]

Marijuana and Hard Drugs

Marijuana and the so-called hard drugs present other, and often graver, legal problems for the campus. They also present graver public relations problems. In 1973, the National Commission on Marijuana and Drug Abuse noted:

> Whatever the reason, there is an obviously strong tendency among university administrators to hide campus drug problems from public view.[18]

A few years later that tendency was observed by Gerald L. Robinson, the personnel director of the University of Pennsylvania. Writing in the *Annals of the American Academy of Social and Political Science*, he said that colleges and

universities "still appear to retain some of their former and traditional protective role when it comes to shielding student drug use from public view"—a
posture, he suggested, that was "not entirely altruistic" but in some degree
designed to protect the institutional public image.[19] The passage of time
probably has ameliorated that problem; the number of campus drug prosecutions reported in the appellate courts in the intervening years indicates that
America's institutions of higher education are no longer looking the other
way concerning student drug abuse.

Possession of illegal drugs varies in criminal seriousness depending on the
drug involved, the amount of it, and the jurisdiction in which the offense
occurs. In fact, a few places treat marijuana possession as a civil offense only,
and many others treat it as a minor misdemeanor and provide that a conviction may be "expunged" from an offender's record after a period of time with
no further offense. In Alaska, the state supreme court effectively decriminalized the possession of small amounts of marijuana by ruling that the privacy
provision in the state constitution prohibited prosecution.[20]

Possession of "hard drugs" is far more serious, but more serious yet is the
selling of drugs—called in most states "delivery of a controlled substance."
With the passage of the so-called schoolyard statute, Congress authorized the
federal courts to enhance the penalties for persons convicted of possessing
hard drugs with the intent to sell, when the offense takes place within 1,000
feet of a school, college, or university.[21] Several courts have held that the law
does not require defendants to know that a drug transaction took place near a
school.[22]

Many state legislatures have followed suit by passing their own schoolyard
statutes, which enhance the state law penalties for drug offenses that occur
near a school or college campus.[23] In one instance, however, an Indiana court
held that the Indiana schoolyard statute, enhancing the penalty for selling
drugs on school property or within 1,000 feet of a school, did not apply to a
university student who was charged with selling marijuana to an undercover
officer from his campus dormitory room. Criminal statutes must be construed
strictly, the court said, and the common meaning of the word "school" does
not include a college or university.[24]

FEDERAL AND STATE EFFORTS TO REDUCE ALCOHOL AND DRUG ABUSE

So far, we have discussed campus alcohol and drug abuse as crimes, which
lawmakers have addressed in the criminal statutes. But federal and state
lawmakers have also passed civil legislation to discourage drug and alcohol
abuse. Specifically, Congress passed the Drug-Free Workplace Act and the
Drug-Free Schools and Communities Act amendments, which obligate col-

leges and universities to take specific steps to discourage alcohol and drug abuse by students and employees. Some state legislatures, recognizing the special problem of alcohol abuse by college students, have passed laws that limit the availability of alcohol on or near college campuses.

Drug-Free Schools and Communities Act Amendments

Under the Drug-Free Schools and Communities Act Amendments of 1989, every college or university that receives federal funds must adopt and implement drug and alcohol policies.[25] Each institution is required to certify to the Department of Education that it has implemented a program designed to prevent the illicit use of drugs and alcohol. At a minimum, an institution's program must:

- prohibit the unlawful possession, use, or distribution of illegal drugs or alcohol on college property or as part of a college activity;
- distribute annually to all students a document describing the health risks associated with using illicit drugs or abusing alcohol; available drug and alcohol counseling programs for students and employees; local, state, and federal legal sanctions, as well as the college's sanctions; and
- establish sanctions for drug and alcohol offenses up to and including expulsion and referral for prosecution.

The act also requires college recipients of federal funds to ensure that their sanctions are consistently enforced and to review their prevention program at least every two years. Through administrative regulations, the Secretary of Education has established sanctions for colleges and universities that fail to comply with the act.[26]

One commentator has pointed out that it is important for college and university administrators to understand that the act does not require institutions to assume new duties to protect students from using illegal drugs or abusing alcohol or to protect third parties from the consequences of students who use drugs or alcohol. Schools should take care that their programs do not unintentionally assume additional duties that could be used as the basis for imposing liability against them if someone is injured as a result of a student's use of alcohol or illegal drugs.[27]

Drug-Free Workplace Act

Passed in 1988, the Drug-Free Workplace Act places specific obligations on all federal contractors and federal grant recipients to take certain specified actions to reduce drug use in the workplace.[28] The act applies to any higher education institution that receives a federal contract or grant, and it requires these institutions to do the following:

- publish a statement notifying employees that the unlawful manufacture, possession, distribution, or use of an illegal drug is prohibited in the workplace and specifying the action that will be taken against an employee who violates this policy;
- establish a drug free awareness program to inform employees of the dangers of drug abuse in the workplace, the institution's policy of maintaining a drug free workplace, drug counseling and rehabilitation programs that may be available to employees, and the penalties that may be imposed against an employee who violates the policy.

In addition, the act requires federal contractors and grant recipients to inform employees that they must notify the employer if they are convicted of any criminal drug violation that occurs in the workplace. The employing institution in turn must notify the appropriate federal funding agency when it learns that one of its employees has been convicted of such a drug offense. Finally, the act requires covered institutions to either sanction an employee convicted of a drug offense in the workplace or require the employee to satisfactorily complete a drug abuse assistance or rehabilitation program.

State Laws Regulating Alcohol on Campus

During the early 1980s, the legal drinking age in several states was 18 or 19, but in 1984, Congress passed legislation authorizing the Secretary of Transportation to withhold federal highway funds to states where the minimum drinking age was under 21.[29] Consequently, all states with lower drinking ages amended their laws, and the uniform drinking age in all states is now 21.[30]

This change has complicated many colleges' alcohol management policies, because institutions now have a mixed group of students—some who can legally drink and some who cannot. College officials debate whether the better policy is to counsel underage students to abstain or to encourage them to drink responsibly, whether or not they have reached the legal drinking age.[31]

In addition to raising the drinking age, some state legislatures have passed specific legislation designed to reduce alcohol abuse on or near college campuses. In Georgia, for example, it is illegal to sell alcoholic beverages within 100 yards of any college campus[32;] and the possession of alcoholic beverages is prohibited on the grounds of any public trade, vocational, or industrial school.[33] West Virginia law specifically prohibits college fraternities or sororities from being licensed to serve alcohol as private clubs.[34] The Washington legislature passed a law prohibiting liquor manufacturers or distributors from conducting promotional activities for liquor on college and university campuses or from engaging in activities that facilitate or promote the consumption of alcoholic beverages by college students.[35] (However, the statute permits the campus sale of alcohol on licensed premises and liquor advertising in campus publications.) And in Mississippi, the consumption of alcoholic beverages is prohibited on any college campus or at any college athletic event.[36]

These statutes are an indication that state legislatures recognize alcohol as a problem for higher education institutions. College officials should familiarize themselves with all state laws regulating alcohol, and particularly those that apply specifically to higher education. They should also urge local authorities to enforce these laws strictly and discourage any tendency on the part of local businesses to wink at the alcohol laws when college students are concerned.

CAMPUS DISCIPLINE, EDUCATION, AND COUNSELING

Campus Discipline

As stated above, the Drug-Free Schools Act and the Drug-Free Workplace Act require college recipients of federal funds to establish sanctions for drug and alcohol offenses that occur on campus. When offenses have borne some relationship to campus life or programs, the courts have been consistent in upholding dismissal of offending students and faculty members. Two institutions, for instance, have dismissed pharmacy students after their convictions on drug charges.

When a Florida A & M student pleaded guilty to possession of cocaine with intent to distribute, the charge was made that he had betrayed the ethical standards expected of pharmacy students. The university's expulsion of the student was upheld by a Florida appeals court, which said that his conduct endangered "the health and safety" of other university students and other members of the academic community.[37]

A University of Maryland pharmacy student was dismissed after one of the pharmacists who oversaw his training charged him with working while in an "impaired condition" due to use of pharmaceuticals and also because the student had pleaded guilty to possession of cocaine in a noncampus-related criminal case. A federal district court upheld the university's action.[38]

In an off-campus offense case, Ferris State University was allowed by a federal court to proceed with campus disciplinary proceedings against a student who was then being charged in criminal court with selling 12.4 grams of marijuana to an undercover deputy. The student had sought to restrain the university from disciplining her, at least pending resolution of the separate criminal charges. The court held that educational institutions have "both a need and a right to formulate their own standards and to enforce them; such enforcement is only coincidentally related to criminal charges and the defense against them."[39]

Faculty conduct has been accorded similar treatment. When an assistant professor of music allowed students in his care on a college trip to use marijuana and alcohol, the college fired him, and the Wyoming Supreme Court upheld the discharge in a 1982 decision.[40] Likewise, a California court approved the dismissal of a community college teacher who had been arrested for participating in the sale of cocaine.[41]

Colleges and universities should be aware, however, that although an employee may be disciplined for an alcohol- or drug-related offense, alcoholics and recovered drug addicts enjoy certain job protections under federal handicap discrimination laws. Under Section 504 of the Rehabilitation Act of 1973,[42] an alcoholic is entitled to protection afforded other handicapped individuals unless the employee's current use of alcohol prevents him or her from performing job duties or current alcohol abuse constitutes a direct threat to property or the safety of others.[43] Under a 1990 amendment, current drug abusers are not covered by the act, but rehabilitated drug addicts who are otherwise qualified to perform their jobs may not be discriminated against because of their history of drug abuse.[44] The Americans with Disabilities Act contains similar provisions.

For example, in a 1993 case, the head basketball coach at Cleveland State University was arrested and charged with driving under the influence and having an open container of alcohol. The coach called a press conference in which he admitted that he had an alcohol problem that required treatment. Two days later, university officials held a press conference where it was announced that the coach had been fired.

Subsequently, the coach was indicted for substance abuse (cocaine) and driving while intoxicated. He received treatment in lieu of conviction pursuant to Ohio law. After successfully completely the treatment program, the criminal charges against him were dismissed. The coach then sued the university and several university officials, claiming a violation of the Rehabilitation Act. According to the coach, his alcoholism did not impair his ability to perform his coaching duties; thus, the university discriminated against him by firing him solely because of his alcohol problem.

On the university's motion to dismiss, a federal district court ruled that the coach's allegation that he had been dismissed solely due to his alcohol abuse satisfied the requirement for a prima facie case under the Rehabilitation Act. The court did, however, authorize the university to file a subsequent motion to dismiss if the university could present evidence that the coach was not qualified for the position or that he was fired for reasons other than his alcoholism.[45]

Campus decision makers should remember that federal antidiscrimination laws do not require institutions to tolerate egregious misbehavior simply because the employee is an alcoholic. In most cases involving very serious misconduct by alcoholics, courts have upheld the employer's decision to discharge the employee.

For example, in a 1993 decision, the Fourth Circuit Court of Appeals upheld the dismissal of an FBI agent for being intoxicated on duty. Employers subject to the Rehabilitation Act must be permitted to dismiss employees for egregious conduct, the court said, regardless of whether the employee is handicapped.

"[I]t plainly appears," the court stated, "that the appellant was fired because of his misconduct, not because of his alcoholism." The agent was notified that he was being dismissed for failure to comply with the FBI's established standard that agents remain mentally and physically fit for duty at all times. "Without attempting to recite in detail the duties of an FBI special agent," the court observed, "it is certain that being intoxicated while on duty will undoubtedly prevent an FBI special agent from being 'mentally and physically fit for duty at all times.' "[46]

Likewise, a federal court rejected the discrimination claim of an alcoholic federal agent who was discharged after he had an automobile accident while driving in an intoxicated condition. A two-year-old child was killed in the accident, and the agent pleaded guilty to vehicular homicide and driving under the influence of alcohol.

In ruling against the agent's discrimination claim, the court said:

> The Rehabilitation Act mandates nondiscrimination against disabled individuals; it does not waive basic prerequisites to service. Engaging in serious criminal acts . . . could disqualify anyone, regardless of ability, from continuing to serve the federal government.[47]

The purpose of the Rehabilitation Act, the federal court continued, was to put persons with disabilities on equal footing with nondisabled persons. "It was not designed to insulate them from disciplinary action which would be taken against any employee regardless of his status."[48] It was clear, the court concluded, that the agent was discharged because he killed a young child, not because he might have been an alcoholic.

Education and Counseling

Although federal antidrug laws require institutions that are federal fund recipients to distribute information about the health risks associated with drug and alcohol abuse and to inform students and employees about available counseling, the laws do not require institutions to develop specific kinds of education or counseling programs to combat drug and alcohol abuse. It is clear, however, that a number of colleges have invested heavily in education and counseling in an effort to cut the rate of substance abuse on their campuses. In the mid-1970s, for example, Brown University appointed an associate dean for problems of chemical dependency, whose responsibilities included efforts to reduce alcohol abuse by faculty.[49] And in 1991, Princeton University's president assigned his chief assistant full time to respond to the problem of campus alcohol abuse.[50]

Educating students about the risks associated with alcohol abuse seems particularly appropriate, because alcohol is so often the root cause of serious accidents involving college students. As news accounts and court cases illustrate, many students have a poor appreciation of their risk of injury when they are intoxicated. For example, a 1991 case described the injuries suffered by an 18-year-old University of Washington student who became intoxicated at a dormitory drinking party and then entered a dormitory elevator with several of his friends. One of the students stalled the elevator between floors and then pried the door open. Following the example of his companions, the student attempted to jump out of the stalled elevator to the floor below but lost his footing and fell 50 feet down the elevator shaft.[51] And in 1990, an inebriated Princeton student lost both legs and his left hand when he climbed atop a commuter train and touched the power line.[52]

Research suggests that providing information about the risks associated with alcohol or drugs may help persuade students not to become substance abusers, particularly if the information is specific.[53] Thus, education programs that teach students about the health and safety risks of drugs and alcohol may cut down on substance abuse and the serious injuries that often accompany it.

CONCLUSION: GROWING PUBLIC CONCERN ABOUT DRUGS AND ALCOHOL

A conservative consistency may be seen in the treatment of substance abuse problems on America's campuses. Criminal activity has been prosecuted vigorously, and the discipline and discharge of miscreant students and employees has been upheld.

Recent federal laws, however, have given colleges and universities added responsibilities with regard to managing campus alcohol and substance abuse. The Drug-Free Schools and Communities Act amendments and the Drug-Free Workplace Act impose an obligation to promulgate substance abuse policies and to distribute information about drugs and alcohol to students and employees. The Rehabilitation Act of 1973 and the Americans with Disabilities Act prevent higher education institutions from discriminating against alcoholics and give recovered drug addicts protection against discrimination. Federal legislation that encouraged states to raise the legal drinking age to 21 have complicated the alcohol policies of universities where on-campus drinking is permitted, since these institutions now have significant numbers of students who legally cannot purchase or consume alcohol.

In addition to this federal legislation, many states have passed tough new laws in an effort to cut down on drug and alcohol abuse. Some of these laws are specifically aimed at reducing alcohol and drug use on college campuses.

Together, an expanding body of state and federal law makes clear that lawmakers and the public want colleges and universities to do more to control alcohol and drugs on their campuses. In the next chapter, we will examine the expanding theories of liability that have been put forward against institutions that fail to meet these rising expectations. As we will see, it is becoming increasingly important for higher education institutions to develop sound risk-management policies to reduce the threat of injury due to campus alcohol or drug abuse.

NOTES

1. John S. Brubacher and Willis Rudy, *Higher Education in Transition*, 3d ed. (New York: Harper & Row, 1976), pp. 51-52.
2. *Bradshaw v. Rawlings*, 612 F.2d 135, 142 (3d Cir. 1979), *cert. denied*, 446 U.S. 909 (1980).
3. U. S. Department of Justice, *Drugs and Crime Facts, 1991*. (Washington, D.C.: U.S. Government Printing Office, 1992).
4. *The Chronicle of Higher Education*, May 21, 1986, p. 36.
5. Charles Dervarics, "Survey Finds Drop in Drug Use by Athletes," *Black Issues in Higher Education*, November 9, 1989, p. 4.
6. See, e.g., *Bally v. Northeastern University*, 403 Mass. 713, 532 N.E.2d 49 (1989).
7. Pub. L. 101-542, Sec. 102.
8. Rosemarie B. Bogal-Allbritten and William L. Allbritten, "The Hidden Victims: Courtship Violence among College Students," 26 *Journal of College Student Personnel* 201 (1985).
9. Susan Dodge, "Campus Crime Linked to Students' Use of Drugs and Alcohol," *The Chronicle of Higher Education*, January 17, 1990, p. A33.
10. Ann Matthews, "The Campus: The Ivory Tower Becomes an Armed Camp," *New York Times Magazine*, March 7, 1993, p. 41.
11. Ibid.
12. *Schmerber v. California*, 384 U.S. 757 (1966).
13. *State v. Taft*, 143 W.Va. 365, 102 S.E.2d 152 (1958).
14. Miss. Code Ann. Section 97-29-47.
15. Frank Morn, Diane Alexander, and Daniel Sadler, "Small Town Police Forces Have Big City Problems," 17 *Campus Law Enforcement Journal* 32 (January 1987).
16. *People v. Castillo*, 70 Cal.2d 264, 74 Cal. Rptr. 385, 449 P.2d 449 (1969).
17. *Evans v. State*, 645 P.2d 155 (Alaska 1982).
18. National Commission on Marijuana and Drug Abuse, *Drug Use in America: Problem in Perspective* (Washington, D.C.: U.S. Government Printing Office, 1973).
19. Gerald L. Robinson and Stephen T. Miller, "Drug Abuse and the College Campus," 417 *Annals of the American Academy of Political and Social Science* 101 (1975).
20. *Raven v. State*, 537 P.2d 494 (Alaska 1975).

21. 21 U.S.C. Sec. 860(a).
22. See, e.g., *United States v. Haynes*, 881 F.2d 586 (8th Cir. 1989).
23. See, e.g., La. Rev. Stat. Sec. 40.981.3.
24. *Pridgeon v. State*, 569 N.E. 2d 722 (Ind. App. 1991).
25. 20 U.S.C. Sec. 1145g.
26. 34 C.F.R. Sec. 86.5.
27. Eugene D. Gulland, *Universities, Colleges and the Abuse of Alcohol and Drugs: An Update of the American Council on Education's White Paper on Student Alcohol Abuse*, prepared for the American Council on Education (February 1992).
28. 41 U.S.C. Sec. 701 *et seq.*
29. 23 U.S.C. Sec. 158.
30. Donald B. Gehring and Christy P. Geraci, *Alcohol on Campus: A Compendium of the Law and a Guide to Public Policy* (Asheville, NC: College Administration Publications, 1989).
31. Courtney Leatherman, "College Officials Are Split on Alcohol Polices: Some Seek to End Underage Drinking; Others Try to Encourage 'Responsible' Use," *The Chronicle of Higher Education*, January 3, 1990, p. A33.
32. Ga. Code Ann. Sec. 3-3-21(a)(1)(A). For a summary of all states' alcohol laws that affect colleges and universities, consult Gehring and Christy.
33. Ga. Code Ann. Sec. 3-3-21.1(a).
34. W. Va. Code Sec. 60-7-4(c).
35. Wash. Rev. Code Sec. 66.28.160.
36. Miss. Code Ann. Sec. 67-1-37(g).
37. *Wallace v. Florida A&M University*, 433 So.2d 600 (Fla. App. 1983).
38. *Sohmer v. Kinnard*, 535 F.Supp. 50 (D. Md. 1982).
39. *Hart v. Ferris State College*, 557 F. Supp. 1379 (W.D. Mich. 1983).
40. *White v. Board of Trustees*, 648 P.2d 528 (Wyo. 1982), *cert. denied*, 459 U.S. 1107 (1983).
41. *West Valley-Mission Community College District v. Concepcion*, 21 Cal. Rptr.2d 5 (Cal. App. 1993).
42. 29 U.S.C. Sec. 794.
43. 29 U.S.C. Sec. 706(8)(C)(v).
44. 29 U.S.C. Sec. 706(8)(C)(i). The Americans with Disabilities Act, which also prohibits colleges and universities from discriminating against disabled persons, contains language regarding the rights of alcoholics and recovered drug addicts. 42 U.S.C. Sec. 12114.
45. *Mackey v. Cleveland State University*, 837 F. Supp. 1396 (N.D. Ohio 1993).
46. *Little v. Federal Bureau of Investigation*, 1 F.3d 255, 259 (4th Cir. 1993).
47. *Wilber v. Brady*, 780 F.Supp. 837, 840 (D. D.C. 1992)
48. Ibid.
49. Bruce E. Donovan, "Chemical Dependency, Denial, and the Academic Lifestyle," *Academe*, January-February 1990, p. 20.
50. "Alcohol Concern Brings High Level Appointment," *Campus Crime*, May 1991, p. 58.
51. *Houck v. University of Washington*, 60 Wash. App. 189, 803 P.2d 47 (1991).
52. "Alcohol Concern Brings High Level Appointment," p. 58.
53. Gerardo M. Gonzalez and Michael L. Haney, "Perception of Risk as Predictors of Alcohol, Marijuana, and Cocaine Use among College Students," 31 *Journal of College Student Development* 313 (1990).

C H A P T E R

11

• • • • • • • • •

Students, Suds, and Summonses
Strategies for Coping with Campus Alcohol Abuse

As noted in the previous chapter, beverage alcohol, the potent social lubricant, is as inexorably a part of American campus life as text books, professors, and football. Around 90 percent of college and university students drink.[1] From 20 percent to 25 percent of them can be categorized as being heavy drinkers or as having a drinking problem,[2] and one study reported that 7 percent were alcoholic.[3]

As discussed in chapter 10, with alcohol abuse comes campus problems. In the United States, alcohol frequently accompanies criminal and criminal-like activity; the attorney general of California recently estimated that 70 percent of all reported crime in his state is either alcohol or drug related.[4] This statistic probably holds true on college campuses as well. For instance, one study discussed in chapter 2 reported that about half the assailants in campus courtship violence had been drinking, and campus law enforcement officers regularly report, anecdotally, that alcohol is a factor in a large part of campus violence.[5] A nationwide survey conducted by Towson State University indicated that more than half of the persons involved in campus vandalism had been using alcohol.[6]

In addition to the discipline and safety problems related to campus alcohol abuse, developments in the law of civil liability have made the problem more compelling. In recent years, the victims of alcohol misuse have begun suing higher education institutions, their auxiliaries, and individual administrators

This article originally appeared in *Journal of College Student Development*, Vol. 30, pp. 118–22 (March 1989). Used by permission of *Journal of College Student Development*.

based upon claimed duties of oversight and protection of students and campus guests, even from themselves.

Coping with the problem presents dilemmas for campus administrators. Liberal use of alcohol is, in many ways, a part of college mythos. The beer gardens of "The Student Prince" are not just fictional, and good administration-student relations are not fostered by heavy-handed security and enforcement measures. In addition, administrators must hold "enrollment management"—keeping up the numbers—in mind. Both student recruitment and alumni and public support may be adversely affected by too much publicity about any kind of problem on campus, including criminal-like behavior and problems resulting from alcohol abuse. The "head in the sand" is the easiest posture for campus administrators to assume, yet the magnitude of the present problem will not permit it for long.

STUDENT ALCOHOL ABUSE TODAY

Drunken college students were a problem even in colonial times,[7] and recent studies indicate the problem persists, although one recent major review of data about college alcohol abuse has been critical of the quality of many contemporary studies. As noted earlier, about 90 percent of college students drink at some time.[8]

One sizable national survey conducted by R. C. Engs and D. J. Hanson[9] indicated that 81.9 percent of college students were drinking at least once a year, and that 20.2 percent were heavy drinkers. F. E. Hill and L. A. Bugen,[10] surveying 326 students at the University of Texas in the late 1970s, found that 14.4 percent of the men and 4.9 percent of the women reported getting drunk at least once a week. In a smaller but more recent study by T. A. Seay and T. D. Beck[11] at one university, 45 percent of the students reported that they had increased their drinking since attending college; 21 percent said they mixed alcohol with other drugs, and on the Michigan Alcohol Screen Test (MAST), 7 percent were indicated to be alcoholic, while another 25 percent were classed as problem drinkers.

More than two decades ago, M. LeMay reported a significant relationship between alcohol abuse and poor grades.[12] Several studies suggest there has been little change in drinking habits or problems of college students in recent years, but one recent study did find a decrease in drinking and driving problems.[13]

These data reveal a campus problem of major significance. In addition to the social implications, campus alcohol misuse recently has brought with it legal problems (with concomitant financial problems) for abusers, campus social organizations, and the colleges and universities themselves.

CIVIL LAW AND ALCOHOL ABUSE

When drunkenness has led to another person's injury, the injured party always has been able to bring a civil suit for damages against the drunk who caused it if there was evidence the drunken person acted either intentionally or negligently in causing the harm. But recent years have seen several legal offshoots in such cases; now, a person or institution who improperly furnishes alcohol to an intoxicated person, or who fails in a duty to supervise or police an intoxicated person, may be liable to the injured party as well—even if the injured party is the intoxicated person himself or herself, or the intoxicated person's surviving heirs.

With colleges, the legal theories behind these claims have varied. Some claimants have argued that as a part of the education that students are buying, the college has a duty to care for and protect them, particularly during younger, formative years. Others have claimed liability because institutions failed to enforce laws or their own regulations governing alcohol use by students. These theories have met with mixed results in the courts, and consistent legal principles have not yet been established nationwide.

The necessity of establishing a legal duty on the part of the institution to prevent such injuries presents the greatest legal difficulties for the plaintiffs. Other complications for claimants include legal distinctions between nonfeasance and misfeasance, whether consumption was an independent, intervening cause of injury and questions of sovereign or charitable immunity.[14] Nonetheless, when the potential for such injuries was "foreseeable," liability often now is imposed. This follows the trend in other sorts of cases in which persons have been injured by crimes committed on campus. (See chapter 5.)

Cases establishing institutional liability have involved either failure to police the campus adequately or direct participation in the alcohol abuse by university employees. In *Bearman v. University of Notre Dame*,[15] in which a football fan was injured by a falling drunk in a parking lot "tailgate" area, the university lost because it knew of the danger but did not police the area. A similar principle was involved in *Karbel v. Frances*,[16] which arose when security guards, following policy, ordered a drunk driver to leave the campus; a wreck ensued, and another motorist was severely injured. The New Mexico Court of Appeals said the security force was liable either for failing to arrest the driver or for not taking other steps to prevent his driving. The California Court of Appeals upheld a judgment against the University of California in favor of a man who fell from a balcony after being served alcohol while he was obviously intoxicated at a party sponsored by dormitory resident staff.[17]

The institutions have won the cases that involved purely private drinking by students, even though it was in violation of university rules. In *Baldwin v. Zoradi*[18] and *Campbell v. Trustees of Wabash College*,[19] appellate courts in

California and Indiana declined to hold institutions liable when student drinking in residence halls, without involvement by university personnel, was followed by driving that led to automobile wrecks. Thus, "failure to police" theories have not been extended to a duty to prevent student drinking in residence halls.

Likewise, when there was only limited involvement by university personnel in student drinking, the institutions have won. In Bradshaw v. Rawlings,[20] the U.S. Third Circuit Court of Appeals held that Delaware Valley College was not an insurer of its students' safety, and thus was not liable in a case brought by a student who was left a quadriplegic as a result of an auto wreck after the annual sophomore class picnic. The student was under Pennsylvania's legal drinking age at the time. His suit alleged that because it was well known that drinking occurred at the picnic, and because a faculty member had co-signed a check that was used to buy beer (although the faculty member did not personally attend the picnic), the college owed the student a duty of protection. "What we know as men and women we must not forget as judges," the opinion said, "and this panel of judges is able to bear witness to the fact that beer drinking by college students is a common experience."

Likewise in Beach v. University of Utah,[21] when an intoxicated student wandered away from a biology field trip and was left a quadriplegic after she fell down a rock crevice, the Utah Supreme Court held there was no liability even though her professor had participated in some of the drinking.

The cases involving suits against fraternities have been less consistent. In Ballou v. Sigma Nu,[22] the South Carolina Court of Appeals upheld a judgment for the heirs of a 20-year-old pledge who died after being required to chug-a-lug from a "goblet of truth" filled with liquors and to drink various other alcoholic beverages. At death, his blood alcohol level was .46 percent. Likewise, in an older case, Weiner v. Gamma Phi Chapter of Alpha Tau Omega Fraternity,[23] liability was imposed when the fraternity held a drinking party at an isolated ranch house, and a highway crash followed the party, because it was obvious that those attending would have to drive home.

Fraternities have escaped liability in several other cases. In Fassett v. Poch,[24] a female student who was left a quadriplegic as the result of a wreck following a fraternity party at Villanova University lost her claim against the fraternity. The court said merely "allowing a party on one's premises" did not constitute "furnishing" alcohol under Pennsylvania's "social host" doctrine, which imposes liability on a host who furnishes liquor to a minor, or under the state's Dram Shop Act.

Similarly, in Stein v. Beta Rho Alumni Association,[25] the Oregon Court of Appeals held that the fraternity alumni association, which owned a fraternity house where a boisterous party occurred and a burlesque dancer was injured, was not liable to her for what happened in the house. In Bell v. Alpha Tau

Omega,[26] which involved injuries to a 19-year-old pledge who fell from the fraternity house roof after a drinking party, the Nevada Supreme Court held that the state criminal law against selling alcohol to minors did not cast a civil duty upon those who violated it to care for such intoxicated minors.

In a more recent case, *Millard v. Osborne*,[27] the estate of an 18-year-old freshman student who was killed in an auto accident after drinking heavily at a fraternity house, failed to hold either the national fraternity or the college liable for the student's death. A Pennsylvania court ruled that the national fraternity counseled against the use of alcohol and was not in a position to control the day-to-day actions of its members. As for the college, the court said that it, too, counseled against the use of alcohol. The fact that the college permitted students to drink who were of legal drinking age did not give rise to a special duty to control the actions of underage students who were determined to acquire alcoholic beverages.

Finally, a recent Louisiana case involving alcohol and student injuries illustrates the kinds of circumstances in which universities now find themselves vulnerable to a lawsuit. In *Fox v. Board of Supervisors of Louisiana State University*,[28] a rugby player from St. Olaf College sued Louisiana State University for injuries he suffered during a rugby match on the LSU campus. The student argued that LSU was vicariously liable for his injuries because the LSU rugby club held a cocktail party that lasted into the early morning hours and then scheduled two rugby matches later that day. He also claimed that the LSU club had failed to determine whether the tournament players were properly trained, coached, and supervised.

The Louisiana Supreme Court was not sympathetic to the student's negligence theories. "The fact that a club at LSU invited plaintiff's team to LSU does not make LSU the guardian of all of the participants' safety," the court reasoned. Although the court acknowledged that the university was responsible for maintaining a safe playing field, the student had not claimed any defect in the field. "To require LSU to ensure the athletic ability of everyone utilizing this area would be too onerous," the court concluded.

CRIMINAL LAW AND ALCOHOL USE

Much campus alcohol use is not treated like the crime that it is. State and local criminal laws broadly control the sale, possession, and use of alcoholic beverages. All states punish drunken driving, and most states and many municipalities outlaw drunkenness in places frequented by the public. Many states and municipalities prohibit open containers of alcoholic beverages in motor vehicles, and many municipalities ban the carrying of open containers in a public place. State law in some jurisdictions imposes total prohibition of beverage alcohol upon school, college, and university property, and persons under age 21 cannot purchase or possess any alcoholic beverage.

Every jurisdiction regulates the sale of alcoholic beverages. It is illegal to sell them without a state license, it is illegal to sell them to minors, and, in most places, it is illegal to sell them during certain hours. These provisions may be used to control boisterous parties in some circumstances.

CONCLUSION: A SYSTEMIC RESPONSE

Campus alcohol abuse presents administrators with myriad, sometimes conflicting, problems. Attention focused on campus alcohol abuse may bring the institution adverse publicity. Repressive enforcement of prohibition or other alcohol control laws or regulations may create poor relations with students and, at least during football season, even with alumni. But, when egregious or criminal behavior is tolerated, there may be a loss of morale among campus constituencies because standards of safety and decency are not upheld, and the institution and its administrators may face civil suits from those injured as a result of unchecked alcohol abuse.

There are other negative consequences, as well, when alcohol abuse is ignored. Among them are 1) loss of the deterrent aspect of sanctions—both in providing an example for others that the conduct is not to be tolerated, and in limiting the ability of the offender to repeat the misdeed; 2) loss of an opportunity for rehabilitative services for offenders; and 3) loss of data for rational planning to identify specific campus problems.

Alcohol abuse actually presents colleges and universities with significant educational opportunity. All experience is educative, and the manner in which institutions of higher learning respond to alcohol abuse problems is a part of the educational lesson they are imparting to their students. The response conveys a cogent message about what the institution truly values.

In this light, a successful strategy for dealing with campus alcohol abuse must be one that is grounded in an ethical and educational stance that addresses alcohol abuse as a social problem; the message to students must be that alcohol abuse is dangerous and harmful, and not to be tolerated, much less encouraged, by institutional programs or practices.

An appropriate response to alcohol abuse by an institution of higher education must be a systemic response, which addresses at least the following concerns:

1. Alcohol education should be included in the curriculum or campus activities in a way that all students are exposed to it. Goals would be increasing knowledge about alcohol, fostering responsible attitudes toward alcohol use (including setting standards for responsible drink-

ing), and teaching students how to intervene and help friends who have drinking problems.[29]

2. Clinical intervention resources should be available.
3. Nondrinking extracurricular activities should be provided as an alternative to recreational drinking.
4. Institutions should enforce state and local alcohol control laws when hard violations occur. The prophylactic effect of law enforcement should not be underestimated as a tool in the campus administrator's armamentarium; enforcement carries with it both a deterrent effect and a clear affirmation of institutional policy.
5. Institutions should have reasonable rules and regulations regarding alcohol use or misuse, but they should not have rules or regulations that they will not enforce. The existence of a regulation might be an acknowledgment that the institution recognized the subject of the regulation as a potential problem area, and failure to enforce the regulation might make the institution look all the more negligent.
6. When alcohol is served on campus, the utmost care must be taken to assure that it is done in full compliance with the law and good judgment. Facilities such as campus pubs present paradoxes. They provide controlled atmospheres in which responsible drinking can be fostered, and they make it unnecessary for students to seek other, uncontrolled places to drink off-campus (with resultant drunk driving). Yet, by their very existence, campus pubs may be seen as giving a stamp of approval to drinking. Anytime a college or university becomes a commercial vendor of alcohol, liability risks are increased.

Drinking by college students is not going to disappear, just as drinking by adults in our society is not going to cease. Beverage alcohol is widely used and even applauded as a social lubricant and tranquilizer at the same time that alcohol abuse brings many grievous social problems. If the goal of education is to enable a person to successfully cope with his or her environment, colleges and universities are confronted by urgent opportunity in the field of alcohol awareness.

NOTES

1.   F. E. Hill and L. A. Bugen, "A Survey of Drinking Behavior among College Students," 20 *Journal of College Student Personnel* 236-43 (1979); R. Saltz and D. Elandt, "College Student Drinking Studies, 1976-1985," 13 *Contemporary Drug Problems* 117-59 (1986).
2.   R. C. Engs and D. J. Hanson, "The Drinking Patterns and Problems of College Students: 1983," 32 *Journal of Alcohol and Drug Education* 65-83 (1985); T. A. Seay and T. D. Beck, "Alcoholism among College Students," 25 *Journal of College Student Personnel* 90-92 (1984).

3. Seay and Beck, 90-92.
4. 3 *School Safety* (Winter, 1987). (published by the National School Safety Center, Pepperdine University, Encino, Calif.).
5. R. B. Bogal-Allbritten and W. I. Allbritten, "The Hidden Victims: Courtship Violence among College Students," 26 *Journal of College Student Personnel* 201-04 (1985).
6. "Campus Violence Survey" (unpublished compilation), Office of Student Services, Towson State University, 1987.
7. J. S. Brubacher and W. Rudy, *Higher Education in Transition*, 3d ed. (New York: Harper and Row, 1976), pp. 54-57.
8. R. Saltz and D. Elandt, "College Student Drinking Studies, 1976-1985," 13 *Contemporary Drug Problems* 117-59 (1986).
9. Engs and Hanson, 65-83.
10. Hill and Bugen, 236-43.
11. Seay and Beck, 90-92.
12. M. Lemay, "College Disciplinary Referrals for Drinking," 29 *Quarterly Journal of Studies on Alcohol* 939-42 (1968).
13. D. J. Hanson and R. C. Engs, "College Students' Drinking," 58 *Psychological Reports* 276-78 (1986).
14. T. M McLean, "Tort Liability of Colleges and Universities for Injuries Resulting from Student Alcohol Consumption," 14 *Journal of College and University Law* 399-416 (1987).
15. 453 N.E.2d 1196 (Ind. App. 1983).
16. 709 P.2d 190 (N.M.App. 1985).
17. 125 Cal.App.3d 646, 178 Cal.Rptr. 185 (1981).
18. 123 Cal.App.3d 275, 176 Cal.Rptr. 809 (1981).
19. 495 N.E.2d 227 (Ind.App. 1986).
20. 612 F.2d 135 (3rd Cir. 1979).
21. 726 P.2d 413 (Utah 1986).
22. 352 S.E.2d 488 (S.Car.App. 1986).
23. 485 P.2d 18 (Ore. 1971).
24. 625 F.Supp. 324 (E.D.PA. 1985).
25. 621 P.2d 632 (Ore.App 1980).
26. 642 P.2d 161 (Nev. 1982).
27. 611 A.2d 715 (Pa. Super. 1992).
28. 576 S.2d 978 (La. 1991).
29. A. Cherry, "Undergraduate Alcohol Misuses: Suggested Strategies for Prevention and Early Detection," 32 *Journal of Alcohol and Drug Education* 1-6 (1987).

CHAPTER

Firing the Miscreant Employee

While academic freedom demands that faculty have real job security, of tantamount importance in the delivery of quality education is the capacity of a college or university to fire a truly bad employee. This capacity is particularly needed where an employee has engaged in criminal or criminal-like conduct. Termination of an employee, however, is not always easily accomplished today, and a bungled attempt to fire someone can be expensive and disastrous for institutional morale.

The traditional rule in American law has been that an employee hired for an indefinite term could be discharged by the employer at any time with or without cause or explanation. This often harsh rule reflected the free-for-all business climate of the young American nation, but now the complexities and wealth of the modern age have led the courts and the legislatures to moderate the rule significantly.

In higher education, of course, the concept of tenure was developed to assure that professors could speak freely in the marketplace of ideas without undue fear of losing their jobs because they offended someone or some societal convention. Its origins have been traced to the High Middle Ages.[1]

Tenure exists today in many, but certainly not all, institutions of higher learning. Where it does exist, it has been created by state statutes, employment contracts, institutional policies, or collective bargaining agreements. In essence, tenure provides that a professor may not be fired except for financial exigencies, termination or reduction of programs, or good cause.

Many employees on campus do not have tenure. Noninstructional staff generally do not acquire tenure, and faculty members in their probationary period—usually five to seven years—have not yet earned tenure. This is not to say that they are "at will" employees who may be capriciously fired, however. Today, no one can be fired for certain "bad" reasons, and probationary faculty often are entitled to a certain period of notice and a hearing before termination or nonrenewal, and, under some policies, a showing that the action was not arbitrary or capricious.

WISE EMPLOYMENT PRACTICES

Prudent institutional administrators will have established a personnel management system that sets forth, up front, what is expected of employees, then monitors their work to see whether it meets expectations and gives them "feedback" on deficiencies so that they can improve. If an employee is to be discharged for cause, the employer must be able to prove that the cause exists. If the cause consists of an accumulation of small failures, such as absenteeism, tardiness, or failure to do small things reasonably required in the job, a thorough record of events, appraisals, discussions, and admonitions is critical to a supportable personnel decision that can withstand review in the courts.

It is preferable that faculty and professional staff be included in the process of establishing professional competencies, in the process of monitoring compliance, and in the employment decision-making process. Participatory governance enhances institutional morale, deters lawsuits, and reduces judicial intervention. In the last analysis, however, it is the institutional administrators who must administrate, and campus policies must not paralyze or choke administration.

Evaluators of employees must be trained to make an honest and objective appraisal. The evaluator must be a person who has been in a position to have actual and accurate knowledge of the employee's work, and the evaluator must consider only those things that bear some relationship to the job and the employment setting. Evaluators must recognize that if they overrate an employee to avoid conflict or out of sympathy, both the evaluator and the institution are not going to be able to claim differently about the employee later. If a poor employee gets worse, there may not be sufficient legal grounds for termination if earlier evaluations by supervisors reflected that the employee was competent and adequate. And, one very poor evaluation often is not credible after a history of good evaluations—it looks as if the new, negative evaluation is some sort of personal vendetta.

Of course, a "track record" of an employee's performance is not necessary for every sort of discharge for cause. One discrete incident of gross insubordination, criminal conduct, or an action that endangers other persons probably will be entirely sufficient cause for an immediate termination. Specific grounds for discharge will be discussed later in this chapter.

In any event, it is important to have institutional policies set forth, usually in an employee handbook, which specify the expectations of employment, the grounds for discipline and discharge, and the procedures to be followed. One caveat must be remembered, however: once an institution has rules, it usually will be bound to follow them.[2] Thorough review of employment policies by competent legal counsel is a must, or an institution that truly needs to discipline an employee may find itself trapped in a box of its own making. Further, this review should be made before the policies are promulgated, because they may be held to be a binding term of the employment relationship, which the institution cannot unilaterally change.[3]

Wise administrators will include in personnel handbooks a clear statement that the institution reserves the right to alter the terms of the handbook as circumstances may require. Also, it should be specified that the handbook is not itself a part of the employment contract, but merely a general guide to personnel policies and employee benefits. Some companies even require that employees sign a card acknowledging receipt of the employee handbook and declaring that its contents are not terms of employment, and that the employer may revise it at any time.

"BAD" REASONS FOR DISCHARGE

Regardless of their employment status, the law provides that employees may not be discharged for certain sorts of matters. For instance, in most states, statutes provide that a person cannot be fired for taking military reserve leave, performing jury duty, or making a claim for worker's compensation because of a job-related injury. At least one state precludes the firing of public college or university employees for "political reasons."[4]

Congress has outlawed similar kinds of "retaliatory" discharges for the exercise of various federally protected rights: retaliation for union-organizing activity;[5] exercise of rights under the federal wage and hour laws;[6] and reporting of violations under the Occupational Health and Safety Act,[7] the Asbestos School Hazard Detection and Control Act,[8] and the Clean Air Act.[9] The Consumer Credit Protection Act prohibits discharge of a person because his or her wages have been subjected to garnishment for any one indebtedness.[10] The Veterans Reemployment Act provides that returning veterans cannot be discharged within their first year of employment except for cause.[11]

Discrimination on the basis of race, sex, age, religion, national origin, or handicap is prohibited under various federal and state laws. Title VII of the Civil Rights Act of 1964[12] prohibits employment discrimination on the basis of race, color, religion, sex, or national origin. Employment practices that result in disparate treatment of a particular class of persons protected by the act can constitute discrimination under the act; an employer can justify disparate treatment only on the basis of a bona fide occupational qualification bearing a reasonable relationship to the job in question.

Age Discrimination

Age discrimination claims are becoming common in higher education. Under federal law, colleges and universities cannot discriminate in employment on the basis of age against persons who are 40 years old or older.[13] Prohibited aspects include discrimination in advertising, interviewing, hiring, promotion, leaves, discipline, work conditions, layoff, transfer, discharge, job referral, and fringe benefits. The plaintiff must prove that age played only some small role in the adverse employment action to win the suit. To escape liability, an employer must show that the action was taken on the basis of a reasonable factor other than age, or another bona fide occupational qualification.

Millsaps College terminated two janitors, one aged 59, the other 55. Their supervisor had been inconsistent in his statements as to why they had been terminated, but the jury accepted the college's explanation that the firing had been for poor job performance, and not on the basis of age. The decision was affirmed on appeal.[14] However, the University of Oklahoma failed in its efforts to show that a 59-year-old female cartographer was not discriminated against on the basis of age in the process of selecting a new cartography section chief. A 36-year-old had been selected by a faculty committee, but a district court jury had found there was age bias in the selection process. The trial judge had set aside the jury's verdict, saying it was based only on "murky theories," but the verdict in favor of the older claimant was reinstated by the Tenth U.S. Circuit Court of Appeals.[15] In an unusual case in which a 40-year-old teacher accused the University of Georgia of favoring an *older* employee, the Eleventh Circuit Court of Appeals upheld a jury's decision that the university had retaliated against the teacher after he complained when an older teacher was assigned two classes while he was assigned only one class.[16]

Age discrimination law is a complicated area that affects the whole range of institutional decisions involving hiring, termination, compensation, and retirement programs. Recent cases illustrate the danger of failing to understand the legal rights of older employees. For example, a federal court concluded that Howard University had violated federal age discrimination laws by failing to promote a university administrator, based partly on a finding that the university's handbook contained an erroneous statement of law regarding the mandatory retirement age for nonfaculty employees. The fact that the handbook was not changed after the Equal Employment Opportunity Commission advised the university that it had misstated the law was an indication to the court that the university was insensitive to age discrimination issues.[17]

In another age discrimination case, a letter from a college president to a music teacher, explaining why her tenure request was being denied, was cited by the court as evidence of possible age-based discrimination. Writing to the nearly 60-year-old teacher, the president explained that recent federal legislation eliminating a mandatory retirement age might undesirably constrain institutional flexibility if she were granted tenure. The court considered the president's letter to be a direct reference to age and one that bore on the possible existence of discriminatory intent.[18]

Institutional Good Faith

A claim of discrimination is easily raised by an employee who is being disciplined or terminated if he or she is a member of one of the protected groups, and thus employers must have extensive documentation of legitimate grounds for dismissal to rebut the discrimination defense. Evidence of the institution's good faith will be helpful. The Eighth U.S. Circuit Court of Appeals has held that evidence that an institution developed and was implementing an affirmative action plan was relevant to questions of discriminatory intent under a Title VII claim.[19]

Whistle Blowers and Free Speech

Another "bad" ground for discharge in many states is a discharge made in retaliation for the exercise of some important public policy principle by the employee. This policy protects people who are fired because they "blow the whistle," or because they refuse to break the law for their employer. Examples include a bank employee who was fired because he brought to light violations of federal and state consumer protection laws,[20] an energy company employee who was terminated because he refused to participate in an illegal scheme to fix retail gasoline prices,[21] and a railroad employee who refused to alter pollution sample reports to the state antipollution agency.[22]

In the same vein, public employees are protected from being fired because they have exercised basic rights under the First Amendment, especially the rights to free speech and association. Suits alleging discharge because of exercise of free speech rights are commonplace in the field of employment law, and are among the most problematic for employers. These so-called Section 1983 actions are based upon the federal Civil Rights Act of 1872.[23] The act creates a right to sue for money damages anytime a person is deprived of a constitutional right by someone acting "under color" of state law—in other words, by any state official.

The U.S. Supreme Court established the right of public employees to bring such suits in the case of *Pickering v. Board of Education,* decided in 1968.[24] Pickering had been fired after he sent a local newspaper a letter to the editor that was critical of the school board. The Court held that a public employee who was fired or suffered other adverse employment consequences for engaging in protected speech could maintain a "1983" damage suit against those who fired him or her in violation of First Amendment rights.

However, the Supreme Court made clear that a public employee's right to speak out on public issues is not absolute. In *Pickering*, the Court recognized that there were occasions in which a public employer had a legitimate interest in sanctioning employees for criticizing their superiors and co-workers. Thus, the Court established a balancing test whereby the employee's right to speak on issues related to employment were weighed against the government agency's need for promoting efficiency in the workplace.

Because a disgruntled employee often has been critical of his employer and superiors prior to discharge, it is easy for an employee to suggest that the discharge was a result of the criticism, and therefore a violation of free speech rights. In a 1983 decision, the Supreme Court refined the *Pickering* balancing test to make clear that free speech concerns were minimal if the employee was only speaking out on internal employee grievances, not on matters of public concern. In *Connick v. Myers*,[25] a disgruntled assistant district attorney circulated a questionnaire among fellow employees asking them to comment on office policy and morale. When the district attorney learned about the questionnaire, he fired the assistant; and she sued on First Amendment grounds.

The Supreme Court ruled that the assistant prosecutor's questionnaire did not involve a matter of public concern, and thus her First Amendment rights were not violated. "When employee expression cannot be fairly considered as relating to any matter of political, social, or other concern to the community," the Court said, "government officials should enjoy wide latitude in managing their offices, without intrusive oversight by the judiciary in the name of the First Amendment." Even if a dismissal decision is characterized as unreasonable or mistaken, the Court continued, it should not be subject to judicial review, absent some violation of statute, regulation, or tenure provision.[26]

Pickering and *Connick* have been applied in dozens of cases in which public employees, including college and university employees, have claimed they were discharged or sanctioned in retaliation for engaging in protected speech. In all cases, the courts ask whether the public employee's speech involves a matter of public concern. If it does, they then balance the employee's constitutional right to engage in the speech against the public employer's interest in maintaining the efficiency of the workplace.

For example, where an untenured librarian at West Virginia Northern Community College had been critical of plans by her superiors to remodel the library, the West Virginia courts found that the nonrenewal of her employment was a result of her exercise of free speech concerning the library, a public matter, and awarded her damages for the discharge.[27] Likewise, when City University of New York deprived a professor of his department chairmanship after he made an off-campus speech that was critical of specific ethnic groups, he sued for reinstatement, claiming his First Amendment rights were violated. A federal trial court upheld a jury verdict for the professor, even though the court described some of the professor's statements as "hateful, poisonous, and reprehensible." The speech was constitutionally protected, the court reasoned, and the university had not shown that the professor's remarks hampered the efficient operation of the university.[28] On appeal, the trial court's decision was affirmed with some modification.[29]

On the other hand, a federal court upheld Auburn University's decision to transfer a tenured professor to another department, even though the transfer was a response to constitutionally protected speech. The professor, a member of the mechanical engineering department, had contributed to a sharp, written critique of the department and the department head. Specifically, the critique pointed to weaknesses in the mechanical engineering curriculum, inadequate facilities, a low faculty-to-student ratio, and the poor performance of Auburn graduates on the professional licensing examination for engineers.

The court determined that the professor and other contributors to the critique were sincere and that the critique contained some constitutionally protected speech. Nevertheless, when the court applied the *Pickering* balancing test to weigh the professor's free speech interest against the university's need to maintain an efficient mechanical engineering department, it concluded that the university's interest outweighed that of the professor.

The court pointed out that the critique, which characterized the department head as dictatorial and inflexible, was produced on the eve of the department's accreditation review and that it distracted faculty and students from the primary academic tasks of education and research. Furthermore, the critique contributed to a lack of harmony among the faculty, interfered substantially with the regular operation of the department, and hampered communication between the department head and faculty members. These facts, the court concluded, justified university administrators in transferring the professor to another department.[30]

Likewise, in a school district case, a Texas school board suspended the school superintendent shortly after new board members were elected over the superintendent's active and public opposition. The superintendent sued, claiming his constitutionally protected right to free speech was violated.

Although the superintendent's political involvement in the election touched on matters of public concern, a federal appeals court denied the superintendent's claim. The court reasoned that the superintendent occupied a confidential relationship and a high-level policy-making position in his relationship with the school board. His involvement as a political partisan in the school board election campaign precluded an effective working relationship with the board after the election.[31]

In several cases, courts have rejected the free speech defenses of employees who challenged university sanctions, finding that the speech they engaged in was not a matter of public concern. For example, a Louisiana Tech University professor claimed he was discriminated against with regard to pay increases and teaching assignments because he had expressed his concern about lowering academic standards. The professor sued for violation of his First Amendment rights, but a federal court dismissed the case.

On appeal, the Fifth Circuit Court of Appeals upheld the trial court's decision, based on the conclusion that the speech in question was not a matter of public concern. "[I]nterfaculty disputes arise daily over teaching assignments, room assignments, administrative duties, classroom equipment, teacher recognition, and a host of other relatively trivial matters," the court wrote, but federal courts were not the place to resolve these disagreements. "We have neither the competency nor the resources to undertake to micromanage the administration of thousands of state educational institutions." Although the professor had characterized his speech as motivated by concern for academic excellence, the court decided that the primary motivation was nothing more than personal concerns about the work environment and teaching assignments.[32]

Likewise, a federal court found no issue of public concern in a lawsuit between the University of Wisconsin—Oshkosh and a professor who was demoted for allegedly giving a student an unfair grade and for writing insulting and demeaning letters to the student in an effort to extract an apology from her. Thus, the court dismissed the professor's lawsuit claiming a violation of his First Amendment right to academic freedom. On appeal, the Seventh Circuit Court of Appeals upheld the trial court's decision.[33]

Although the speech must involve a matter of public concern to be the subject of a Section 1983 suit, it is immaterial that the speech was made in private. The issue is not where the speech was made, or to whom, but whether the content involved a matter of public concern. Thus, criticism of administration policies voiced to administrators in a private setting will still be protected.[34]

It should be remembered that Section 1983 suits are available only in cases of public employment, because only the conduct of employers who act "under color" of state law are covered. However, in many jurisdictions, private employers can be sued for wrongful discharge if they fire employees on grounds that violate public policy, including the dismissal of an employee for exercising basic constitutional rights.[35] For example, a veterinarian sued Washington University, a private institution in Missouri, alleging he had been wrongfully discharged in retaliation for reporting the university's violation of the Animal Welfare Act (AWA). The veterinarian's claim was buttressed by a federal regulation that specifically prohibited reprisals against employees who reported AWA violations. A Missouri appellate court allowed the suit to proceed, holding that at-will employees could sue if they are discharged for reasons that violate a law, a regulation, or a constitutional provision.[36]

Not all states recognize this legal theory, however. Accordingly, an ophthalmologist faculty member at the New York Medical College lost her wrongful discharge suit against that private institution because New York does not recognize such an action. The physician had been fired after she suggested, in an interview in the *New York Times*, that some student seats in the medical school had been "sold" in exchange for contributions of $100,000.[37]

Strategies for the Defense

Obviously, employees who are terminated for legitimate reasons may try to characterize their termination as discriminatory or retaliatory because of the class they are in or because they have exercised some important, protected right. For many, this defense will be the only way available for them to contest the loss of their jobs. Litigation over such issues is highly fact intensive, and points up the necessity for an airtight case of discharge on legitimate grounds. Employers must be prepared to rebut the suggestion that discrimination or retaliation was any factor in the termination, and to show that it was independently justified and that the same decision would have been made in the absence of the factor of the protected speech or class. If this can be done, the discharge will succeed.

DUE PROCESS

Whether a person has tenure or not, many public employees are entitled to procedural "due process"—meaning notice and a hearing—before being discharged. This right to due process does not create any right to keep a job or create any substantive standards for a termination. It means only that the person is entitled to notice of the reasons for the termination and an opportunity to have a hearing at which he or she can dispute any relevant facts.

This right is grounded in the Fourteenth Amendment, which provides that government shall not deprive a person of "life, liberty, or property without due process of law," and thus involves public employees with either "property" or "liberty" interests in their jobs.

Property Interest in a Job

Simply having a job is not in itself a protected "property" interest, but the courts have held that where a person has some valid expectation that the job will continue for some specific period of time—an "expectation of continued employment"—there is a property interest that will be protected by due process. The due process requirement is simply a check on arbitrary or capricious action by public employers.

It is to be noted that an ostensibly private college or university might, if it receives a significant amount of state funding, be held to be a public employer under the "state action" doctrine and thus required to give due process.[38] However, the courts have been loath to invade the domain of private education and have regularly turned back such challenges to private educational institutions.[39]

Who has a legitimate "expectation of continued employment?" It cannot be a mere unilateral expectation by the employee; the employer must have done some explicit thing indicating that the employment was not at will, and that the employee could expect the employment to be permanent or to last for a specific period of time.[40]

Tenured and term employees. Clearly, a person who holds tenure has such an expectation. Likewise, nontenured faculty are guaranteed, in many institutions, that they will be rehired for the ensuing year unless they receive notice to the contrary by a certain specified date. Absent of such a timely notice of nonrenewal, they have an expectation of continued employment for the ensuing year. In some cases, an expectation has been created, explicitly or impliedly, by promises made by personnel officers, superiors, or by provisions in employee handbooks indicating that the employment was to be permanent.[41]

De facto tenure. The Supreme Court held in _Perry v. Sindermann_ that a professor of government who had worked for nine years in the Texas public higher education system and had held his present position in the system at Odessa Junior College for four years had relied upon oral and written representations that satisfactory performance would be rewarded with continuing employment, and that thus he had an expectation of continuing employment and was entitled to notice and a hearing before nonrenewal.[42] The court described the situation alleged by Sindermann as "de facto tenure."

In _Perry_ the college did not have a formal tenure program; numerous appellate decisions have distinguished the _Perry_ case by emphasizing that an institution with an established tenure program would not allow for a finding of de facto tenure. Thus, a promise by a department chair that a new professor would receive tenure "as a matter of course" would not create an implied right to tenure when the institution had a formal, published tenure process.[43]

Other conditions of employment. The fact that a public employee has a property interest in a particular job does not entitle that employee to due process every time some aspect of the job is changed. In a 1990 case, the Fourth Circuit Court of Appeals held that the transfer of a tenured professor from one department to another, without loss of rank or pay, did not implicate any property interest protected by the Due Process Clause.[44] Likewise, a federal court decided that a University of Tennessee faculty member's demotion from department chairman to professor did not involve a protected property interest in employment.[45] And yet another federal court ruled that a change in a graduate student's duties from a teaching position to a position in which she was not primarily responsible for teaching did not deprive her of a constitutionally protected property interest.[46]

Liberty Interest Claims

Besides having a right to due process because a "property" interest is present through an expectation of continuing employment, a public employee also may have a right to due process on the basis of a "liberty" interest that is infringed. How can one's "liberty" be infringed by being disciplined or fired? It is, the courts have said, if it impairs the employee's ability to move elsewhere and get another job. To succeed, such a claim probably would have to be founded upon defamatory remarks about an employee, made public in a reckless or malicious way, so as to place a "stigma" upon him or her. In *Roth v. Board of Regents,* the U.S. Supreme Court made clear that a mere failure to rehire an employee, when he remained as free as before to seek other employment, would not constitute a deprivation of a liberty interest.[47] Should such an improper, stigmatizing case be established, however, it would give rise not only to due process entitlement, but it could also be the basis of a Section 1983 suit for damages (discussed earlier in this chapter).

In *Ortwein v. Mackey,* the Fifth U.S. Circuit Court of Appeals held that the liberty interests of a nontenured tennis instructor at the University of South Florida were not abridged when he was not rehired and the university did not make any information about him public, "other than in connection with the defense" of the legal action.[48] In a rare decision in favor of a faculty member on a liberty interest issue, the Eighth U.S. Circuit Court of Appeals held in *Wellner v. Minnesota State Junior College Board* that charges of racism against an instructor did constitute a stigmatization sufficient to entitle him to a due process hearing before termination.[49] Wellner had been a nontenured physical education instructor and wrestling coach at Metropolitan State Junior College when charges arose that he held bias toward blacks, and his teaching appointment was not renewed. The appeals court noted that the charges diminished his chances of securing other employment, because prospective employers would have access to the file. The appeals court gave him back pay, and ordered that the material in his file referring to the charges of racism be expunged.

Due Process Requirements

What are the standards required by due process? At a minimum, the employee should have notice of the action to be taken and the reasons for it and a hearing before an unbiased tribunal or fact finder at which the employee can challenge any factual errors and present relevant evidence of his or her own. The notice must be given far enough in advance of the hearing so that the employee has adequate time to prepare. The employee is not entitled to an extensive checklist of procedural rights or a full-blown adversarial trial, but the hearing should be such as will achieve a fair result.

In a 1985 opinion, *Cleveland Board of Education v. Loudermill*,[50] the Supreme Court indicated that in most instances public employees are entitled to some sort of due process hearing before they are terminated. The Court made clear that an employee's pretermination hearing need not be elaborate if a more formal hearing is scheduled after termination. At a minimum, however, an employee is entitled—prior to termination—to either oral or written notice of the charges, an explanation of the employer's evidence, and an opportunity for the employee to present his or her side of the story.

The Consequences when Due Process Is Denied

As we have seen, the right to due process does not, in itself, create any additional right to retain one's job. What, then, is the penalty if due process is not accorded? Failure to grant due process may result in a Section 1983 suit that can grant reinstatement and award lost wages and fringe benefits, as well as attorney fees and costs of court. If it can be shown that the employer's action was malicious or wanton, punitive damages may be awarded. After reinstatement, the employer is free to terminate or nonrenew the employee upon the same grounds as were available before, but only after the requisite notice and hearing have been accorded, or waived, by the employee. Obviously, such a mistake not only may cost an employer considerable sums of money, but it also can gravely damage institutional morale, because the administration is made to appear impotent in the eyes of other employees. Prudence dictates that, if there is any question about an employee's entitlement to due process, it should be granted. What little time and trouble are lost far outweigh the cost of an erroneous denial.

FINANCIAL EXIGENCY AND PROGRAM DISCONTINUANCE

Tenured, probationary, and "at will" employees may be terminated at any time because of a genuine financial exigency or program discontinuance. For example, the Wisconsin Court of Appeals ruled that the University of Wisconsin Board of Regents had the power to terminate employees for reasons of financial exigency, even though the authority was not expressly granted by law. Such authority was implied, the court said, under the board's general statutory powers.[51] Likewise, the Fourth Circuit Court of Appeals recognized Goucher College's inherent power to terminate a tenured professor for financial reasons, even though the college's by-laws were silent on the subject.[52]

Of course, public employers must afford those who have an expectation of continuing employment a due process hearing even if the termination is based on a program discontinuance or financial exigency. One court has held that a university's decision to eliminate a program required only the barest procedural protection, since the university had a strong interest in pursuing its academic mission as it deemed best. With regard to terminating individual faculty members from the eliminated programs, however, the court determined that greater procedural safeguards were required. Faculty members are tenured to the institution, not a particular department, the court reasoned; and professors from an eliminated program were entitled to "a meaningful opportunity to demonstrate that, even if his or her program was to be discontinued and the number of faculty positions associated with that program eliminated, he or she should nevertheless be retained to teach in a field in which he or she is qualified."[53]

Moreover, financial exigency or program discontinuance cannot be used as a mere subterfuge for the termination of an unwanted employee. If a terminated employee raises the issue of bad faith, the courts will look behind the college's claim to see if there was some abstruse motivation.

The 1940 statement of the American Association of University Professors (AAUP), which has become the standard for many tenure plans, provides that terminations for financial exigency must be "demonstrably bona fide." In 1976, the AAUP further defined a demonstrably bona fide financial exigency to be "an imminent financial crisis which threatens the survival of the institution as a whole and which cannot be alleviated by less drastic means." The American Council on Education has refused to concur in this definition because it appears to require that the institution be on the brink of bankruptcy, and it might preclude program restructuring that could allow the institution to survive.

Not surprisingly, faculty members sometimes argue that an institution should have pursued alternatives to terminating employees when responding to a financial crisis. For example, when Bloomfield College experienced financial woes and laid off tenured professors under a claim of financial exigency, the professors countered that the college could have refinanced its debt service and sold the "Knoll Golf Club," a 322-acre property worth more than $5 million. They further complained that other new faculty had been hired in the same time period in which they were terminated. The superior court reinstated the professors, finding that sale of the property was "an available alternative" to the abrogation of tenure. The court also held that the college had failed to demonstrate, by a preponderance of the evidence, that its action was in good faith related to a condition of financial exigency.

The Appellate Division of the Superior Court affirmed, although contradicting the trial court on two key points. The appellate judges said that the decision whether to sell the Knoll property was one properly left to the college administration, and further held that the college had, in fact, demonstrated that it was suffering a bona fide financial exigency. Nevertheless, the court said, the college had the further burden of showing that the abrogation of tenure was a bona fide response to the financial exigency. Hinting that perhaps the new faculty had been hired as cheaper replacements for the terminated professors, the court said the college had failed to prove bona fide causation for the terminations, and therefore it affirmed the holding for the professors.

In the absence of bad faith, most courts will not substitute their judgment for that of college officials when it comes to the way an institution responds to a financial crisis. Thus, one court said that a terminated professor was not entitled to have a jury decide whether a financially pressed college should have invaded capital assets or sold land it was holding for a better price. Furthermore, the court said that the existence of a financial exigency should be determined by the adequacy of a college's operating funds rather than its capital assets.[54]

TERMINATION FOR CAUSE

Tenured professors and nontenured professors who are working under a contract for a specific term or in a year in which a nonrenewal notice was not given can be fired only for good cause, financial exigency, or program discontinuance. If the institution fires them for any other reason, they are entitled to damages for breach of contract. Professors at public institutions are entitled to due process—a notice and a hearing—before the termination.

Vagueness

What is good cause? Better institutional policies will contain a thorough definition of cause sufficient for termination. A basic premise of due process of law is that standards must be defined with sufficient precision that persons affected can know what conduct is prohibited, and that decision makers can apply the standards with evenhandedness. Accordingly, a simple policy statement that a person may be terminated for "good cause" or "adequate cause" might be so vague and overbroad that the courts would find, in the case of public institutions, that it denied due process of law or, in the case of private institutions, that it was unconscionable or simply unenforceable as a contract term.

In *Keyishian v. Board of Regents*, the U.S. Supreme Court held that faculty at a public institution could not be dismissed because they refused to sign a certificate stating that they were not and never had been communists.[55] The Court held that the requirement violated the professors' right to freedom of association, but further said that the certificate was overbroad and left uncertain what conduct was proscribed. Such a situation, the opinion said, would "cast a pall of orthodoxy over the classroom."

For the most part, however, in close calls on vagueness issues the courts have favored higher education institutions and have looked to see how the institutions have interpreted and applied the questioned provisions. In *Adamian v. Jacobsen*, the Ninth U.S. Circuit Court of Appeals held that only a narrow interpretation and application of the code provision requiring faculty "to exercise appropriate restraint [and] show respect for the opinion of others" would be able to pass constitutional muster.[56] On remand, the trial court found that the university had interpreted the phrase in a manner consistent with AAUP guidelines, and thus it upheld the professor's dismissal based on his conduct during a campus demonstration. On a second appeal, the Ninth Circuit Court affirmed and held that, as interpreted and applied, the phrase was not overbroad, and the university's action did not interfere with the faculty member's rights to freedom of speech and association.[57]

In *Korf v. Ball State University*,[58] the Seventh U.S. Circuit Court of Appeals declared that an institution's policy need not specify every type of impermissible conduct so long as the interpretation of what is unacceptable is consistent with reasonable professional standards and capable of being understood by the faculty member. In that case, a music professor charged with making homosexual advances toward his students was dismissed under an ethics provision that prohibited exploitation of students and required professors to respect students and adhere to a proper role as counselor.

Giving universities an even stronger hand, the Fifth U.S. Circuit Court of Appeals has held that the term "adequate cause" as a ground for termination is not too vague to meet due process standards. In *Garrett v. Mathews*, a tenured mathematics professor at the University of Alabama had contested his discipline on specific allegations of insubordination and dereliction of duty.[59] The appellate court affirmed the discipline, simply stating that the term "adequate cause" in the faculty handbook, as the ground for the discipline, met due process standards.

Finally, in a 1992 case, the Third Circuit Court of Appeals ruled that a Rutgers University regulation requiring "sound scholarship and competent teaching" gave a tenured chemistry professor adequate notice that certain behavior could lead to dismissal, even though it was not directly related to teaching or research. The professor was charged with a variety of misconduct, including an allegation that he verbally abused and intimidated two visiting Chinese scholars, compelling them to perform domestic service for the professor. He was also charged with some improprieties concerning federal research funds and payroll records, and with submitting an individual's application to graduate school, knowing it contained a questionable recommendation letter.

Although the trial court considered the professor's alleged misconduct to be "alien to any concept of how civilized professionals should comport themselves," it ruled that the university's regulation was too vague to give the professor notice of prohibited behavior.[60] On appeal, however, the Third Circuit Court ruled that the professor should have known that the regulation encompassed more than actual teaching or research skills. "It is not unfair or unforeseeable for a tenured professor to be expected to behave decently towards students," the court wrote, or to be "truthful and forthcoming" when dealing with payroll records, federal research funds, or applications for academic positions.[61]

In a noneducation case, the U.S. Supreme Court sustained a provision that authorized dismissal of a federal employee for "such cause as will promote the efficiency of the service." The ruling came in a case in which an employee of the Office of Economic Opportunity had been discharged after he had accused his superiors of taking bribes, but had been unable to back up the accusation.[62] More recently, the Supreme Court rejected a high school student's argument that school rules did not give him adequate notice that a lewd speech at a school assembly would subject him to discipline. Maintaining security and order in the schools required a certain amount of flexibility in school disciplinary procedures, the Court wrote. "Given the school's need to be able to impose disciplinary sanctions for a wide range of unanticipated conduct disruptive of the educational process, the school disciplinary rules need not be as detailed as a criminal code which imposes criminal sanctions."[63]

Relationship to the Workplace

Apart from issues of vagueness and overbreadth in stated grounds, what sorts of things are typically cited as valid reasons for discipline and termination? In most employment settings, the grounds must relate directly to the workplace and not merely involve the private life of an employee. Faculty at colleges and universities, like public school teachers, are somewhat different, because of their role in formulating the full personhood of the students entrusted to them. If their private lives affect their ability to perform in the educational setting, private actions may be the subject of discipline.

This principle is illustrated by a case involving the dismissal of a community college psychology teacher after she was convicted for possession of marijuana and cocaine that had been found in her home. The teacher appealed the dismissal, arguing that the conviction, standing alone, did not constitute just cause for her termination.

An Iowa court disagreed, finding sufficient evidence to support a finding by the college board of directors that the teacher was unable to perform her professional duties because of her conduct and the criminal conviction. The directors had concluded that the teacher's leadership and role model effectiveness had been undermined by the events. The court also upheld the college board's finding that the college's reputation would be negatively impacted if the teacher were retained.[64]

Immorality

Immoral or unethical conduct is often cited as grounds for dismissal. In a typical case, a male community college faculty member was found partially nude one night parked in a car with one of his female students, and he fled from a police officer who discovered them; the California Court of Appeals noted that the level of notoriety certain to result from the matter could be presumed to affect teaching fitness.[65] Similar holdings have come recently from federal appeals courts upholding the firings of a Ball State University music professor (discussed earlier in this chapter and in chapter 7) for making homosexual advances to students,[66] of a tenured chemistry professor at the University of Texas at El Paso for sexual harassment of students, [67] and of a tenured professor of veterinary medicine at Oklahoma State (discussed in chapter 7) for soliciting homosexual activity in a restroom of the student union building.[68]

Immorality and unethical conduct are not limited to sexual misconduct; they can include criminal conduct or a violation of professional ethical standards. Where a teaching psychologist pleaded guilty to Medicaid fraud in his private practice, he was dismissed from his university post on grounds of immorality[69] (This case is discussed in more detail in chapter 9); and where a faculty member lied to the college about holding various degrees, the Colorado Court of Appeals found the "misrepresentation" sufficient to warrant dismissal, because the situation was an embarrassment to the university and would perhaps jeopardize its accreditation.[70] (See chapter 9).

But, the Florida courts set aside the dismissal of a tenured female psychology instructor at Saint Johns River Junior College on grounds of immoral conduct because her "indiscretions" were a private matter, and there was not a sufficient showing that it impaired the institution's operations. The instructor had been charged with immorality, misconduct in office, and willful neglect of duty. It was alleged that she used profanity and made sexual references in class, drank heavily at a student's home, asked a student to have an affair with her ex-husband, and committed other acts of misbehavior. The Florida Court of Appeals distinguished the standard to be applied to the professor's conduct from that applicable to a public school teacher. "If a school teacher is responsible for teaching students in their formative years and commits acts of immorality after school hours, such acts may be indirectly related to misconduct in office," the court said. But, in the case of a college professor, conduct must be viewed in the context of "more liberal, open, robust college surroundings." The court said her actions were mere "indiscretions" that could not constitute sufficient grounds for dismissal from an institution of higher education.[71]

A California college also failed in an attempt to fire a professor for alleged sex-related misconduct. The courts found that two of the alleged acts of sexual harassment occurred too long ago to permit disciplinary action and the remaining charge did not support a "pattern or practice" of sexual harassment, as had been alleged by the institution. The court ordered the professor reinstated.[72]

Incompetence

Incompetency, or misfeasance, can warrant dismissal if a specific lack of ability renders the employee unable to perform his or her duties. This ground may be difficult to prove, particularly in the case of a faculty member, because competency in an academic field and teaching methods are such subjective matters. Generally, a discharge on this ground can be sustained only if there is an abundance of defensible data upon which evaluations of competence have been based, the person has been afforded an opportunity for remediation, and specific, objective standards have been established that the person has been unable to meet.

Still, where evidence exists, colleges may terminate professors for incompetence. A tenured professor at Fayetteville State University was terminated on charges of lack of class preparation, poor teaching, and poor relations with students.[73] A Dickinson College teacher lost an employment discrimination suit after a federal court ruled that her contract was not renewed because of poor teaching and her inability to work as a "team player" with colleagues.[74] The Third U.S. Circuit Court of Appeals upheld the nonrenewal of a professor in his fifth year of teaching at Mansfield State College, based upon his intransigence in dealing with superiors and unfavorable evaluations of his teaching by students and other faculty. He had been given previous notice of specific deficiencies, but there was no improvement in performance.[75] In a case discussed earlier in this chapter, Rutgers University discharged a tenured chemistry professor for failure to adhere to "sound scholarship and competent teaching," based on allegations that included the mistreatment of visiting foreign scholars and inappropriate handling of federal research funds and payroll records. The university's action was upheld on appeal.[76] Furthermore, the California Court of Appeals has held that a chemistry professor charged with incompetence was not deprived of any rights by being required to perform a number of experiments at a hearing.[77]

At some institutions, employees can only be dismissed for "just cause," a term that is generally interpreted to include incompetence. For example, the South Dakota School of Mines and Technology brought dismissal proceedings against a tenured associate librarian on several grounds, including incompetence and flagrant neglect of duty. As a member of the faculty union, the librarian was covered by a collective bargaining agreement between the union and the school; and this agreement specified that union members could only be fired for "just cause."

The South Dakota Supreme Court ruled that the school had established just cause by producing evidence that the librarian lacked the skills to perform his job, lacked the interest or ability to obtain those skills, and was unable to cooperate and interact with supervisors and staff members. Although the librarian had been put on a plan of improvement, the court ruled that the school was entitled to dismiss him before the plan had run its course, based on evidence that he had made no effort to comply with the plan.[78]

Neglect of Duty

Neglect of duty can justify dismissal for cause. Faculty and staff are charged with express and implied obligations in their employment, and failure to meet those obligations can properly result in termination. If sufficient documentation exists, absenteeism and tardiness in classroom teaching by a professor can certainly be grounds for dismissal. Professors are not free to leave their classrooms unattended, even to travel elsewhere to exercise free speech rights.[79] Other types of neglect, such as failure to meet office hours or perform community service, may be more difficult to prove, unless clear standards were enunciated up front and good documentation of failures exists.

Administrators have various duties, and failure to perform them can constitute neglect. Where the chairman of the mathematics department at a community college failed to implement a required evaluation of his administrative performance, as required by the college handbook and the chair's contract, he was not rehired. The Oregon Court of Appeals found that the chair had not met his required duties and said he was not in a position to complain about his nonreappointment to the post.[80]

Failure to account for the expenditure of funds and submit project reports can constitute neglect of duty. When a tenured faculty member at Eastern Michigan University failed to report, as required by university regulations, on sponsored biology research grants, his dismissal was affirmed by the federal courts.[81]

Failure to supervise students can likewise be neglect of an implied duty. As described in chapter 10, where a music professor allowed students on a college trip to drink alcoholic beverages and smoke marijuana, the Wyoming courts held he had a contractual obligation to provide supervision of the students, and his failure justified dismissal.[82]

Insubordination

Insubordination consists of a defiant attitude of noncompliance or a willful failure to conform with legitimate direction. Contumacious conduct is a stubborn refusal to do that which has been ordered by legitimate authority. Both are grounds for termination for cause if the behavior adversely affects the institution or fulfillment of its mission. Insubordination cannot, however, consist merely of an exercise of a free speech right by an employee, making known his or her views on a matter of public concern.

The courts have upheld terminations for insubordination in the following cases: a Kent State University faculty member who "flout[ed] the authority" of the music department director and assistant director and refused to meet his scheduled classes;[83] a faculty member at Indiana University of Pennsylvania who made persistent criticisms that amounted to verbal attacks against university administrators;[84] and a microbiology instructor at Lake City Community College who refused his dean's instruction that he conduct his lectures in a certain auditorium and told the dean, with an accompaniment of expletives, "Hell, no, I won't do it, and I'll fight you all the way, if you try to make me . . . !"[85]

A tenured faculty member at Central Washington University ignored a dean's denial of a request for a leave of absence to deliver a professional paper at a conference in Israel. He took the trip anyway, and as a result missed the beginning of the semester and was dismissed. The Court of Appeals of Washington, noting a history of absenteeism by the professor, rejected the professor's claim that his conduct was protected by a privilege of academic freedom, and upheld the termination.[86]

A rule of reasonableness will be applied in determining what duties are required in a job. A federal court in Alabama held that a professor's failure to open mail from his superior and to comply with a superior's request that he supply a list of publications constituted dereliction of duty and insubordination. The court noted that opening the mail and supplying the list were not written requirements of the job, but said, "Not showing up for class naked is not a written job requirement either. Some things go without saying."[87] Making a similar point, the Seventh Circuit Court of Appeals wrote that a college was not required to adopt detailed rules before it could discipline a professor for giving an unfair grade and for sending insulting and demeaning letters to a student. "For example," the court observed, "a professor could properly be disciplined for assigning grades on the basis of hair color, even if no rule to that effect had been previously announced."[88]

Free speech defense. Employees disciplined for insubordination often assert a free speech defense. For instance, a tenured education professor at the University of Colorado refused to administer a standardized faculty evaluation form to her students, based on her belief that teaching and learning could not be evaluated by a standardized approach. When the university responded by withholding her merit pay increase, she sued, arguing that the university had violated her First Amendment right to academic freedom.

A federal district court dismissed her suit. The evidence was clear, the court said, that the professor's merit pay increase was not denied because of her teaching methods or the opinions she expressed. Rather, it was withheld because she refused to comply with the university's teacher evaluation policy. "[A]lthough [the professor] may have a constitutionally protected right under the First Amendment to disagree with the university's policies," the court wrote, "she has no right to evidence her disagreement by failing to perform the duty imposed upon her as a condition of employment."[89]

The position of nontenured art professor at Stephen F. Austin State University was not renewed after his department chair characterized his actions as insubordinate. A federal district court said the conduct in question amounted to a protected exercise of free speech, and held for the instructor. However, the Fifth U.S. Circuit Court of Appeals reversed, citing testimony from university officials that the instructor had yelled at a female employee who was explaining a policy, had used improper language and was generally rude, and had, on one occasion, refused to assign a grade for a student in his graduate art class after being directed to do so by the departmental chair.[90]

Profanity in the classroom was the basis of a similar decision by the Fifth Circuit Court of Appeals, *Martin v. Parrish*.[91] An economics instructor at Midland College was dismissed after he failed to heed directives from his superiors to cease using profanity in his classes. The instructor had used such words as "bullshit," "hell," "damn," "Goddamn," and "sucks," chiefly as he was berating the classes for what he thought was poor academic performance. Despite being warned orally and in writing to cease using such language, he made such statements in class as "the attitude of the class sucks"; "You may think economics is a bunch of bullshit"; and "If you don't like the way I teach this Goddamn course, there is the door." The comments drew student complaints, and the college fired him.

After the discharge, he sued, claiming deprivation of his First Amendment right to free speech, abridgment of academic freedom, and denials of due process and equal protection. The federal district court dismissed the suit, holding that the profanity was not constitutionally protected. The appeals court affirmed, holding that Martin's actions were not a citizen's comments upon matters of public concern, but only an employee's comments upon matters of personal interest. The court said that a college teacher has no First Amendment right to use profane language in the classroom solely for the purpose of belittling and "cussing out" students, and characterized Martin's actions as a deliberate, superfluous attack on a "captive audience" with no academic purpose or justification.

Nor do public university professors have a constitutional right to air their religious views in their classes. In *Bishop v. Aronov*, a University of Alabama professor who taught in the College of Education occasionally made references to his religious beliefs during instructional time. The professor prefaced his remarks as personal "bias," and he did not engage in prayer, read Bible passages, or hand out religious tracts. On one occasion, shortly prior to final exams, he scheduled an optional class for one of his courses, where he lectured on and discussed "Evidences of God in Human Physiology." Attendance was voluntary and did not affect grades.

After receiving complaints from some of the professor's students, the department head sent the professor a memorandum, directing him not to interject his religious beliefs during instructional periods and to cease holding optional classes where the "Christian perspective" on an academic topic is delivered. The professor challenged the directive in federal court, claiming a violation of his right to free speech and right to free exercise of his religion.

Although the professor prevailed in the trial court, the Eleventh Circuit Court of Appeals reversed. First, the appellate court ruled that the professor's classroom was not an open forum for unrestricted free speech. Instead, during instructional time, the classroom was specifically reserved for teaching a university course for credit. Second, the court ruled that the department head's memorandum was not vague or unconstitutionally overbroad. On the contrary, the directive was sufficiently clear and narrowly focused to put the professor on notice as to what he could and could not do during instructional time and optional classes and did not restrict the professor's right to engage in other protected speech.

Finally, the court ruled that the University of Alabama had not violated the professor's constitutional rights by restricting his speech in the classroom and prohibiting optional classes that had a religious content. Under its authority to control the content of the curriculum, the university's conclusions about course content were entitled to hold sway over an individual professor's judgment.[92]

Martin and *Aronov* are especially significant because each opinion relied on a Supreme Court case that restricted free speech rights in the public school setting. In *Martin*, the Fifth Circuit Court of Appeals cited *Bethel School District No. 403 v. Fraser*[93] to support its holding that indecent language and profanity may be regulated in the university classroom. In *Bethel*, the Supreme Court had ruled that a school district could sanction a high school student who made a lewd and offensive speech at a school assembly.

In *Aronov*, the Eleventh Circuit Court of Appeals relied on *Hazelwood School District v. Kuhlmeier*[94] to uphold the University of Alabama's restrictions on a professor's in-class speech. In *Hazelwood*, the Supreme Court had upheld the censorship of a school newspaper by school authorities. *Hazelwood*, the *Aronov* court said, stood for the proposition that a school's basic education mission gives it the authority to reasonably restrict in-class speech that it could not censor outside the classroom.

Although *Aronov* and *Martin* appear to give universities greater authority to regulate a professor's classroom expression, two recent cases suggest that this authority is considerably diminished when a university sanctions a professor for engaging in off-campus speech. In *Levin v. Harleston*,[95] administrators of City University of New York created an alternative class for students who might want to transfer out of a professor's class after he made much-publicized written statements suggesting that the average black person was not as intelligent as the average white person.[96] The university also created an ad hoc committee to determine whether the professor's racial views affected his teaching ability.

The professor sued, claiming that the creation of an alternative class section stigmatized him solely because of his expression of ideas and that the formation of the special committee had a chilling effect on his First Amendment rights. The professor prevailed at the trial level, and on appeal, the judgment in his favor was in large part affirmed. Although the university argued that the professor's expression outside the classroom harmed students and the educational process within the classroom, the Second Circuit Court of Appeals noted that the evidence did not support the university's argument. Thus, the creation of an alternative section, which encouraged the professor's class size to shrink, was a First Amendment violation. The court also declared that the commencement of disciplinary proceedings or the threat of their commencement, if based solely on the professor's constitutionally protected off-campus statements, violated the professor's First Amendment rights.

In a second case, involving the same university, the Second Circuit Court of Appeals upheld a jury decision that university officials had unfairly removed a professor from his position as chair of the Black Studies Department in retaliation for off-campus statements that the university president described as anti-Semitic. According to the court, the university had not presented persuasive evidence that the professor's remark either disrupted the university or interfered with his duties as department chair. (Subsequently, the Supreme Court remanded the case back to the Second Circuit for further consideration.)[97]

To summarize, when faculty members or other university employees claim they are being discharged or sanctioned for engaging in protected speech, the courts will apply the *Pickering* balancing test, weighing the employee's interest in free expression against the university's interest in maintaining efficient service. A trend may be emerging in the cases to treat college classrooms more like classrooms in public schools, where the courts have restricted free speech rights considerably. But, the courts have provided considerable protection against sanctions for professors who express controversial views outside the classroom, even if the views might be characterized as racist. Above all, the courts seem increasingly reluctant to find free speech issues in cases involving internal squabbles among faculty members over issues that excite little, if any, interest outside the walls of academe. Unless the employee's speech involves a matter of public concern, the courts will not interfere with the university's personnel decisions on First Amendment grounds.

CONCLUSION: THE PERFECT POLICY

A review of the cases discussed in this chapter points up three important considerations for college and university administrators who must deal with a bad employee: 1) all the available evidence must have been marshaled and thoroughly examined before any personnel decision is made; 2) all defenses potentially available to the employee must be weighed before any personnel decision is made; and 3) the statutes, policies, and contractual terms that govern the employment relationship must be scrutinized to ascertain that the facts of the case fit an available ground for discipline or termination.

The importance of having well-defined job requirements and grounds for employee discipline or removal cannot be overstated. At private institutions, grounds for discipline and discharge usually are spelled out in employment contracts or collective bargaining agreements. At public institutions, they typically are established by statute and policy adopted by the governing board of the institution or system, and often are further enunciated in employee handbooks. If employees have notice of changes, rules generally can be changed from one contract period to another, for valid reason, and even during a contract period, so long as there is no due process loss of substantive rights.[98]

What should be included in a good policy? Certainly grounds that incorporate nonfeasance and neglect of duty should be included to cover people who simply do not do their jobs. Incompetency and misfeasance should be included to cover those who do their jobs poorly. Insubordination and contumacious conduct should be included to cover people who do not obey legitimate orders and direction. Another set of grounds should include malfeasance, defined as conviction of any felony or misdemeanor involving moral turpitude. Moral turpitude, as a legal term, includes not only sex offenses but also acts of dishonesty or cheating. These grounds should include not only conviction, but also simply the commission of any act that would constitute a felony or misdemeanor involving moral turpitude under the laws of the state in which the institution is located. A provision of this latter sort would empower the institution to take disciplinary action for such an offense even though an actual criminal prosecution is delayed or not pursued at all.

Other specific grounds found in many employment contracts include absence or tardiness, destruction of the employer's property, intoxication on the job, willful disregard of the employer's interests, fighting on the job, dishonesty, and theft. Such terms may or may not be appropriate in individual college or university policies; some may be appropriate for staff employees but not for faculty.

In a time of increasing fiscal pressures on colleges and universities, it is also a good idea to develop a policy for terminating faculty or staff due to financial exigency or program discontinuance. Such a policy should clearly define the conditions that can trigger these kinds of layoffs and should set forth the criteria for deciding which positions will be eliminated.[99]

Policy should also include an internal grievance procedure. A basic principle of administrative law is that aggrieved persons cannot go to court until they have exhausted their administrative remedies, and a good internal procedure may resolve the problem more quickly, at less expense, and with less damage all around. But, faculty committees sometimes develop policies and evaluate cases from a posture strongly sympathetic to accused faculty members. Administrators want to make certain that such on-campus procedures do not tie their hands and prevent them from doing what properly must be done.

NOTES

1. Walter P. Metzgar, "Academic Tenure in America: A Historical Essay," in *Faculty Tenure: A Report and Recommendations by the Commission on Academic Tenure in Higher Education*, edited by William R. Keast (San Francisco: Jossey-Bass, 1973).

2. *Nzomo v. Vermont State Colleges*, 136 Vt. 97, 385 A.2d 1099 (1978). However, not every failure to conform to technical requirements of policies will amount to a denial of due process. *Levitt v. University of Texas at El Paso*, 759 F.2d 1224 (5th Cir. 1985), *cert. denied sub. nom., Levitt v. Monroe*, 106 U.S. 599 (1986); *Piacitelli v. Southern Utah State College*, 636 P.2d 1063 (Utah 1981).

3. *Zuelsdorf v. University of Alaska, Fairbanks*, 794 P.2d 932 (Alaska 1990); *Moore v. Utah Technical College*, 727 P.2d 634 (Utah 1986); *United California Bank v. Prudential Insurance Co.*, 140 Ariz. 238, 258, 681 P.2d 390, 410 (Ariz. App. 1983); *Lancaster v. Arizona Board of Regents*, 143 Ariz. 451, 459, 694 P.2d 281, 289 (Ariz. App. 1984); *Boyce v. Umpaua Community College*, 67 Or. App. 629, 680 P.2d 671, 675 (1984). This is not to say that an institution cannot change the procedures set forth in it policies,

however, so long as there is no due process loss of substantive rights. *Garrett v. Mathews*, 625 F.2d 658 (5th Cir. 1980).
4. Section 37-101-13(f), Mississippi Code.
5. 29 U.S.C. 158.
6. 29 U.S.C. 215(a)(3).
7. 29 U.S.C. 660(c).
8. 20 U.S.C. 3608.
9. 42 U.S.C. 7622(a).
10. 15 U.S.C. 1674(a).
11. 38 U.S.C. 2012, 2021(b)(1).
12. 42 U.S.C. 2000(e) *et seq.*
13. 29 U.S.C. 621-634.
14. *Lewis v. Millsaps College*, 759 F.2d 1239 (5th Cir. 1985).
15. *EEOC v. University of Oklahoma*, 774 F.2d 999 (10th Cir. 1985), *cert. denied*, 475 U.S. 1120 (1986); see the district court opinion at 554 F.Supp. 735 (W.D. Okla. 1982).
16. *Edwards v. Board of Regents of University of Georgia*, 2 F.3d 382 (11th Cir. 1993).
17. *Ware v. Howard University, Inc.*, 816 F.Supp. 737, 751-52 (D.D.C. 1993).
18. *Puppel v. Illinois Benedictine College*, 731 F.Supp. 310 (N.D. Ill. 1990).
19. *Craik v. University of Minnesota*, 731 F.2d 465 (8th Cir. 1984).
20. *Harless v. First National Bank in Fairmont*, 289 S.E.2d 692 (W.Va. 1982).
21. *Tameny v. Atlantic Richfield Co.*, 27 Cal.3d 167, 164 Cal.Rptr. 839, 610 P.2d 1330 (1980).
22. *Trombetta v. Detroit, Toledo & Ironton Railroad Co.*, 81 Mich.App. 489, 265 N.W.2d 385 (1978).
23. 42 U.S.C. 1983.
24. 391 U.S. 563, 88 S. Ct. 1731, 20 L.Ed. 2d 811 (1968).
25. 461 U.S. 138, 103 S.Ct. 1684 (1983).
26. *Id.*, 103 S. Ct. at 1689-91.
27. *Orr v. Crowder*, 315 S.E.2d 593 (W.Va. 1983), *cert. denied*, 469 U.S. 981 (1984).
28. *Jeffries v. Harleston*, 828 F.Supp. 1066, 1071 (S.D.N.Y. 1993).
29. *Jeffries v. Harleston*, 21 F.3d 1238 (2nd Cir. 1994).
30. *Maples v. Martin*, 858 F.2d 1546 (11th Cir. 1988).
31. *Kinsey v. Salado Independent School District*, 950 F.2d 988 (5th Cir.), *cert. denied*, 112 S. Ct. 2225 (1992).
32. *Dorsett v. Board of Trustees for State Colleges and Universities*, 940 F.2d 121, 123-24 (5th Cir. 1991).
33. *Keen v. Penson*, 970 F.2d 252 (7th Cir. 1992).
34. *Givhan v. Western Line Consolidated School District*, 439 U.S. 410, 99 S.Ct. 693, 58 L.Ed.2d 619 (1979).
35. See, for example, *Novesel v. Nationwide Insurance Co.*, 721 F.2d 894 (3d Cir. 1983); *Luedtke v. Nabors Alaska Drilling, Inc.*, 678 P.2d 1123 (Alaska 1989); *Martin Marietta Corp. v. Lorenz*, 823 P.2d 100 (Colo. 1992); *Brockmeyer v. Dun & Bradstreet*, 113 Wis. 2d 561, 335 N.W.2d 834 (1983).
36. *Luethans v. Washington University*, 838 S.W.2d 117 (Mo. App. 1992).
37. *Boniuk v. New York Medical College*, 535 F.Supp. 1353 (S.D.N.Y.), *aff'd* 741 F.2d 111 (2d Cir. 1982).

38. See Krynicky v. University of Pittsburgh, 742 F.2d 94 (3d Cir. 1984), cert. denied, 471 U.S. 1015 (1985), which held that the university received sufficient public support as to be acting "under color of" state law.

39. Rendell-Baker v. Kohn, 457 U.S. 830, 102 S.Ct. 2764, 75 L.Ed. 2d 418 (1981); Powe v. Miles, 407 F.2d 73 (1968).

40. See Orr v. Crowder, 315 S.E. 2d 593 (W. Va 1993), cert. denied, 469 U.S. 981 (1984).

41. Goodman v. Board of Trustees of Community College District, 511 F.Supp. 602 (N.D. Ill. 1981); Toussaint v. Blue Cross and Blue Shield, 408 Mich. 579, 292 N.W.2d 880 (Mich. 1980). See also Adelson v. Regents University of California, 128 Cal. App. 3d 891, 180 Cal. Rptr. 676 (1982); Marwil v. Baker, 499 F.Supp. 560 (E.D. Mich. 1980).

42. Perry v. Sindermann, 408 U.S. 593, 92 S.Ct. 2694, 33 L.Ed. 570 (1972). See also Soni v. Board of Trustees, 513 F.2d 347 (6th Cir. 1975), cert. denied, 426 U.S. 919 (1976).

43. Davis v. Oregon State University, 591 F.2d 493 (9th Circ. 1978); see also Haimowitz v. University of Nevada, 579 F.2d 526 (9th Cir. 1978).

44. Huang v. Board of Governors of University of North Carolina, 902 F.2d 1134 (4th Cir. 1990). See also, Maples v. Martin, 858 F.2d 1546, 1550-51 (11th Cir. 1988).

45. Garvie v. Jackson, 845 F.2d 647, 651 (6th Cir. 1988).

46. Kelleher v. Flawn, 761 F.2d 1079, 1086-87 (5th Cir. 1985).

47. 408 U.S. 564, 92 S.Ct. 2701, 33 L.Ed.2d 548 (1972).

48. 511 F.2d 696 (5th Cir. 1975).

49. 487 F.2d 153 (8th Cir. 1973).

50. 470 U.S. 532, 105 S.Ct. 1487, 84 L.Ed.2d 494 (1985).

51. Graney v. Board of Regents, 92 Wis. 2d 745, 286 N.W.2d 138, 145 (Wis. App. 1979).

52. Krotkoff v. Goucher College, 585 F.2d 675 (4th Cir. 1978).

53. Texas Faculty Association v. University of Texas at Dallas, 946 F.2d 379, 387 (5th Cir. 1991).

54. Krotkoff, 585 F.2d.d at 681.

55. 385 U.S. 589, 87 S.Ct. 675, 17 L.Ed.2d 629 (1967).

56. 523 F.2d 929 (9th Cir. 1975).

57. Adamian v. Lombardi, 608 F.2d 1224 (9th Cir. 1979), cert. denied, 446 U.S. 938 (1980).

58. 726 F.2d 1222 (7th Cir. 1984).

59. 625 F.2d 658 (5th Cir. 1980).

60. San Filippo v. Bongiovanni, 743 F. Supp. 327, 338 (D. N.J. 1990).

61. San Filippo v. Bongiovanni, 961 F.2d 1125, 1137 (3rd Cir.), cert. denied, 113 S.Ct. 305 (1992).

62. Arnett v. Kennedy, 416 U.S.l 134, 94 S.Ct. 1633, 40 L.Ed.2d 15 (1974).

63. Bethel School District No. 403 v. Fraser, 478 U.S. 657, 686, 106 S.Ct. 3159, 3166 (1986).

64. Board of Directors of Des Moines Area Community College v. Simons, 493 N.W.2d 879 (Iowa App. 1992).

65. Board of Trustees of Compton Junior College District v. Stubblefield, 16 Cal.App.3d 820, 94 Cal.Rptr. 318 (1971).

66. Korf v. Ball State University, 726 F.2d 1222 (7th Cir. 1984).

67. Levitt v. University of Texas at El Paso, 759 F.2d 1224 (5th Cir.), cert. denied sub nom., Levitt v. Monroe, 474 U.S. 1034 (1985).

68. Corstvet v. Boger, 757 F.2d 223 (10th Cir. 1985).

69. Samaan v. Trustees of California State University and Colleges, 150 Cal.App.3d 646, 197 Cal.Rptr. 856 (3 Dist. 1983).

70. *Denberg v. Loretto Heights College*, 694 P.2d 375 (Colo. App. 1984).
71. *Texton v. Hancock*, 359 So.2d 895 (Fla. Dist. Ct. App. 1978), *cert. denied*, 366 So.2d 881 (Fla. 1979).
72. *Brown v. California State Personnel Board*, 166 Cal. App. 3d 1151, 213 Cal.Rptr. 53 (1985).
73. *Jawa v. Fayetteville State University*, 426 F.Supp. 218 (E.D.N.C. 1976), *aff'd*, 584 F.2d 976 (4th Cir. 197), *cert. denied*, 440 U.S. 974 (1979).
74. *Garvey v. Dickinson College*, 775 F.Supp. 788 (M.D.Pa. 1991).
75. *Chung v. Park*, 514 F.2d 382 (3d Cir. 1975), *cert. denied*, 423 U.S. 948 (1975).
76. *San Filippo v. Bongiovanni*, 961 F.2d 1125, 1137 (3rd Cir. 1992), *cert. denied*, 113 S.Ct. 305.
77. *Bevil v. Brisco*, 165 Cal. App. 3d 812, 212 Cal.Rptr. 36 (1985).
78. *McCauley v. South Dakota School of Mines and Technology*, 488 N.W.2d 53 (S.D. 1992).
79. *Stastny v. Board of Trustees of Central Washington University*, 32 Wash. App. 239, 647 P.2d 496 (1982), *cert. denied*, 460 U.S. 1071 (1982); *Kalme v. West Virginia Board of Regents*, 539 F.2d 1346, 1348 (4th Cir. 1976); *Akyeampong v. Coppin State College*, 538 F.Supp. 986, 909 (D.Md. 1982), *aff'd*, 725 F.2d 673 (4th Cir. 1983).
80. *Zink v. Lane Community College*, 34 Or. App. 251, 578 P.2d 471(1978).
81. *Bates v. Sponberg*, 547 F.2d 325 (6th Cir. 1976).
82. *White v. Board of Trustees*, 648 P.2d 528 (Wyo. 1982), *cert. denied*, 459 US.1107 (1983).
83. *Smith v. Kent State University*, 696 F.2d 476, 479 (6th Cir. 1983).
84. *Roseman v. Indiana University of Pennsylvania*, 520 F.2d 1364 (3d Cir. 1975), *cert. denied*, 424 U.S. 921 (1976).
85. *Adams v. Lake City Community College*, 404 So.2d 148 (Fla. Dist. Ct. App. 1981).
86. *Stastny v. Board of Trustees of Central Washington University*, 647 P.2d 496 (Wash. App. 1982), *cert. denied*, 460 U.S. 1071 (1983).
87. *Garrett v. Mathews*, 474 F.Supp. 594 (N.D. Ala. 1979), *aff'd*, 625 F.2d 658 (5th Cir.1980).
88. *Keen v. Penson*, 970 F.2d 252, 259 (7th Cir. 1992).
89. *Wirsing v. Board of Regents of University of Colorado*, 739 F.Supp. 551 (D.Colo. 1990), *aff'd*, 945 F.2d 412 (10th Cir. 1991), *cert. denied*, 112 S. Ct. 1264 (1992). See also *Shaw v. Board of Trustees of Frederick Community College*, 549 F.2d 929 (4th Cir. 1976).
90. *Hillis v. Stephen F. Austin State University*, 665 F.2d 547, *cert. denied*, 457 U.S. 1106 (1982).
91. 805 F.2d 583 (5th Cir. 1986).
92. *Bishop v. Aronov*, 926 F.2d 1066 (11th Cir. 1991).
93. 478 U.S. 675, 106 S.Ct. 359, 92 L.Ed.2d (1986).
94. 484 U.S. 260, 108 S.Ct. 562, 98 L.Ed.2d 592 (1988).
95. 966 F.2d 85 (2d Cir. 1992).
96. Quotations from the professor's writings are contained in the trial court's opinion in the case, *Levin v. Harleston*, 770 F.Supp. 895 (S.D.N.Y. 1991).
97. *Jeffries v. Harleston*, 828 F.Supp. 1066 (S.D.N.Y 1993), *modified*, 21 F.3d 1238 (2nd Cir); *vacated, remanded*, ____ U.S. ____, 115 S. Ct. (1994).
98. *Garrett v. Mathews*, 625 F.2d 658 (5th Cir. 1980).
99. Marybeth K. Saunders, "Developing a Financial Exigency Policy for Terminating Personnel," 65 *Educational Record* 42-44 (1984).

C H A P T E R
13

Victims

Technically, in a criminal case, the person injured or robbed is not the victim of the crime. Rather, the victim is the commonwealth of all the people, gathered together in their government. Illustrative of this situation are the facts that the government is the plaintiff in all criminal cases, and, in most jurisdictions, criminal indictments must not only spell out in detail the unlawful act that the defendant is accused of performing, but must end with the words ". . . and against the peace and dignity of the state."

Likewise, the individual human victim of a crime does not "own" the prosecution. Although, as a practical matter, authorities often do not pursue a criminal prosecution where the individual victim does not wish to "press charges," in fact, the wishes of the individual victim are totally immaterial legally, and a criminal prosecution certainly can move forward even though the individual victim has no interest in pursuing it or wishes it all forgotten.

This posture of crime and the criminal justice system probably is the reason that the individual victim often has been called the "forgotten person" in the process. But changes in that unhappy situation are beginning to occur today.

THE VICTIM AS THE FORGOTTEN PERSON

The Department of Justice reports that there are more than 34 million criminal victimizations a year in our country. In a typical recent year, more than 15.7 million households were victimized by burglary, larceny, or automobile theft. More than 6.4 million Americans were the victims of violent crime, including more than 5 million cases of assault and 173,000 victims of rapes.[1] The annual loss of property runs into the billions, and the resultant mental and emotional suffering is immeasurable.

With the victims so numerous, and, in most cases, their innocences so obvious, it is paradoxical that the criminal justice system has moved boldly in recent decades to protect the rights of the accused defendant but has treated the victims with callous indifference, at least until the past few years. The goal of good government should be to ensure that all citizens are treated justly and decently, not just those accused of committing crimes.

What problems have victims faced? Often, they have been forced to deal with huge and impersonal bureaucracies—the police and court systems— entirely on their own. They have been subjected to sometimes callous and humiliating questioning by police, and they have been required to fill out numerous forms and then to attend court hearings that frequently are postponed at the last minute, with little or no notice to them. They have been forced to wait in dirty, smoky, smelly, and sometimes unsafe police stations and courthouses for hours and days while proceedings drag on and have had to sustain additional financial losses because of missed work, costs of transportation, and so on, with their only compensation being a paltry daily witness fee. They have been subjected to humiliation and ignominy when cross-examined by counsel for the defendant. Very often, charges have been reduced or even dismissed by prosecutors without the victim having had any say in the matter, and many times the victim is not even informed of the event.

The victim of every sort of crime suffers some form of psychic pain as well as property loss or physical pain, and thus every crime victim can benefit from assistance of some type. There are, however, two classes of cases, rape and domestic violence, that present special needs for assistance.

Rape Victims

It is sometimes said that a rape victim is raped twice—once in the original assault and a second time when she takes the witness stand in her assailant's trial. In *Trauma and Recovery*, Judith Herman explains why this is so. "[A]n adversarial legal system," Herman writes, "is of necessity a hostile environment; it is organized as a battlefield in which strategies of aggressive argument and psychological attack replace those of physical force." A rape victim is rarely prepared for judicial proceedings that often seem like a second attack against her. And even if she is, the nature of the criminal justice system, with its strong emphasis on the rights of the accused, may put her at a disadvantage when seeking justice. Indeed, Herman writes, "If one set out by design to devise a system for provoking intrusive post-traumatic symptoms [in rape victims], one could not do better than a court of law."[2]

Fortunately, the law has been changed in most jurisdictions in recent years to aid rape victims who press charges against their assailants. Formerly, if the defendant claimed that the woman had consented to the sexual act, the rape victim's past sexual history could be paraded before the jury, because it was thought that her morals and past conduct would shed some light on whether she had consented or not. Chiefly as a result of a campaign by the National Organization for Women, most states in recent years have modified their laws and evidentiary rules so that a victim's past sexual behavior is held immaterial, and thus cannot be brought out at the trial.[3] Most states recognize two exceptions under the new rule. Where semen or some physical injury was found on the victim after the alleged attack, recent sexual activity with another person can be shown if there is a suggestion that the other man was the source of the semen or injury, and not the defendant. Also, past sexual activity with the defendant can be shown if the defendant has claimed consent, as willing sexual acts with the defendant in the past may well be relevant to whether the victim consented this time.[4]

Colleges and universities can do little to make the criminal courts more hospitable to rape victims, but they can do a great deal to provide victims with support within the campus community. First, colleges can provide trained counselors, including counselors trained in the most prevalent form of sexual assault on campus—acquaintance rape. Colleges can also make available victim's assistance advocates to help the victim decide whether to seek legal recourse and to assist her in her encounters with the criminal justice system. In addition, colleges can make sure that trained medical personnel are available at campus health care facilities to provide emergency treatment and collect evidence if necessary to assist in a criminal prosecution.[5]

Domestic Violence Victims

Domestic violence, which includes violence against spouses, intimate sexual partners, and children, presents special needs. For one thing, the victim may not be able to return home because of continuing danger. Most communities now provide spouse abuse shelters, which are open to unmarried as well as married persons. In some cases these shelters have provided temporary living quarters for college women who have been abused by their boyfriends. The welfare or human services agencies in every state now are empowered to provide "protective services" intervention for children or helpless adults who are the victims of physical violence, and youth courts likewise can intervene to protect children who fall under the classification of abused or neglected children.

Quite often in the past the victims of abuse by boyfriends or spouses did not "press charges" because to do so would have made their lives worse. They had no life options. If the husband was in jail, he could not work and provide for the family; the woman all too often had no independent means of livelihood for herself and the children. Further, it was often thought that retaliation would be certain, and that the woman would just be further endangering herself if she called police and encouraged prosecution of the case. A study by the National Institute of Justice and the Minneapolis Police Department belied the latter belief, however. The study found that 16 percent of the women who reported domestic violence to the police were assaulted a second time, but 23 percent of those who did not call police suffered a second assault. When the assailant was the victim's spouse, the statistics were even higher: the woman was 41 percent less likely to be assaulted again if she called police than if not. Moreover, it appeared from a controlled study that the likelihood of repeat conduct was reduced if the assailant was arrested, rather than just "given advice" by the police or ordered to stay away from the home for eight hours. Only 19 percent of domestic assault assailants who were arrested committed another assault within the following six-month period, while 33 percent of those who were advised did, and 37 percent of those who were told to stay away did. The researchers concluded that, in domestic assault cases, police should make an arrest "unless there are good, clear reasons why an arrest would be counterproductive."[6]

Later research, however, challenged the Minneapolis study and suggested that arresting the abuser is no panacea for the problem of domestic violence. Researchers studying the police response to domestic violence in Milwaukee, Wisconsin, found that arrests made some kinds of people *more* violent against their cohabitants. Specifically, the study found that arrest made employed, married, high school graduate, or white suspects less likely to have a repeat incident of domestic violence. For unemployed men, unmarried men, high school dropouts, or black suspects, however, an arrest for domestic violence was associated with increased reports of violence Overall, the Milwaukee researchers found no evidence of a long-term effect of arrest on domestic violence.[7] Researchers studying the police response to domestic violence in Charlotte, North Carolina, reached similar conclusions.[8]

Some commentators have argued that arrest should continue to be employed, even if it is ultimately ineffective, as a way of demonstrating society's intolerance for domestic assaults.[9] Another commentator noted that the Milwaukee and Charlotte research demonstrated that there is no single method of preventing domestic violence. Therefore, he wrote, society must allow the nation's crisis intervention workers, including the police, the flexibility to select the most appropriate resource and strategy for any given case.[10]

Victims' Rights Laws

Reforms in court procedures have come to many states in recent years as a result of heightened awareness of the victim as the forgotten person in the system. New statutes now have changed many old, less-sensitive practices.

Formerly, a victim's stolen property, or other property that would be needed for evidence at the defendant's trial, had to be held by police until the trial, which could be months or years after the crime itself. The new codes in many states require that the property be returned to the victim, if it can be photographed and otherwise accurately represented and depicted at the trial, or if the victim can later produce it for the trial. Often, case dispositions were made by plea bargain, and the victim was not consulted. In many states now, prosecutors cannot enter into any plea bargain until the victim is notified and has an opportunity to give his or her views on the proposal. Often, after a plea bargain or conviction, the judge would sentence the defendant without consulting the victim. Now, judges in many states are required to have a "victim impact statement" prepared before sentencing and to consult it. Such a statement details the physical, emotional, and financial impact the crime has had on the victim, or on the family of a homicide victim, as well as ways in which restitution might be helpful, and it states whether any attempt at restitution has been made by the defendant. In some states, such as West Virginia, the victim has to be notified that he or she has a right to appear in person before the judge to express his or her view before the sentencing.

Victims' Rights Organizations

Whether they suffer physical injury and/or property loss, crime victims need both immediate and long-term support to recover from the crime that was perpetrated against them. The National Organization for Victims Rights has identified eight stages of the criminal justice process and the assistance a victim needs during each stage, beginning with the crime itself and ending after the perpetrator has been convicted. In the early stages, a victim may require emergency medical treatment, crisis counseling, and perhaps some security measures to prevent the perpetrator from repeating the violation. If an arrest is made, the victim will need to be kept informed of the status of the case and to be oriented to the criminal justice system. If it is necessary to testify, the victim may need child care and transportation. Finally, if the perpetrator is convicted of the crime, the victim may need assistance in preparing a victim impact statement to aid the court in sentencing, along with information about options for obtaining restitution.[11]

In recent years, victims' assistance groups have been formed in every state to perform some of these services. Mothers Against Drunk Drivers (MADD), Parents of Murdered Children, local rape crisis centers, and child advocacy groups provide various kinds of assistance to crime victims. In his recent book, *First Get Mad, Then Get Justice*, Charles G. Brown provides a state-by-state listing of these organizations, along with an excellent explanation of how the criminal justice system works from the victim's perspective.[12]

INTIMIDATION OF WITNESSES OR VICTIMS

Without a doubt many victims fear retribution from some source, even without any specific threat, when they take their case into the criminal justice system. Sometimes specific threats are made against victims in an attempt to get them to drop the charges, or against witnesses to encourage them not to testify or to alter the content of their testimony. Threats and abuse of this sort sometimes even occur on college and university campuses in student disciplinary proceedings (see chapter 2).

Intimidation of witnesses or victims in criminal cases is illegal. If it happens during or closely related to judicial proceedings, it can constitute contempt of court, and if it happens before a trial, it constitutes obstruction of justice and, in some jurisdictions, comes under other special "witness tampering" statutes. If there is actual or attempted violence, it can be prosecuted like any other assault, battery, or homicide case. If the defendant is out on bail when the intimidation is attempted, bail can be immediately revoked and the person jailed until trial. Any attempt at intimidation should be reported to police or the prosecutor immediately. Campus disciplinary codes should contain similar protections that clearly forbid any attempt to intimidate witnesses or interfere with campus disciplinary processes, and everyone involved should be so informed when the proceedings commence.

Protection and Relocation

In a criminal case if a threat presents imminent danger, police can provide 24-hour protection, and in some cases they can actually temporarily relocate witnesses and their families for their safety. In major cases, federal authorities can even provide a permanent new identity for witnesses whose lives may continue to be in danger. Under the Organized Crime Control Act of 1970 and the Witness Security Reform Act of 1984,[13] the U.S. Marshal's Service operates a top-secret relocation program for witnesses and their families, which includes giving them new names, complete with supporting documents, as well as assistance with housing, employment, medical services, and other social services. This program can be used for witnesses in both state and federal prosecutions, but usually it is utilized only in organized crime cases.

Bail: Right Back on the Street

Release of criminals on bail presents problems in some cases where victims or witnesses fear retaliation or intimidation. Because every person is presumed innocent until proven guilty in a trial, our American system is loath to deprive anyone of liberty before trial, unless it appears that he or she is unlikely to return for the trial. As stated earlier, the only purpose of bail is to assure that the accused will return for the trial; it is not to be any sort of punishment in itself. In many states, the right to bail in a reasonable amount is guaranteed, except in capital cases where the proof of guilt is great. However, in recent years, because of several odious cases of retaliatory violence by persons shortly after their release on bail, Congress and a number of state legislatures have enacted stiffer pretrial detention procedures for cases where there is credible evidence that the accused will present a danger to others if he or she is released before trial. Under these new statutes, courts can consider the effect of pretrial release on victims or witnesses in determining whether to admit the accused to bail.

COMPENSATION AND RESTITUTION

Victims of crime have always had a right to bring a private damage suit against the criminal for the victims' losses in the crime, including pain and suffering. Most criminals, of course, are impecunious and likely to remain so, and thus private damage awards are nearly always uncollectible and not worth the effort.

In recent years, there has been a growing public awareness that some public provision could be made to compensate crime victims for losses that are not otherwise reimbursed. Perhaps implicit in the willingness of legislatures to enact such statutes is a recognition both that society has a duty to provide for its citizens in need and that crime represents some sort of societal failure. Accordingly, the states have established programs to pay victims for certain personal expenses resulting from violent crimes, within dollar ceilings established by the legislatures. These programs do not cover the value of property stolen or damaged by crime, chiefly because the cost of doing so would be staggering. In any event, significant property losses are often insured against.

Congress passed the Victims of Crime Act in 1984,[14] which provided grants to states that established victims' compensation programs meeting federal criteria. Encouraged by this legislation, all 50 states had a victims' compensation program in place by 1991. Across the country, these programs make at least some provision to compensate for loss of support—meaning wages or income lost as a result of injury inflicted during the crime—and for out-of-pocket expenditures, including medical bills, and, in the case of a homicide, funeral expenses.[15] As noted above, these programs generally do not compensate victims for property that has been stolen or damaged in the commission of crime, nor do they pay for the intangibles of pain and suffering experienced by a victim. Neither do they provide compensation for crimes that were covered by some other compensatory source, such as private insurance, unemployment compensation, and the like. Under these compensation programs, it is immaterial whether the criminals are caught or whether they are prosecuted. If the conduct producing the injury constituted a crime, the victim will be eligible to some form of compensation.

Restitution by the Offender

Another, and in some cases better, source of compensation for crime victims is court-ordered restitution as a part of the disposition of criminal cases, following a conviction or plea bargain. Under newly beefed-up statutes in all the states, criminal courts can require restitution as a term of probation. It can include a requirement that the defendant return stolen property to the victim, compensate the victim for property losses and other expenses resulting from the crime, and, in some cases, even require that the defendant perform certain services for the victim. If a defendant fails to make the required payments through bad faith, his or her probation can be revoked and the person may be incarcerated for the duration of the assigned sentence.

In many cases, court-ordered restitution will have several advantages over state crime victim compensation programs. Restitution can cover losses from theft and property damage crimes, unlike the crime victim compensation programs, which are limited to crimes of violence. In addition, in court-ordered restitution there are no limits on the amounts that can be recovered, whereas crime victim compensation statutes have dollar ceilings. But, there may be disadvantages. Restitution can be effective only to the extent that the criminal can repay. If the criminal is in prison, or is unable to work at gainful employment, his or her ability to make restitution will probably be minuscule or nonexistent. In addition, the victim may not want to have any continued dealings with the criminal, however remote.

The courts have come to look on court-ordered restitution programs with favor, and the practice of requiring restitution is growing rapidly in many jurisdictions. The courts in many jurisdictions are vigorously enforcing restitution orders, and the Supreme Court of the United States exhibited its approbation of the practice when it held that court-ordered restitution in a criminal proceeding cannot be discharged by the criminal-obligor in a bankruptcy proceeding.[16]

CONCLUSION: REMEMBERING THE VICTIM

New legal developments are providing a variety of assistance for crime victims. Those who work with college and university students and employees who have been victimized by crime should be aware of the remedies available to help a victim through a difficult and sometimes tragic period. Witnesses, too, need support as they perform their duties as citizens.

Institutions can be victims, too. While most of the victim assistance programs are couched in terms of assistance for individual citizens, their benefits sometimes can be available to institutions as well. Colleges and universities could certainly benefit from court-ordered restitution programs established as a part of probation, particularly in cases of "white collar" crimes such as embezzlement and theft by employees who have financial resources and future earnings potential, and in cases involving students who damage institutional property.

NOTES

1. U.S. Department of Justice, Bureau of Justice Statistics. *Criminal Victimization in the United States, 1991* (Washington, D.C.: U.S. Department of Justice, 1992).
2. Judith Herman, *Trauma and Recovery* (New York: Basic Books, 1991), p. 72.
3. Forty-eight states have passed rape shield laws. For a listing of these laws, see Harriet Galvin, "Shielding Rape Victims in the State and Federal Courts: A Proposal for the Second Decade, 70 *Minnesota Law Review*. pp. 906-07 (1986).
4. Ibid. pp. 818-24.
5. Carol Bohmer and Andrea Parrot, *Sexual Assault on Campus, The Problem and the Solution* (New York: Lexington Books, 1993), pp. 206-13.
6. National Institute of Justice, *Domestic Violence* (Washington, D.C.: Government Printing Office, 1987).
7. Lawrence W. Sherman, Janell D. Schmidt, Dennis P. Rogan, Douglas A. Smith, Patrick R. Gartin, Ellen G. Cohn, Dean J. Collins, and Anthony R. Bacich, "The Variable Effects of Arrest on Criminal Careers: The Milwaukee Domestic Violence Experiment," 83 *Journal of Criminal Law and Criminology* 167-69 (1992).
8. J. David Hirschel and Ira W. Hutchison III, "Female Spouse Abuse and the Police Response: The Charlotte, North Carolina, Experiment," 83 *Journal of Criminal Law and Criminology* 115-19 (1992).
9. Ibid., p. 119.
10. David Mitchell, "Contemporary Police Practices in Domestic Violence Cases: Arresting the Abuser: Is It Enough?" 83 *Journal of Criminal Law and Criminology* 248 (1992).
11. National Institute of Justice, *Serving Crime Victims and Witnesses* (Washington, D.C.: Government Printing Office, 1987), p. 3.
12. Charles G. Brown, *First Get Mad, Then Get Justice*. (New York: Birch Lane Press, 1993).
13. 18 U.S.C. 3521.
14. 42 U.S.C. 10601, *et seq.*
15. National Institute of Justice. *Compensating Crime Victims: A Summary of Policies and Practices* (Washington, D.C.: Government Printing Office, 1992).
16. *Kelly v. Robinson*, 107 S.Ct. 353 (1986).

CHAPTER

14

Responding to a Crime Incident
A Practical Guide for Campus Decision Makers

I n an earlier time, college presidents, deans, and faculties could run things pretty much as they liked, constrained only by tradition and good manners. The student was a suppliant, taking what was dealt. No more. That relationship has been replaced by the concept of student as citizen and consumer, a person who simply is buying a service. If the student becomes a consumer, the college becomes a vendor, and the two parties now must deal at arm's length. And, at least where public institutions are concerned, the college must deal as government, affording due process of law.[1]

Add to this new institution-student relationship the complexities of modern life, the size of our institutions, and the fact of crime in our society today, and the implications for campus decision makers are enormous. Institutions owe a duty to provide their students and employees reasonable safety in their persons and property. Mishandling of campus crime has massive implications for student and faculty recruitment and retention, alumni and press relations, and, in the case of public institutions, for legislative appropriations. In addition, administrators who bungle crime matters may expose their institutions and themselves to extensive liability in civil damage suits.

RESPONSIBILITY FOR DEALING WITH CAMPUS CRIME

Who are the decision makers who must respond to the campus crime problem? As always, responsibility resides at the top. Campus governing boards and presidents must ensure both that adequate data are being gathered and analyzed to provide the necessary foresight for crime avoidance and that institutional constituencies are cooperating to achieve those ends. Campus security, student affairs and housing, personnel, and physical plant administrators all have major roles in dealing with campus crime. "Turf" problems and disciplinary jealousies may hinder a systematic response to campus crime; some may feel their prerogatives and fields of expertise are being usurped and withhold support. Others may incorrectly assume the problem is being addressed by others. For these reasons, top-level administrative coordination and oversight are an absolute necessity.

The American Council on Education has published a resource document on campus security in which the need to assign security tasks to specific individuals is stressed, including the designation of responsible individuals to be on call for security emergencies.[2] According to the document, campus administrators must ensure that the following security concerns receive attention:

1. Security needs are taken into account in the design, maintenance, and operation of the institution's buildings, grounds, and equipment.
2. Students and other members of the institutional community are adequately informed about security risks and procedures.
3. Security personnel are adequately screened, trained, equipped, and supervised by the institution or its contractor.
4. The number of security personnel used is adequate to perform the functions assigned to the department. If no security personnel are used, the campus should be made reasonably secure by other means.
5. Data regarding security incidents are collected and receive periodic administrative review.

It should go without saying that institutional policies and disciplinary codes should have been promulgated long before they are needed. On many campuses, however, these policies exist piecemeal, and coordination of the ones that deal with campus crime is a function of top-level administration. One aspect of policy review critical to dealing with campus crime is clear assignment of decision making so that fateful decisions are not left by default to lower-level supervisors or campus security officers when the unexpected happens.

University Counsel

The assistance of university counsel is an absolute must in developing adequate policies and codes, and in evaluating campus risk factors. A word of caution: Just because someone is a lawyer is no assurance that he or she is skilled in matters of this sort. College and university law is a specialty, and competent counsel is needed. Someone fresh out of law school might be of some help, but not much. Law school is basically an endurance contest, in which skills at legal research are acquired. Law school certainly does not teach anyone to practice law, nor does it give the kind of savvy that is needed to size up and respond to campus problems.

Ideally, a campus lawyer would have at least five years of experience actually practicing law, and would be well versed in the legal fields of personnel, negligence, and, if it is a public institution, governmental operations. Obviously, familiarity with academe is desirable; the nuances and subtleties of campus life might otherwise be foreign, and perhaps problematic. A persuasive personality is important; much of a lawyer's work is negotiation, and the ability to daunt one's opposition often averts problems or turns potential losses into wins. Strong trial experience would be a real plus, even if the lawyer will not actually handle cases in court; someone who has not actually been a litigator will probably not be very good at evaluating potential court cases or preparing them for trial. Experience on the staff of a prosecuting attorney is among the best sort of experience for work in a public agency or institution.

A lawyer can be hired in two ways: either as a full-time staff member or under an hourly fee arrangement with a lawyer or law firm in private practice. Many institutions are finding that the former is less expensive; lawyers can be hired for the same sort of salary paid other administrators, and they can handle many campus duties, such as affirmative action officer, hearings officer, and so on, in addition to review and negotiation of contracts, leases, and personnel decisions. In some cases, lawyers are given half-time appointments as faculty members in fields in which they can teach, such as business or administration, criminal justice, or political science.

Most public institutions are represented by the state attorney general. While the staffs of attorneys general often include many excellent lawyers, they typically are spread far too thin. In some states, one, two, or a handful of lawyers are assigned to represent the entire state higher education system. The inadequacies of such an arrangement are obvious; the lawyers will have their hands full trying to keep up with existing litigation, will have little time to answer run-of-the-mill questions, and will have no time for a "preventive medicine" approach to campus legal problems. While attorneys general zealously guard their turf, they usually are glad to get some help so long as it does not threaten their ultimate authority. Accordingly, many public institutions have begun to hire lawyers as members of the university administration, giving them a title such as "executive assistant to the president." This lawyer then can handle day-to-day matters for the campus and act as liaison to the attorney general's office for litigation. In some cases, the attorney general may want to give the campus lawyer a special appointment as an assistant attorney general to handle specific campus litigation, with the understanding that the attorney general will retain ultimate responsibility and control over the matter.

In addition to a lawyer, the services of a professional risk manager can be of great help in assessing potential dangers in campus operations. Larger campuses, of course, have long had access to such services, but smaller institutions often have not. One good resource can be insurance companies and agencies that provide risk management consultation as a part of their services.

Changing the Law

Last, campus decision makers should keep in mind that onerous law and legal processes can be changed. So long as they remain within constitutional bounds, Congress and the state legislatures can alter substantive legal standards, court processes, principles of legal liability, and even insurance practices. College and university presidents and board members normally maintain relationships with political leaders for reasons related to appropriations, grants, and the like; these channels should likewise be used to seek appropriate changes in legal policies that hinder institutions in accomplishing their missions.

CAMPUS DISCIPLINE AND THE CRIMINAL

Where is the proper split between formal criminal charges and on-campus disciplinary proceedings? What if the two overlap? Often a student's egregious conduct will simultaneously violate both the state's criminal laws and the institution's code of student conduct. In other cases, a student may run afoul of the criminal laws, but in a manner and place not directly related to the college. How should campus decision makers respond?

It is entirely possible, and in many cases appropriate, for state and local criminal charges and campus disciplinary code proceedings to be maintained simultaneously against the same student, over the same matter. It is well-settled law that one does not, in itself, foreclose the other.[3]

Deference to the Criminal Courts

Where formal criminal charges are brought first, it probably is wise for college officials to examine the situation, seek advice from university counsel, and consult with the prosecuting attorney who is handling the matter before moving ahead. There are several reasons why this procedure is advisable.

First, it is possible that the campus action might adversely affect the formal criminal case, and thus the college or university might want to defer action on the matter until the criminal case is concluded, particularly if it will be resolved promptly. Because procedure is less formal at campus disciplinary hearings[4] and a person can be called as a witness against himself or herself, a student's constitutional rights against self-incrimination and freedom from unreasonable search and seizure in a subsequent criminal trial might be jeopardized by participation in the earlier campus proceeding. On the one hand, this situation could unfairly compromise an accused. On the other, it is conceivable that it might lead to the acquittal of a clearly guilty person, should a court hold that the basic unfairness would constitute a denial of due process of law.

In addition, the legal doctrine of collateral estoppel might be used to halt a criminal prosecution if the same issues were resolved in the defendant's favor in a related disciplinary proceeding at a state institution. Collateral estoppel bars relitigation of issues that have already been resolved between the parties, and if the state was unable to prevail in a civil proceeding with its lower burden of proof—proof of guilt by a mere preponderance of the evidence—then it could not be expected to meet the higher burden of proof beyond a reasonable doubt in a criminal proceeding.[5] Thus, were a student acquitted by a campus disciplinary panel, subsequent criminal proceedings might be estopped. It is quite rare, but there have been cases where courts held that acquittal in administrative proceedings brought by the state estopped subsequent criminal proceedings on the same matter.

Resolution of the matter by the courts. A second reason the institution may wish to defer disciplinary action is that the criminal case may resolve the matter by itself. If the student is acquitted, the institution may choose to drop the matter at that point, and a lot of trouble is avoided. On the other hand, if the student is convicted in criminal court or enters into a pretrial "diversion" arrangement or a plea bargain, withdrawal from the college or university may be arranged as one of the terms of the arrangement or probation. Pretrial diversion is a new sort of informal probation used in minor offenses; under it, an offender receives counseling or guidance, makes restitution, and meets other terms, and if he or she keeps a clean record for a period of time, the criminal charge simply is dropped. Like probation for a convicted offender, this arrangement readily lends itself to special terms desired by the college or university.

Cases in Which the College Must Move Quickly

Of course, if an erring student presents an immediate threat to campus safety, the institution must move boldly and quickly to exclude him or her. If the student is incarcerated, any immediate problem of the student's presence on campus is made moot, but the institution probably will want to pursue dismissal procedures so that the student cannot reappear at a later date and be entitled to automatic reenrollment. To make such a dismissal valid, caution must be taken to ensure that the suspension or expulsion is made for valid grounds under campus policy. Institutional policies or disciplinary codes should include a provision that a student may be excluded from the campus for the commission of any act or conviction of any crime that demonstrates that the student is a danger to the health or safety of others in the college community.

A 1987 study of campus violence by Towson State University revealed that 7 percent of the 764 colleges and universities sampled did not have policies that made possible an immediate suspension of a dangerous student.[6] In most cases, due process of law requires a "predeprivation" hearing.[7] However, in a case involving secondary students, the Supreme Court said that "[s]tudents whose presence poses a danger to persons or property or an ongoing threat of disrupting the academic process may be immediately removed from school."[8] Institutions that do not provide for immediate suspension in appropriate cases are remiss in their obligations to protect other members of the college community and may be creating civil liability for themselves.

What kind of circumstances might justify the suspension of a university student prior to a hearing? In *Davis v. Mann*, school authorities dismissed a dental student from a residency program before the student was provided a hearing, which the student argued was a denial of his right to due process. The court agreed that in most circumstances a student should receive a pre-termination rather than a post-termination hearing. Nevertheless, the court noted that the rule had some exceptions. In the case before the court, school authorities suspected the student of providing substandard care to patients, including two occasions in which his treatment allegedly could have caused serious harm. Given the dental school's interest in providing proper treatment for its patients and protecting their safety, the court concluded that immediate dismissal prior to a hearing was justified.[9]

Some institutions take the position that campus disciplinary actions should almost always move forward, regardless of pending criminal proceedings.[10] Criminal cases sometimes move very slowly, often taking more than a year to conclude. Even if an accused student presents no physical danger, the student's presence can be disruptive to campus activities. As one University of Maryland official explained, "On campus, where the violators, victims, and potential witnesses may be living close together, going to classes together, we don't want to wait a year [before beginning the campus disciplinary process]."[11]

In addition, fast disciplinary action can provide a way for a college or university to express its concern about campus security and criminal behavior. A campus administrator at the University of Texas at Austin stated his institution's policy whenever a serious infraction occurred. "Historically," he said, "more often than not we have waited for criminal charges to be disposed of before we proceeded. But with charges serious enough to warrant something like a permanent expulsion from the university, we want to get it done quickly. And particularly where a death is involved, we want the world to know [we] take it seriously."[12]

Attorney Participation in Campus Disciplinary Hearings

For the most part, courts have upheld the right of a student to have an attorney when defending against charges in a campus disciplinary proceeding, particularly if criminal charges are also pending over the same allegations. One federal appeals court, in the case of *Gabrilowitz v. Newman*, required the University of Rhode Island to permit a student charged with attempted rape of a female student to have counsel at his disciplinary hearing, even though university policy precluded lawyers at such hearings. To deprive him of counsel at the campus hearing deprived him of constitutional due process of law, the court held, because the evidence adduced against him at the hearing might be used against him in the criminal trial. The court noted that all the student was asking was that he be allowed the advice of counsel "when he throws his college degree into the balance against a possible loss of liberty." The opinion acknowledged that academic institutions have a significant interest in maintaining student disciplinary procedures and said the limited role of counsel it was requiring "would not be very intrusive. Counsel would be present only to safeguard appellee's rights at the criminal proceeding, not to affect the outcome of the disciplinary hearing. . . . Counsel should, however, be available to consult with appellee at all stages of the hearing, especially while appellee is being questioned."[13]

This approach received collateral approbation from another federal appeals court in a marijuana case involving a midshipman at the United States Naval Academy.[14] Similarly, where a midshipman at the Massachusetts Maritime Academy faced criminal charges of possession of hashish and amphetamines in New Orleans as well as academy drug charges, a federal trial court halted the academy's expulsion proceedings against him until either he could have right to counsel in the campus proceedings or the criminal charge was finally resolved.[15]

More recently, however, in *Osteen v. Henley*,[16] a varsity football player at Northern Illinois University, accused of assaulting two students outside a bar, lost his argument that he was denied the constitutional right to counsel at a university expulsion hearing. "Even if a student has a constitutional right to *consult* counsel . . . ," the Seventh Circuit Court of Appeals wrote, "we do not think he is entitled to be represented in the sense of having a lawyer who is permitted to examine or cross-examine witnesses, to submit and object to documents, to address the tribunal, and otherwise to perform the traditional function of a trial lawyer." To recognize such a right, the court continued, would turn campus disciplinary hearings into adversarial litigation. "The university would have to hire its own lawyer to prosecute these cases and no doubt lawyers would also be dragged in—from the law faculty or elsewhere—to serve as judges."[17] In the court's opinion, all this would increase the cost of the hearings and encourage bureaucratization of higher education.

Moreover, the court observed, the risk that the student was unjustly expelled was trivial. Indeed, it pointed out, the university would seem to have no incentive to rig disciplinary proceedings against a student whom it had wanted so much that it had given him an athletic scholarship. Finally, the court ruled that the consequences of an error—a two-year suspension—were not so serious as to justify all the due process protection afforded litigants in court.

Does *Osteen* conflict with *Gabrilowitz* and other court opinions that recognized a student's right to consult an attorney in a campus hearing? Probably not. As the Seventh Circuit Court pointed out in *Osteen*, the football player was not denied the right to *consult* counsel in the disciplinary proceedings, only the right to full courtroom-style legal representation. Had the athlete been denied all access to a lawyer, *Osteen* might have been decided differently.

What then is the prudent thing to do with regard to permitting students to be represented by lawyers at campus disciplinary proceedings? When a student faces criminal charges while campus disciplinary proceedings are taking place, it seems wise to permit the student to have counsel present, at least for purposes of consultation. Indeed, one commentator has argued that there is a compelling constitutional rationale for permitting a student's counsel to have at least limited participation at *any* disciplinary proceeding, without regard to whether criminal charges are pending.[18]

More active attorney involvement does not seem warranted by the present state of the law. The same commentator also noted that courts have generally granted universities the right to determine the bounds of attorney involvement in campus disciplinary proceedings. In a 1987 case, for example, two veterinary students accused of cheating on an examination attended a disciplinary hearing accompanied by counsel, but neither they nor their counsel were permitted to directly cross-examine adverse witnesses. Instead, all questions were posed through a presiding officer, who then directed the questions to the witnesses. The Eleventh Circuit Court of Appeals found no constitutional infirmity with this procedure, although it acknowledged that the opportunity to directly question the witnesses might have been valuable to the accused students.[19]

Off-Campus Criminal Behavior

A related issue is whether an institution may exclude a student for criminal conduct that has no nexus with the campus or collegiate activities. Obviously, basic constitutional rights of property in education, equal protection of the laws, and due process of law, on the one hand, and preservation of institutional safety, morale, and reputation, on the other, are involved in this issue.

It was argued by one campus observer during the 1960s that the mere fact that a person committing a crime is also a student gives the university no grounds for imposing discipline. "The private life of a student is his own affair; the non-university connected conduct of a student is not the affair of a university . . . (unless it involves) protecting the whole university community against dangers which particular students may have shown themselves to constitute."[20] A Vietnam-era policy statement by the American Civil Liberties Union, while upholding the right of students to demonstrate to the point of arrest on political issues, acknowledged that a college might take internal punitive measures against a student when "he has acted in a way which adversely affects or seriously interferes with its normal educational function, or which injures or endangers the welfare of any of its members."[21]

The courts, however, have given broad backing to the right of institutions to dismiss students for serious off-campus misconduct. In 1982, a Pennsylvania court upheld the suspension of a student at Clarion State College who had been convicted by a campus conduct board of trespass and improper behavior at a private party at an off-campus residence. The court declared: "obviously, a college has a vital interest in the character of its students, and may regard off-campus behavior as a reflection of a student's character and his fitness to be a member of the student body."[22] A federal court in Virginia in 1976 upheld the constitutionality of a Virginia Tech policy that permitted sanctions for off-campus drug possession by students. The policy in question created an irrebuttable presumption that off-campus drug possession detrimentally affected university life.[23] Several decades ago, the Texas Court of Civil Appeals upheld the suspension of a West Texas State University student for speeding off-campus. He had earlier been placed on probation for speeding on the campus.[24]

In 1989, the attorney general of Maryland issued an opinion involving the University of Maryland that agreed with the approach of the courts. The opinion held that the university was empowered to discipline students for off-campus misconduct that was detrimental to university interests, including drug offenses and disruptive, assaultive behavior.[25]

The same principles should apply to private schools as apply to public institutions, subject to any provisions to the contrary in an institution's rules or contracts with its students. Private institutions, especially religiously affiliated ones, usually have broad powers to exclude students for private conduct, so long as the institutions follow their own rules and conduct codes.

Discipline of Employees

Similar principles govern the handling of criminal matters involving faculty and other campus employees. While student codes obviously do not apply, employee handbooks, collective bargaining agreements, governing board policies, and the like often establish rights and procedures that affect employee discipline.

Occasionally, a higher education institution may allow an employee who is accused of some impropriety to resign rather than proceed with a disciplinary hearing or termination procedures. It is sometimes in the best interest of the institution and the employee to resolve an incident in this way. For example, the facts may be so tangled that a clear determination of culpability may seem unlikely; or the publicity over the allegations may have been so intense that the employee can no longer be effective, regardless of the outcome of any fact-finding proceeding. It is customary in these instances for the interested parties to prepare and sign a settlement agreement that spells out their rights and obligations.

Campus officials and their counsel should remember that a public institution's settlement agreements are considered public documents under many states' open records laws and must be disclosed if a request is made by the press or a member of the public. For example, when the University of Maine entered into a confidential settlement agreement with a former basketball coach, the Maine Supreme Court ruled that the agreement had to be made available to a publishing company that requested it. (One section of the agreement, concerning medical information about the former employee, was protected from disclosure by a statutory exception to Maine's open records law.) "[T]he public has a right to know the terms upon which a public employer has settled with a resigning contract employee," the Maine court said.[26]

University counsel should draft any settlement agreement as if the terms will ultimately be made available to the press. And the campus executive who authorizes such an agreement should consider the public reaction if the settlement terms become public knowledge. Generous terms to a departing employee may make sense to an institution based on the facts of a particular case or the cost of pursuing litigation, particularly if it is assumed that the settlement terms are kept secret. Settlement terms may be difficult to justify, however, if they are reported in the press and the public interprets the institution's settlement provisions as unjust enrichment to an employee who departs under a cloud of controversy.[27]

Finally, college officials should be careful when negotiating with an employee about the terms of a termination not to appear to be pressuring an employee to resign. For example, in a Florida case, a school principal supposedly told a teacher he would recommend her dismissal unless she accepted an unpaid leave of absence. A Florida appellate court ruled that a forced leave of absence under those terms was "tantamount to an unlawful firing or dismissal," and awarded the teacher back pay for the period of the unpaid leave.[28]

STUDENT CRIME RECORDS—OPEN OR CLOSED?

The competing natures of public records and student privacy rights may clash when it comes to campus crime. Most public records and other official activities are open to public scrutiny under so-called state sunshine laws and federal and state freedom of information statutes. The citizenry's "right to know" is zealously asserted by the news media. At the same time, some state education laws protect student privacy, and all concerned with educational administration are aware of the pervasive presence of the Family Rights and Privacy Act (FERPA), often called the Buckley Amendment.[29] In essence, it prevents educational institutions from releasing personally identifiable information in "educational records" about a student to most third parties without the student's permission.

What FERPA Does and Does Not Cover

Just how far-reaching is FERPA? First of all, it does not preclude release of "directory information" about a student, which, the act provides, encompasses a student's name, address, telephone number, date and place of birth, major field of study, participation in officially recognized activities and sports—including weight and height of members of athletic teams—date of attendance, degrees and awards received, and the most recent educational agency or institution attended by the student. However, every institution is required to give "public notice" of the categories of such information it designates as "directory information" and must allow a reasonable period of time after such notice for a student to inform the institution that any or all of the information designated should not be released.

Other sorts of information from educational records cannot be released, under FERPA, without student consent, except in two kinds of special cases. First, information in educational records may be released in response to a subpoena or court order. Even then, the institution must take reasonable steps to notify the student or parent in advance of compliance with the order or subpoena. Accordingly, several cases have held that this legislation does not prohibit release of information where it is needed as evidence in a criminal proceeding.[30] The other exception is an emergency situation that presents physical danger to other persons. The federal regulations interpreting the act allow release, even without a court order or subpoena, to appropriate parties in a health or safety emergency if disclosure of the information is necessary for safeguarding human health or life.[31] This provision would appear to justify disregard of FERPA limitations in a bona fide emergency that immediately threatens human safety.

Law Enforcement and FERPA

A further wrinkle exists as to records kept by campus police or security forces. In its original form, FERPA stated that records kept by a campus "law enforcement unit" were not covered by the law if four qualifications were met. First, the records had to be maintained solely for law enforcement purposes. Second, the security unit could not have access to regular institutional educational records. Third, law enforcement records had to be kept "apart" from regular institutional educational records. Fourth, the law enforcement records could "not [be] made available to persons other than law enforcement officials of the same jurisdiction."

FERPA's provision for dealing with campus law enforcement records was poorly drawn and difficult to interpret. Several universities relied on it, however, as the basis for refusing to disclose campus police records about crimes in which students were involved. Institutions were supported in their position by the U.S. Department of Education, which took the position in several instances that the release of campus crime records containing person-ally identifiable student information could lead to the loss of federal funds.[32]

By the early 1990s, campus and professional journalists had begun suing to obtain access to campus crime records. In addition, there was growing senti-ment that the public had a right to know the details of campus criminal activity that involved students. Some critics of FERPA charged that colleges and universities were using the law to hide significant campus crime problems from the public.

In a 1991 decision, *Bauer v. Kincaid*,[33] a federal trial judge decided that campus crime records were not educational records under FERPA, and he ordered Southwest Missouri State University to make them available to the editor of the university's student newspaper in compliance with the Missouri open records law. "The fact that the statute specifically exempts records maintained for law enforcement purposes demonstrates that Congress did not intend to treat criminal investigation and incident reports as educational records," the court wrote. The court added that it found nothing in FERPA's legislative history that indicated an intent to prevent the disclosure of campus police records that contained students' names or other personally identifiable information.[34]

The *Bauer* court also found constitutional problems with the position that FERPA granted special privacy status to student criminals, victims, or witnesses. In the court's view, such an interpretation "creates an irrational classification" in violation of the equal protection component of the Fifth Amendment.

Moreover, the court added, withholding access to campus crime records violated the First Amendment, since freedom of speech includes not only the right to speak and print, but also the right to receive information. "It is . . . surely one of the purposes of the First Amendment," the court reasoned, "to enable the public to scrutinize the actions of government through access to government information. . . ."[35]

Shortly after the *Bauer* decision, Congress, with the U.S. Department of Education's support, amended FERPA to state that law enforcement records are not educational records. Thus, it now seems clear that the public's access to crime records is not restricted by FERPA. This legislative development is in harmony with passage of the Student Right-to-Know and Campus Security Act (discussed below), which expresses a policy view that students are entitled to considerable information about the incidence of crime on their campuses to better be able to protect themselves from becoming crime victims.

It should also be noted, that although the press is often the party seeking disclosure of campus records, the press has no more right to information protected by the Buckley Amendment than does any other private party. Nevertheless, if the information is available to the press from a source other than the educational records, the Buckley Amendment is not applicable and the information may be printed.[36]

FERPA and Campus Disciplinary Proceedings

Although the 1992 amendment made clear that law enforcement records are not subject to FERPA, a controversy remained about whether student disciplinary records enjoyed FERPA privacy protection. This controversy is illustrated by a 1993 case in which the University of Georgia's student newspaper tried to obtain the records of a campus disciplinary hearing involving hazing allegations against two fraternities. The newspaper claimed the records were subject to Georgia's open records act and had to be released. The university argued that the records were covered by FERPA's privacy provisions and could not be made public.

In *Red & Black Publishing Company v. Board of Regents*,[37] the Georgia Supreme Court ruled that the documents were public records, which the student newspaper had the right to inspect. Records of campus disciplinary proceedings were not "educational records" under FERPA, the court declared. Rather, they were more akin to records kept for law enforcement purposes, which Congress had specifically exempted from FERPA. Further-more, the Georgia court held that the disciplinary proceedings themselves were covered by Georgia's open meetings act and could not be held in secret. *Red & Black Publishing Company* symbolizes the tension between opposing policy considerations about whether campus disciplinary proceedings should be kept confidential. Some would argue that the public has the right to know how colleges and universities are handling disciplinary matters, just as it has the right to know about campus crime incidents. Publicity helps make sure that student offenders receive equal treatment for similar infractions and that campus crime is not kept hidden to avoid bad publicity. Some university administrators, however, argue that publicizing these proceedings may dis-courage students from filing complaints and detract from the purpose of campus disciplinary procedures, which is to educate and guide a student offender, not just mete out punishment.[38]

The Student Right-to-Know and Campus Security Act contains a provision permitting institutions to make the results of campus disciplinary proceedings known to the victim. And the Ramstad Amendment requires both the accuser and the accused to be notified of the outcome of disciplinary proceedings that allege a sexual assault. In 1995, however, the U.S. Department of Education issued new regulations, making it clear that campus disciplinary records are covered by FERPA and cannot be disclosed to the public without the consent of students involved. The department attempted to reconcile its position with *Red & Black* by noting that the disputed records in that suit involved student organizations, not students.

In short, under the present state of the law, as interpreted by the U.S. Department of Education, student disciplinary records may be disclosed to alleged victims in accordance with the statutory provisions just noted, but they may not be disclosed to a wider audience. The department acknowledged public pressure for full disclosure of these records in the interest of public safety, and it offered to work with Congress to amend FERPA further in the interest of balancing student privacy interests with the public's right to broader access to campus crime information.

Consequences of FERPA Violations

It should be remembered that the Buckley Amendment does not create direct, private legal rights. It is simply a proviso attached to institutional eligibility for federal funding, and the penalty for failure to abide by its terms is that an institution might lose that eligibility.

The courts have been unanimous in holding that FERPA does not give anyone a private right to bring a damage suit against an institution or person who has failed to abide by the terms of the Buckley Amendment.[39] Neverthe-less, a few courts have ruled that FERPA violations can be the basis of an action for damages under 42 U.S.C. Section 1983. In *Fay v. South Colonie Central School District,*[40] the Second Circuit Court of Appeals upheld a judgment under Section 1983 against a school district that had violated FERPA by refusing to provide a father with access to some of his children's educational records. The trial court had awarded the father only nominal damages, but the Second Circuit Court ruled that the father should be allowed to present evidence of his compensatory damages.

In *Tarka v. Cunningham,*[41] in which a University of Texas student filed suit in a dispute over a physics grade, the Fifth Circuit Court also ruled that an action under 42 U.S.C. 1983 could be premised on a claimed FERPA violation. Nevertheless, the court wrote, FERPA does not give a student the right to sue over a professor's grading process, and it affirmed the trial court's dismissal of the student's suit.

At least two other federal trial courts have ruled that a FERPA violation may be the basis for a Section 1983 lawsuit for damages. In the first case, a woman who had been admitted to the University of Arkansas School of Law sought access to campus records concerning a sexual incident in a university dormitory. The trial court dismissed the case, but not before ruling that a plaintiff could assert a FERPA violation as the basis for a lawsuit under Section 1983.[42] In the second case, some students and former students at Rutgers University challenged the manner in which students' names and social security numbers were disseminated. The court ruled that Section 1983 was an appropriate vehicle for challenging a FERPA violation, and it issued a preliminary injunction prohibiting the university from distributing class ros-ters with students' names and undisguised social security numbers affixed.[43]

Individual states may have their own student record privacy statutes or constitutional privacy provisions that apply to student records. For example, a California appellate court has held that under some circumstances a university's improper disclosure of a student's records might create a private right to sue for invasion of privacy under California state laws.[44] Campus decision makers, with consultation from university counsel, should acquaint themselves with state laws and judicial opinions pertaining to student records, as well as local applications of FERPA.

CRIME REPORTING OBLIGATIONS: THE STUDENT RIGHT-TO-KNOW AND CAMPUS SECURITY ACT OF 1990

FERPA, which was passed in 1974, furthers a public policy objective in favor of student privacy. But in 1990, Congress passed legislation that expressed a very different policy objective—the policy that the public has the right to obtain information about campus crime, including crimes that involve stu-dents. In passing the Student Right-to-Know and Campus Security Act,

Congress imposed sweeping obligations on higher education institutions to gather information about crimes that occur on their campuses and to make this information available to students, employees, and the public.

Even before Congress acted, a few states had passed their own campus crime reporting laws, but Congress found that these state efforts lacked uniformity and were inadequate to meet the "campus crime challenge."[45] Described as a "consumer protection bill for students," the act was intended to make campus crime information available to students so that they could take action to protect themselves against becoming victims.[46] The law applies to all colleges and universities that receive federal funds.

Overview of the Campus Security Act

The Student Right-to-Know and Campus Security Act has three parts. First, the act addressed a provision of federal law that prevented colleges and universities from disclosing the results of campus disciplinary hearings. Institutions may now release the hearing results of disciplinary proceedings involving violent crime to the victims of those crimes.[47]

Second, the act requires postsecondary institutions to collect information about campus crime and to publish it on an annual basis. Specifically, institutions are required to disseminate an "annual security report" to students and staff which contains the following information:

- a statement of current campus policies for handling campus crimes or other emergencies, including procedures for receiving reports from students and employees;
- a statement of current policies for maintaining campus security, including security arrangements for campus housing and off-campus housing maintained by fraternities, sororities, or other student organizations;
- a statement of current policies concerning campus law enforcement, including
  a) the enforcement authority of campus security forces and their working relationship with state and local law enforcement agencies; and
  b) policies that encourage prompt and accurate reporting of campus crimes to law enforcement authorities;
- a description of the type and frequency of programs designed to inform students and employees of campus security procedures and to encourage students and employees to take responsibility for their own safety and the safety of others;
- a description of programs designed to inform students and employees about crime prevention;

- a statement of policy concerning the monitoring and recording of criminal activity at off-campus student organizations, such as fraternities and sororities;
- a description of policies and procedures regarding possession, use, and sale of alcoholic beverages and illegal drugs;
- a description of available drug and alcohol abuse programs.

In addition, the annual security report must contain statistics on the occurrence of certain crimes during the current and two preceding school years. Specifically, higher education institutions must provide statistics on murder, forcible and nonforcible sex offenses, robbery, aggravated assault, burglary, and motor vehicle theft. Institutions must also report statistics concerning arrests for liquor law violations, drug abuse violations, and weapons possession.

Furthermore, the Student Right-to-Know and Campus Security Act requires postsecondary institutions to make timely reports to the campus community on major crimes that are brought to the attention of campus or local police and that are considered to be a threat to other students or employees. The law requires not only that these reports be timely but that they be provided "in a manner . . . that will aid in the prevention of similar occurrences."[48]

Finally, the act requires colleges and universities to provide the secretary of education with their crime statistics at the secretary's request. Higher education institutions must comply with the act to continue receiving federal funds.[49] Institutions that fail to comply can be fined $25,000 for every offense.[50]

In April 1994, the U.S. Department of Education issued final regulations pertaining to the Campus Security Act and the Ramstad Amendment (discussed in Chapter 7). These regulations specify that an institution's policies for responding to campus sexual offenses must include a statement that the institution will change a victim's academic and living situations after an alleged sexual offense if the victim so requests and a change is reasonably available. In addition, an institution's disciplinary procedures must give the accuser and the accused the same right to have others present during proceedings involving an alleged sexual offense. The regulations also provide that a victim of a sex offense must be told of the importance of preserving evidence for the proof of a criminal offense.[51]

While federal regulations for the Campus Security Act were being promulgated, a controversy arose in the higher education community about the crime reporting obligations of student service personnel and counselors under the new law. If, on the one hand, these people were excused from reporting, an institution's annual crime report might seriously understate the amount of crime that was actually occurring. On the other hand, some argued that requiring campus counselors to report crimes they learned about in their counseling relationships might jeopardize the confidentiality of communications between counselors and clients.[52]

When it issued the final regulations for the Campus Security Act, the Department of Education resolved these competing interests through a compromise. When they issue their annual crime reports, colleges and universities are required to include crimes reported not only to law enforcement authorities but also crimes reported to campus officials "who have significant responsibility for student and campus activities."[53] Thus, crimes that are reported to deans, residence hall directors, or other staff members involved in student affairs must be included in each institution's annual crime report. Presumably, student counselors have the obligation to contribute to these annual reports as well. However, individuals who have "significant counseling responsibilities" are not required to make contemporaneous reports of crimes they learn about in their counseling relationships. Thus, counselors are exempted from higher education institutions' obligation to make timely reports to the campus community about crimes that may pose a threat to staff or students.

Impact of Campus Security Act on Institutional Liability

In the first annual campus security statements required by the new law, colleges and universities reported 7,500 incidents of violent crime, including 30 murders and more than 1,800 robberies.[54] Large institutions, those having 5,000 students or more, accounted for a larger share of these crime incidents. In their first annual report, the large institutions reported 18 murders and 1,210 robberies. In the second year, large institutions reported 1,353 robberies, up 12 percent, and 17 murders.[55] Nationwide, institutions reported nearly 1,000 rapes the first year.

During the first two years in which crime reports were made, critics charged that some institutions were underreporting their crimes or were simply electing not to make arrests for certain offenses to keep their crime totals down. There were complaints that institutions with aggressive campus police forces made their colleges look bad in comparison with institutions with more lax enforcement policies. Others expressed concern that the raw crime statistics encouraged unfair comparisons between dissimilar institutions, comparing large colleges to small ones, for example, or an urban university with one located in a rural setting.[56]

In addition, by only requiring data about on-campus crime, the new law does not give students information about crime patterns in the neighborhoods around colleges, neighborhoods where a lot of college students often live. One commentator has argued for a change in the law that would require institutions to report off-campus crime statistics, including crimes against students and against the population in general.[57]

It is too early to tell whether the Student Right-to-Know and Campus Security Act will increase colleges' exposure to liability. Although the law does not express that as its purpose, it seems possible that the law's requirements may be cited by plaintiff crime victims as the standard of care, breach of which would form the basis for liability. For example, the law requires institutions to make timely reports to the campus community of crimes that might constitute a danger to others. A college that failed to publicize the presence of a serial rapist, to take one example, might face liability to a victim who could have taken precautions had she been informed that a dangerous sex offender was operating in her area.

And, as one commentator has pointed out, the very fact that institutions are now required to collect data and maintain records about campus crime could be the means of showing that a particular crime was foreseeable. If an institution reported a high number of campus robberies or aggravated assaults, it might be considered to be on notice of a serious crime problem. If it then failed to take action to protect students and staff from crimes that were considered to be foreseeable, liability could be imposed for the injuries that resulted from those crimes.[58]

LIBEL, SLANDER, AND CAMPUS CRIME

Akin to campus crime record problems are issues of defamation that may result from accusations of criminal wrongdoing. People are sometimes hesitant to report criminal behavior because they are afraid of being sued for defamation. While some such risk is admittedly always a possibility, so long as good faith and good judgment are used, the risk of losing such a suit is certainly minimal.

Defamation may be defined simply as false words that tend to injure the reputation of another. A spoken defamation is called slander; a written defamation is known as a libel. There must be a "publication"—some sort of communication of the defamatory words to a third party. No defamation is committed when the communication is only between two parties, no matter how harsh or untrue the words that are said, because no injury to reputation results.

Injury to someone's feelings is not a libel or slander, nor are words that are clearly understood to be in jest. For example, in a New Jersey case, a faculty member brought a defamation suit against a school and school officials based on a picture appearing in the student yearbook that arguably implied she proposed to have sex with another faculty member. The picture depicted the plaintiff sitting next to another teacher and was accompanied by a caption that read "Not tonight Ms. Salek. I have a headache."

The trial court dismissed the suit, and the appellate court affirmed. "There is no libel," the appellate court said, "where, as here, the material is susceptible of only non-defamatory meaning and is clearly understood as being parody, satire, humor, or fantasy."[59]

It is often said that one cannot be successfully sued for defamation for merely expressing an opinion, but in a 1990 case, the Supreme Court let it be known that this may not always be true. In *Milkovich v. Lorain Journal Co.*,[60] the Court made clear that an expression of opinion that implies a false, factual assertion enjoys no constitutional protection. In other words, a person does not escape liability for libel or slander simply by attaching the words "in my opinion . . ." to an otherwise actionable defamatory statement.

Defenses to Defamation Claims

There are a number of defenses to a defamation charge, the best-known one being that the thing said was the truth. In most states, the truth is an absolute defense; something that is true about someone, though harmful to that person, does not legally defame. In recent years, however, some courts have come to recognize a new type of legal claim, invasion of privacy, which can, in some limited cases, affix liability upon someone who recklessly or maliciously discloses private facts about another person, even if they are true.

Consent is another defense to a defamation claim. If the person injured by the information is the one who actually caused it to be published to the third party or parties, then he or she has consented. For instance, one who asks someone else to write a letter of recommendation concerning him or her to a prospective employer will probably be held to have consented to what is in the letter, so long as it does not contain malicious falsehoods.

The law divides defamed people into two categories, private citizens and public figures. When a person voluntarily thrusts himself or herself into the public eye, by seeking or holding public office or otherwise becoming a well-known public figure, he or she must expect to be the object of criticism from the press and other citizens. For the public figure to recover for a defamation, it must be shown that the defamer acted with specific malice toward the person, malice being actual knowledge that the statement was false, or with reckless disregard for whether it was true or not. Private citizens need not prove that the defamation was published with malice; merely that it was false and harmful will usually suffice.

High-level college and university administrators probably fall into the public figure category; and thus they would not win a defamation suit unless the false statement about them was maliciously made. With regard to professors, the law is less clear. Courts have split on the question of whether secondary school teachers are public officials for defamation purposes,[61] although one recent court has held that they are.[62] A federal court in

Louisiana ruled that a basketball coach at Delgado Community College was not a public figure for purposes of a defamation suit.[63] Certainly professors would fit within the public figure category if they stepped onto the public stage or became well known.

While not technically a defense, mitigation will improve a defendant's position and reduce potential damages. Mitigation usually consists of a retraction, published to the same audience that heard the original defamatory material.

Qualified Privilege

In addition to the traditional defenses, a sort of immunity from defamation actions exists under the "qualified privilege" doctrine for many persons who make the questioned statements as part of their business. This defense is available to persons who act in good faith, on matters of official or business concern, and who communicate the information only by proper limited means to proper parties who likewise have a legitimate reason for hearing it. Thus, persons who in good faith pass along to appropriate officials reports of wrongdoing about a person would be entitled to claim "qualified privilege" if the information later turned out to be erroneous, and a defamation action were brought. In a campus setting, the doctrine probably would apply to students who reported crimes or campus offenses and administrators who passed the information along to other officials, so long as the communications were made only to persons who needed to know.

The qualified privilege doctrine, then, centers in good faith and communication to a limited number of people who need to know the information. If there is proof of malice, the qualified privilege defense is not available. In one campus case, *Melton v. Bow*, it was held that the defense was not available to an administrator who made false accusations about a student.[64] Ultimately, the Georgia Supreme Court upheld the jury's award of $200,000 against the administrator. The case began when the student, Bow, reported he had received a W-2 tax form for earnings as a student at the University of Georgia at a time when he was no longer working there. Even after a university investigation showed that another person, an embezzler, was responsible, a university official continued to make defamatory statements about Bow to numerous persons not officially involved in the matter. Among the accusations were that Bow had stolen hot plates from a laboratory, was a liar, and was in trouble with the Internal Revenue Service. The court's opinion noted that the defense is available to public administrators who are carrying out their duties, so long as the communications are made only to proper persons; it is not available where the communications are "a mere cloak for venting private malice."

Other Issues in Campus Defamation

An additional campus problem resulting from defamation suits against persons who bring criminal charges is the provision of counsel for student defendants. Occasionally, a student who accuses another of wrongdoing will wind up being sued for defamation over the accusation, along with university administrators who acted upon the report. At public institutions, the campus administrators who are sued in such cases usually will be represented by the attorney general or other attorneys for the state, but these lawyers generally are prohibited from representing students, because students are not state employees. Several states are now exploring the possibility of changing state law so that the attorney general can defend the students in such cases; other states are looking at provision of insurance that will pay legal costs as a part of campus student services. If students are indigent, they may qualify for representation by legal aid attorneys.

A corollary issue is the payment of judgments in such a case. Should a student or administrator lose a defamation case, he or she might have to pay the judgment personally because insurance policies, and state law in the case of public institutions, sometimes preclude payment for actions that were "intentional" wrongs, rather than just negligent acts. Defamation might be categorized as an intentional wrong. Special insurance coverage can be purchased for defamation claims, and administrators would be wise to review the protection that is available to them for defamation claims through their employment or under personal policies.

COMMUNITY RELATIONS AND CAMPUS CRIME

A campus crime can be big news, and higher education leaders can expect to be contacted by the press about any serious crime that affects their institution. A terse "no comment" or the failure to be forthcoming may give the impression that the institution is trying to hide bad news from the public.

One commentator noted that most education administrators were trained in research techniques, and they are often reluctant to comment about matters that are still being investigated. "They tend to be cautious, to want to wait until all the facts are in and analyzed."[65] University officials should remember that news reporters need to get up-to-date information as it becomes available to do their jobs. Unanswered telephone calls and cryptic responses to reporters' questions may create bad press relations that will last beyond the current crisis. University officials should also bear in mind that the public has the right to be kept informed about the way a public institution responds to unfolding events.

This commentator also pointed out that education administrators often appear to speak defensively about a crisis when their first communication is a response to outside questions. "Administrators who make it a point to bring up an issue first can introduce it in the tone and context most comfortable to the organization and the spokesperson."[66]

Of course, as the preceding pages have pointed out, campus decision makers are often constrained in what they can say about a recent crime. A victim's privacy, fairness to the accused, the need to avoid jeopardizing a criminal investigation, and reasonable concerns about defamation all weigh in favor of caution when communicating with the public about a campus crime incident. Nevertheless, within these constraints there is often a great deal of information that a university can and should convey. For example, publicizing the institution's response to a criminal act may reassure various constituencies that appropriate action is being taken. And, perhaps more importantly, a serious crime incident can provide an opportunity for campus leaders to educate students and staff about ways they can avoid becoming a victim of a similar incident in the future.

MAKING IT WORSE: INCRIMINATING ONESELF

Probably the worst thing that a campus decision maker could do in the handling of campus crime would be to so interfere in the processes of public justice that he or she becomes a criminal too. Potential problems develop where crimes are not reported to proper authorities, or where an attempt is made to avoid or thwart a criminal investigation or prosecution.

At ancient common law, a person who stifled a prosecution by failing to report a crime in return for a reward or a bribe was guilty of the crime itself as an accessory after the fact. Those who actively concealed a crime without receiving "consideration"—a compensation or reward—for it could be guilty of a separate crime called "misprision."[67]

Today, punishment as an accessory or for misprision has largely been replaced by state statutes against compounding crimes or obstructing justice. In some instances, such as child abuse, state statutes now make it a criminal offense to fail to report a possible crime even though no consideration is received for the failure. In the past, charges of this sort were rare. Yet, with the great increase in crime in our society and the interest that many organizations and institutions in our society, particularly high-profile institutions like colleges and universities, have in avoiding adverse publicity, it is predictable that instances of attempted coverups will come to light and result in prosecution. The "consideration" received by a campus administrator for covering up a crime need not be money; any personal advantage or benefit could be sufficient to bring a coverup within the purview of the misprision-type statutes.

The Tendency to Hush It Up

College and university administrators have many reasons to want to avoid adverse publicity about their institutions. Reports of crime on campus discourage potential students and faculty members, and everyone in the business today knows the necessity of "keeping up the numbers" of enrollees in order to justify budgets and programs. Criminal investigations take up much time and are fraught with potential disaster for an administrator who bungles things or "misspeaks" to the press. Thus, it might be very attractive to administrators to try to cover up a cheating scandal, drug abuse or sexual assault by an athletic star, or even embezzlement by institutional employees, but campus decision makers must remember that they do so at their own peril.

Obstruction, Perjury, and Extortion

Closely related to misprision is the crime of obstruction of justice. The offense applies to those who hinder the criminal justice process, such as by destroying evidence or persuading witnesses not to appear. The University of Maryland's basketball coach, Charles "Lefty" Driesell, was investigated by the Prince George's County Grand Jury for possibly obstructing justice by tampering with evidence after the drug death of star player Len Bias. The grand jury did not indict, but the state's attorney called Driesell's actions in the matter "stupid."[68]

Perjury—the willful giving of false information under oath—is a related problem area. Perjury is an extremely serious felony. Likewise, subornation of perjury—the procuring of someone to testify falsely—is an equally serious felony. Statutes against "false swearing" are similar and apply to any statement made under oath, not just in court, but even in a notarized document.

The handling of criminal matters on campus provides one other potential problem area for the administrator: the risk of being accused of extortion. American law precludes imprisonment for civil debt, and using the threat of a criminal prosecution as a club to force someone to pay money or do anything else could constitute criminal extortion. At the same time, extortionate behavior may result in civil liability. For example, some courts have condemned the routine use by merchants of criminal "bad check" warrants to collect on checks that have been "bounced" by a bank, unless it can be shown the check was given with true criminal intent. After all, checks may "bounce" as a result of other, noncriminal factors, such as a mistake by the bank, an innocent error in the person's accounting, and so forth. When a man committed suicide with a shotgun after a constable arrived to arrest him on such a "bad check" warrant, the Mississippi Supreme Court ruled that the man's heirs could collect in a malicious prosecution suit.[69] The court labeled the matter a misuse of the criminal courts to collect private, civil debts.

CONCLUSION

When a serious crime takes place on campus, college decision makers must respond quickly. If the perpetrator is a student or employee, the institution must decide whether to begin the campus disciplinary process or await the outcome of criminal proceedings. If the decision is to move forward with campus discipline, care must be taken to ensure that wrongdoing is competently investigated and aggressively pursued, while at the same time maintaining a fair and objective hearing process where an accused student or employee can present a defense.

If a campus crime poses a continuing threat to others, the Student Right-to-Know and Campus Security Act requires campus officials to inform the entire campus community about what occurred. If the crime is a sex offense, federal law requires the institution to provide the victim with specific information, including the existence of counseling services, options for reporting the crime to law enforcement authorities, and the importance of preserving evidence for prosecution.

Finally, campus administrators and law enforcement officers will be asked to field questions from the press, parents, and the public; this effort will require a delicate balance of informing the public about matters of legitimate concern while protecting, to the maximum extent possible, the privacy of crime victims and the accused.

This whole process will go more smoothly if preparations for responding to a crime are made before it occurs. First, it is wise to settle on an institutional policy about what kinds of infractions will be resolved internally and what kinds will be turned over to the police. This policy is especially important in cases involving sexual misconduct, where it is clear that serious offenses should be handled primarily by the criminal authorities. Hearing procedures for students and employees should be in place, and the people who serve as investigators, tribunals, and appellate officers should be trained in their responsibilities and thoroughly understand their roles.

Even an institution too small to have a press officer should select some campus employee to handle communications with the press. This person need not be a public relations specialist, but he or she should be comfortable answering questions from reporters, skilled in developing press releases or other public communications, and capable of explaining the college's obligations to protect the privacy of the victim and the accused as well as its obligation to provide due process to any student or employee who is subjected to campus discipline.

More and more, what can and cannot be disclosed to the public about campus crime is determined by legal considerations: FERPA, the Student Right-to-Know and Campus Security Act, defamation law, and state open records laws. Campus administrators and their legal counsels must become familiar with these legal constraints if they are to successfully navigate through the shoals of conflicting legal and policy considerations: the public's right to know about campus crime and the privacy rights of students and staff members, whether they are crime victims, witnesses, or the accused.

NOTES

1. See Gerard A. Fowler, "The Legal Relationship between the American College Student and the College: An Historical Perspective and the Renewal of a Proposal," 13 *Journal of Law and Education* 401-16 (July 1984).
2. "Achieving Reasonable Campus Security," Resource Document No. 2 (Washington, D.C.: American Council on Education, 1985).
3. *Hart v. Ferris State College,* 557 F.Supp. 1379 (W.D. Mich. 1983); *Nzuve v. Castleton State College,* 335 A.2d 321 (Vt. 1975); *Paine v. Board of Regents,* 355 F.Supp. 199 (W.D. Texas 1972), *aff'd,* 474 F.2d 1397 (5th Cir. 1973); *Furutani v. Ewigleban,* 297 F.Supp. 1163 (N.D. Cal. 1969). See also *Picozzi v. Sandalow,* 623 F.Supp. 1571 (E.D. Mich. 1986), *aff'd without op.,* 827 F.2d 770 (6th Cir. 1987).
4. It has been noted that college disciplinary regulations need not be drawn with the same precision as a criminal code. *Shamloo v. Mississippi State Board of Trustees of Institutions of Higher Learning,* 620 F.2d 516 (5th Cir. 1980).
5. Charles H. Whitebread and Christopher Slobogin, *Criminal Procedure,* 2d ed. (Mineola, N.Y.: Foundation Press, 1986), Sec. 30.04(3), p. 745.
6. "Campus Violence Survey" (unpublished compilation), Office of Student Services, Towson State University, 1987.
7. *Cleveland Board of Education v. Loudermill,* 470 U.S. 532, 105 S. Ct. 1487, 84 L. Ed.2d 494 (1985).
8. *Goss v. Lopez,* 419 U.S. 565, 582 (1975).
9. *Davis v. Mann,* 721 F. Supp. 796 (S.D. Miss. 1988).
10. One model disciplinary code provides that campus disciplinary action "will normally proceed" during pendency of criminal charges. Gary Pavela, "Limiting the 'Pursuit of Perfect Justice,' on Campus: A Proposed Code of Student Conduct," 6 *Journal of College and University Law* 137-60 (1980).
11. Cheryl M. Fields, "When Students Face Serious Criminal Charges, Some Colleges Await Court Action, Others Mete Out Quick Discipline," *The Chronicle of Higher Education,* March 18, 1987, p. 41.
12. Ibid.
13. *Gabrilowitz v. Newman,* 582 F.2d 100 (1st Cir. 1978).
14. *Wimmer v. Lehman,* 705 F.2d 1402 (4th Cir.), *cert. denied,* 464 U.S. 992 (1983).
15. *McLaughlin v. Massachusetts Maritime Academy,* 564 F. Supp. 809 (D. Mass. 1983).
16. 13 F.3d 221 (7th Cir. 1993).
17. *Id.* at 225.
18. "Note, Due Process Rights in Student Disciplinary Matters," *14 Journal of College and University Law* 359, 375 (1987).
19. *Nash v. Auburn University,* 812 F.2d 655 (11th Cir. 1987).
20. Sanford H. Kadish, *Freedom and Order in the University,* edited by Samuel Gorovitz (Cleveland: Western Reserve, 1967), p. 139.

21. "Academic Freedom and Civil Liberties of Students in Colleges and Universities" (Washington, D.C.: American Civil Liberties Union, 1967).
22. *Kusnir v. Leach*, 439 A.2d 223 (Pa. Cmwlth. 1982).
23. *Krasnow v. Virginia Polytechnic Institute and State University*, 414 F.Supp. 55 (W.D. Va. 1976), *aff'd*, 551 F.2d 591 (4th Cir. 1977).
24. *Cornette v. Aldridge*, 408 S.W.2d 935 (Tex. Civ. App. 1966).
25. Opinion of the attorney general of Maryland, January 23, 1989.
26. *Guy Gannett Publishing Company v. University of Maine*, 555 A.2d 470, 473 (Me. 1989).
27. See Richard Fossey, Jeffrey Sultanik, and Perry Zirkel, "Are School Districts' Settlement Agreements Legally Enforceable?" 67 *Education Law Reporter* 1011-19 (1991).
28. *Krueger v. School District of Hernando County*, 540 So.2d 180 (Fla. App. 1989).
29. 20 U.S.C. Sec. 1232g.
30. *In Re Grand Jury Subpoena Served New York Law School*, 448 F. Supp. 822 (S.D. N.Y. 1978); *State v. Birdsall*, 568 P.2d 1094 (Ariz. App. 1977).
31. 34 C.F.R. 99.36
32. E. Gerald Ogg, "Student Records Privacy and Campus Crime Reporting: The Buckley Amendment after Bauer," 13 *Communications and the Law* 39, 53 (1991).
33. 759 F.Supp. 575 (W.D. Mo. 1991).
34. *Id.* at 590-91.
35. *Id.* at 594.
36. *Frasca v. Andrews*, 463 F.Supp. 1043 (E.D.N.Y. 1979).
37. 427 S.E.2d 257 (Ga. 1993).
38. Dennis Gregory, "Misguided Campaigns for the Release of Students' Disciplinary Records," *The Chronicle of Higher Education*, April 27, 1994, p. B1.
39. See, for example, *Fay v. South Colonie Central School District*, 802 F.2d 21 (2d Cir. 1986); *Klein Independent School District v. Mattox*, 830 F.2d 576 (5th Cir. 1987), *cert. denied*, 458 U.S. 1008 (1988); *Girardier v. Webster College*, 563 F.2d 1267 (8th Cir. 1977). See also, T. Page Johnson, "Managing Student Records: The Courts and the Family Educational Rights and Privacy Act of 1974," 79 *Education Law Reporter* 1-18 (1993).
40. 802 F.2d 21 (2d Cir. 1986).
41. 917 F.2d 890 (5th Cir. 1990).
42. *Norwood v. Slammons*, 788 F.Supp. 1020 (W.D. Ark. 1991).
43. *Krebs v. Rutgers*, 797 F. Supp. 1246 (D. N.J. 1992).
44. *Porten v. University of San Francisco*, 64 Cal. App. 3d 825, 134 Cal. Rptr. 839 (1976).
45. Note, "Forewarned is Forearmed: The Crime Awareness and Campus Security Act of 1990 and the Future of Institutional Liability for Student Victimization," 43 *Case Western Reserve Law Review* 525, 560 (1993).
46. Ibid, p. 561.
47. As amended, 20 U.S.C. Sec. 1232g(b)(6) now states: "Nothing in this section shall be construed to prohibit an institution of post-secondary education from disclosing, to an alleged victim of any crime of violence . . . the results of any disciplinary proceeding conducted by such institution against the alleged perpetrator of such crime with respect to such crime."
48. 20 U.S.C. Sec. 1092(f)(3).
49. 20 U.S.C. Sec. 1094(d)(12)(A)(B).
50. 20 U.S.C. Sec. 1094(c)(2)(B).
51. 34 CFR § 668 (a)(12).

52. Douglas Lederman, "Colleges Must List Crimes Reported to Counselors, U.S. Says," *The Chronicle of Higher Education*, May 4, 1994, p. A32.
53. 34 CFR § 688.47(f).
54. Douglas Lederman, "Colleges Report 7,500 Violent Crimes on Their Campuses in First Annual Statements Required under Federal Law," *The Chronicle of Higher Education*, January 20, 1993, p. A32.
55. Douglas Lederman, "Crime on the Campuses," *The Chronicle of Higher Education*, February 2, 1994, p. A31.
56. Ibid.
57. Note, "Forewarned is Forearmed: The Crime Awareness and Campus Security Act of 1990 and the Future of Institutional Liability for Student Victimization," 43 *Case Western Reserve Law Review* 525, 571 (1993).
58. Ibid., pp. 578-82.
59. *Salek v. Passaic Collegiate School*, 605 A.2d 276, 278 (N.J. Super. 1992).
60. 497 U.S. 1, 110 S. Ct. 2695 (1990).
61. Eugene C. Bjorklun, "Are Teachers Public Officials for Defamation Purposes?" 80 *Education Law Reporter* 527 (1993).
62. *Kelley v. Bonney*, 221 Conn. 549, 606 A.2d 693 (1992); see also, *Johnson v. Southwestern Newspapers Corp.*, 855 S.W.2d 182 (Tex. App. 1993), which held that a schoolteacher was not a public figure, but that a teacher who had assumed additional responsibilities as coach and athletic director was a public figure.
63. *Folse v. Delgado Community College*, 776 F. Supp. 1133 (E.D. La. 1991).
64. 241 Ga. 629, 247 S.E.2d 100, *cert. denied*, 439 U.S. 985 (1978).
65. Pat Howlett, "Speak Out . . . And Up . . . And Early . . . And Well," *Thrust*, April 1987, 19.
66. Ibid.
67. 15A *Am. Jur.* 2d. Compounding Crimes, pp. 767-69 (1974).
68. United Press International report, *Sunday Gazette-Mail* (Charleston, W.Va.), August 31, 1986, p. 14C.
69. *State for the Use and Benefit of Richardson v. Edgeworth*, 214 So.2d 579 (Miss. 1968).

CHAPTER 15

· · · · · · · ·

Conclusion

"Pray give Us Order": Developing a Comprehensive Response to Campus Crime

B y tradition, the sheriff of Middlesex County attends each commencement ceremony at Harvard University. The ceremony begins when the marshal of the university turns to the sheriff and says, "Mr. Sheriff, Pray give us order." The sheriff responds by rapping his staff three times on the platform and announcing, "The meeting will be in order." This quaint ritual hearkens back to a bygone century when Harvard's commencement day was an occasion for drinking and riotous behavior, and the sheriff's presence was required to prevent disruption.

The sheriff's admonition is a reminder that the problem of campus crime for American colleges and universities is as old as the institutions themselves. Indeed, today's campus decision makers face many of the same problems encountered by their predecessors. In particular, crimes that are connected with alcohol or aggressive sexual behavior have always been a part of the campus crime scene. To the extent that institutions can teach students to use alcohol responsibly and to behave respectfully and sensitively to the opposite sex, they will have taken a major step toward reducing crime on their campuses.

Although some crime problems have remained unchanged over the years, new ones have emerged. For example, the dramatic growth in federally funded campus research has brought new opportunities for fraud and abuse. Institutions have found it necessary to develop more sophisticated monitoring and review processes for these research activities. Computer crime is another relatively new phenomenon, and it too has required campus law enforcement authorities to become more sophisticated.

Another recent development has been the proliferation of federal legislation that dictates how higher education institutions must respond to the campus crime threat. The Student-Right-To-Know and Campus Security Act, FERPA, and the Ramstad Amendment are a few prominent examples of federal legislation in this area. Campus decision makers must be familiar with this legislation in order to comply with these new federal mandates.

Finally, courts have shown themselves increasingly willing to hold colleges and universities liable for any injuries caused by crime incidents that were foreseeable to campus authorities. By no means has there been a floodgate of litigation in this area, and courts are still quite deferential to decisions made by higher education institutions. Nevertheless, an institution's exposure to liability for campus rape or an alcohol-related injury has increased in the last 20 years.

All these developments require the nation's colleges and universities to develop a comprehensive program to prevent campus crime and to deal with it when it occurs. Such a program must include education, victims' services, compliance with federal mandates, liability containment, sophisticated crime investigation techniques, and due process procedures for adjudicating charges of wrongdoing against students and employees. Employees from virtually every segment of an institution's workforce will have some responsibility for crime prevention or crime response, from campus security forces to medical staff, student services personnel, groundskeeping and maintenance workers, and housing staff members.

Because of the capacious diversity among American institutions of higher learning, it is difficult to offer general recommendations about crime prevention that will hold true for every campus. Further, the law does not lend itself to black-and-white questions or black-and-white answers; because of the infinite variety of human conduct, legal issues are cast in shades of gray. Nonetheless, the following checklists should be helpful to the decision makers on the typical American campus. The first list deals with ongoing campus concerns and the second with specific responses to actual crime events.

ADMINISTRATIVE OVERSEER CHECKLIST

1. Choose an attorney who is familiar with higher education to be your campus legal counsel. Make sure your legal counsel is readily available when needed.
2. Be familiar with basic principles of criminal law and procedure and the due process rights of students and employees.

3. Consider hiring a risk analyst to review your institution's exposure to liability, particularly with regard to high-risk activities and student use of alcohol.

4. Be acquainted with the laws that affect your campus operations. What is the authority and jurisdiction of your campus security officers? What trespass laws apply on your campus? Do municipal police officers or county sheriff's deputies have jurisdiction on your campus? Consult legal counsel to learn whether your jurisdiction's criminal statutes governing computer fraud are adequate. State laws or local ordinances that need to be changed should be given attention. Campus administrators, trustees, and other representatives can readily influence legislators or council members.

5. Familiarize yourself with your state's liquor laws, particularly with regard to sale and consumption of alcohol by minors.

6. Provide adequate locking, lighting, and patrolling for the campus, paying particular attention to student housing and areas where evening activities take place.

7. Locate parking areas as close as possible to classrooms and workplaces. Have shrubbery and the like, behind which an assailant can hide, been minimized?

8. Review evening class schedules and nighttime work activities to make sure they do not take place in isolated or poorly lit settings.

9. Monitor campus crime incident reports on a regular basis to identify problem areas. Take extra steps to make problem areas safer.

10. Have a process in place to publicize criminal activity that may pose a continuing danger to the campus community, such as the presence of a serial rapist, for example.

11. Put adequate protocols in place for the handling of emergencies by security.

12. Assign a major administrator to be available to respond to campus security emergencies 24 hours a day.

13. Have adequate campus disciplinary policies in place to deal with egregious conduct by students or employees (including a policy against sexual harassment).

14. Take great care in selecting and training campus security officers. "Rambo" types are not needed. Does your institution have an appropriate selection process, and does it provide for both initial and continuing professional training for security?

15. Train security officers and medical staff to deal with campus rapes, including techniques for preserving evidence and interviewing witnesses and victims.

16. Provide training about crime on campus. Students and all employees must be taught how to avoid being victimized, and administrators must be trained both in crime avoidance and in successfully dealing with crime after it occurs.

17. Review your institution's programs for precollege age students, such as summer athletic clinics and academic enrichment programs. Make sure young children are properly supervised at all times and that the employees who work with these children are adequately screened.

CRIME RESPONSE CHECKLIST

1. Decide whether your campus police can handle the incident. Unless your security officers are true professionals with full police powers, do not try to handle serious crime matters on campus.

2. Determine whether your campus police should handle the incident. Turning it over to an outside police agency can prevent any later criticism that the institution tried to cover something up to avoid scandal, or that it bungled the case.

3. Do not fail to report a crime for fear of being sued. It is not defamatory of anyone to pass along evidence or information about a possible crime to police or prosecutors for their professional investigation. In fact, failure to report a crime may be a crime itself. Good faith actions usually enjoy immunity.

4. Never delay dealing with a crime report. Time is of the essence in investigating and responding.

5. Be cautious in revealing information about a criminal investigation to the press. If student information is involved, the so-called Buckley Amendment may apply.

6. Remember that, in most cases, you can move ahead with institutional disciplinary proceedings against an errant student or employee, even though formal criminal charges also are proceeding. Regular disciplinary procedures should be complied with, however. Even an accused criminal is entitled to due process of law (notice of substance of the charge, a forum in which to present a response or rebuttal, and basic fairness of process). But, emergency steps are always justified to keep others safe from a person who clearly presents a physical danger.

7. When in doubt, err on the side of prudence.

8. Never, never, never get involved in a coverup.

INDEX

· · · · · · · · ·

Compiled by James Minkin

---

*n refers to the endnote that contains the case citation.

ISBN 0-89774-846-8

90000